LUIF Dictionaries

Tan Kheng Yeang

Order this book online at www.trafford.com
or email orders@trafford.com

Most Trafford titles are also available at major online book retailers.

Printed in the United States of America.

ISBN: 978-1-4669-6500-3 (sc)
ISBN: 978-1-4669-6498-3 (hc)
ISBN: 978-1-4669-6499-0 (e)

Library of Congress Control Number: 2013909770

Trafford rev. 08/08/2013

www.trafford.com

North America & international
toll-free: 1 888 232 4444 (USA & Canada)
fax: 812 355 4082

Other books by Tan Kheng Yeang

Fiction

Novels

Conflict in the Home

Sauce of Life

Struggle Toward Extinction

Motivating Forces

Poetry

Diverse Modes

Poems (Flowery Country/Sun and Rain/Grains of Sand)

Non-Fiction

Memoir

Dark Days

Philosophy

Intrinsic to Universe

The Material Structure

Sayings

Reduced Reflections

Linguistics

LUIF: A New Language

Acknowledgements

The author wishes to thank Ms. Judith Sogor and Ms. Valerie Cameron for their invaluable assistance in preparing the manuscript of this book for publication.

Contents

Introduction

There are three dictionaries in this book: a *Luif-English Classified Dictionary*, a *Luif-English Alphabetical Dictionary*, and an *English-Luif Alphabetical Dictionary*. All three contain the same words of Luif, numbering about four thousand and comprising all the basic words as well as a considerable number of composite words together with some secondary meanings and phrases.

In the English-Luif Classified Dictionary, the Luif words with their English equivalents are tabulated according to their meaning. The basic words are underlined. Certain resultant words whose original parts of speech and primary meanings are evident may not be listed under their original parts of speech. As an example, a verb prefixed by *o* to signify its use in the passive may be classified as a qualifier instead of a verb, the reason being its employment principally as a qualifier.

In the Luif-English Dictionary, the Luif words are defined so that the specific meanings contemplated are manifest. The English equivalents are also furnished. A Luif word may be invested with more than one meaning. Primary meanings are given first; then come secondary meanings in descending order of proximity to the primary meanings. Only the secondary meanings of some resultant words may be recorded, the unequivocal primary meanings being omitted. The

Luif words are systematically arranged strictly in accordance with the order of the letters in the Luif alphabet.

In the English-Luif Dictionary, where the English words are tabulated in alphabetical order according to the order of the letters in the English alphabet, the objective is not to elucidate English terms but to find the nearest equivalents for Luif words. It is a way of rendering the meaning of a Luif word. The words in parentheses that follow the English words are intended to pinpoint the particular sense envisaged. When the comment is just the term *Luif*, the English word refers to what is peculiar to Luif. Words separated from the entry by a comma are either synonyms or indicate that the meaning is subsumed in that of the Luif word. Explanations enclosed in parentheses may be appended to certain Luif words.

I

Luif-English Classified Dictionary

Connectives

I. Position

va	at
zle.va	touching
hê	on or above
hê.êz	above
hê.mi	on
hsa-hê	up
lô	under
lô.mi	under (touching)
lô.êz	below
hsa-lô	down
nu	in
za	outside
ba	middle
ba	between
dê	through
val.dê	along
lên.dê	across
jô	near
jû	next
dluô.jô	beside
jaz-jô	about (here and there nearby)
jaz.fe	around
gu	far
al	front
vuô.ud	opposite
êh	behind
un	hither (on this side)

ôv .... beyond (on that side)
êz .... from
ud .... to
ud.nu .... into
êz .... away, off
zma.fe .... beginning of
grê.fe .... end of
êh .... before, previous
al .... after

II. Nature of Relationship

fe .... of (belonging to)
mi .... with (possessed of)
sê.mi .... without
ro .... including
flua.ro .... for example
pa.ro .... excluding
sû .... amongst
mi .... together
zvê.mi .... in presence of
pe .... besides (in addition to)
ci .... except
ko .... by (indicating the agent)
mi .... using, by means of
tû .... for (in favour of)
tû.pa .... pro and con
vuô.tû .... instead
ih .... as
im .... according to
pue.dê .... via, by way of
suêf.ud .... against, versus

of .... become
es .... concerning
fe-mi .... related
sag-tû .... worth (equal in value to)
ûp .... like (similar)

III. Addition of Ideas

ne .... and
li .... and not
vo .... or
hû .... though
ze .... but
sê.ris.tû .... nevertheless, notwithstanding
gi .... than
tid.sa .... whatever
tid.rô .... wherever
tid.su .... whenever
tid.ca .... however
tid.um .... whoever
do .... while
lêr.do .... as long as
vêu.êz .... since
jû .... after this
hum.jû .... and immediately
hum.su .... as soon as
lêr.jû .... long afterwards
ol .... until
ih .... that (denoting the idea following)
sme.ih .... that is, i.e.
kêu.ih .... namely, viz.
hne.ih .... considering

jeûp.ih	lest
en	because
nzo.ûz	therefore
ûz	thus
ib	in order to
og	if
ci	unless

IV. Interrogative Terms

sa	what
fê	whether (what reply)
rô	where (what place)
jô.rô	whereabouts
su	when (what time)
sa.mul	what condition
ca	how (what manner)
ku	why (what reason)
sa.hzô	what cause
sa.lbu	what result
cu	which (what thing)
um	who (what person)
ôs	whose (of what person or thing)
sa.kêg	what type
sa.fleu	which one
sa.ril	how many
sa.sor	how much

Qualifiers

I. Space and Time

1. Space

val-lên-zal	dimension
val	long
nôh	short
lên	broad
huv	narrow
zal	thick
dêl	thin
jêh-laz	altitude
jêh	high
ban	low
vrôih-bôz	sea level
ban, cûg-ban	shallow
jêh, cûg-jêh	deep
zên.gun	size
zên	big
gun	small
rud.gun	petty
rseut-kêg	miniature
vêi	minute (size)
pa.dba.gun	infinitesimal
jav	shape
buv	regular shape
buv	symmetrical
kûs.dluô	equilateral
troi-jav	definite

nê.laz ... series of points
laz ... point
ûp-ba ... focus
nêz ... line
pca-nêz ... axis
drô-nêz ... crease
dê-kûs ... parallel
blêa ... tapering
hôj ... area (extent)
lub ... volume (content)
nad ... straight
fiûl-guz-nêz ... perpendicular
nad-jêh ... steep
êz-nad ... oblique, leaning
êz-fzi ... sloping
guz-zfê-nêz ... diagonal
vêg ... curved
mloû.vêg ... undulating, zigzag
fe-vêg ... spiral
nu-vêg ... concave
za-vêg ... convex
kûs-blêa-vêg ... parabola
jaz ... round (circular)
jaz-val ... circumference
jaz-lên ... diameter
ba-nad ... radius
val-jaz ... ellipse
ius ... oval
bôz ... flat
bôz ... level
tluin ... serrated
guz ... angular

guz ... corner
huv-guz ... acute angle
fiûl-guz ... right angle
lên-guz ... obtuse angle
tau ... geometrical figure
hôj ... plane figure
zêj ... triangular
zab ... quadrilateral
buv-zab ... parallelogram
ûp-gêd ... rhombus
val-gêd ... rectangle
gêd ... square
dôg ... polygon
lub ... solid figure
liûgued ... prism
guz-blêa ... pyramid
hlua ... cube
vlêô ... sphere
jô-vlêô ... spheroid
hvau ... cylinder
blêa ... cone
jluê ... position
grê-dluô ... end
dêl-grê ... tip
dluô ... side
hôj-dluô ... flat side
nêz-dluô ... edge
zfê-nêz ... seam
zlêu ... here
jzua ... there
jzêu ... right side
nlai ... left side

êz-ud .... direction
nad, dê-nad .... direct
fiûl .... vertical
fzi .... horizontal
izuz .... face to face
zoû-hê .... face upwards
hê-lô .... upside down
nu-za .... inside out
hê-rtam .... upstairs
lô-rtam .... downstairs
vlôi .... north
glui .... east
zluû .... south
ldêi .... west

2. Time

vêu.sê.dba .... eternal
vrêu, zlu.lêr .... permanent
sê.grê .... continual, endless
lêr .... long time
vam .... short time
zlu.vam .... temporary
vaekô vam .... as soon as possible
hum .... immediately
siêpi .... extempore
bêr.jôm .... primitive
gu.jôm .... ancient
nôf .... old
has .... young
lêr, hrô.lêr .... old (long in use)
vam, hrô.vam .... new

bêr	early
zam	late
vêu-kôz	anachronism
jôm	past (time)
vam.jôm	recent
dluô-jôm	last (most recent)
vam-ris	just
fe-buf	modern
buf	present (now)
gas	future
vam-fem	about to
jô-hrô	imminent
hum-vam	soon
lac	then
vôp	already
vêu	continuous
dak	time (occasion)
ciam-dak	opportunity
ef.dak	sometimes
côh	seldom
so.dak	often
vrêu	always
lrai	again
dak	repeated
mloû	frequently repeated
su	ever
jrôû	never
vêu.tis	simultaneous
ghal.cel.dak	biannual
tû ghal	per annum

II. Amount

1. Number

ril	number
mov-kol	odd
cel-poh	even
sa	any
fleu	some, a certain
ef.ril	several
rûg	multitudinous
fûl	zero
sen	fraction
sjie-sen	vulgar fraction
o.sjie.pom	numerator
sjie.pom	denominator
foz-sen	decimal fraction
mûn	hundredth (part)
fe.foz	tenth
fe.poh	quarter
fe.kol	third
rev	half
khau.ril	integer
mov	one
cel	two
kol	three
poh	four
ken	five
pin	six
cûn	seven
tev	eight
rez	nine

foz .... ten
mij .... hundred
sod .... thousand
rûg .... ten thousand
cez .... hundred million
cel jû cel .... two by two
tû mij .... per cent
poz .... first
zma-jroi .... elementary
kûz .... chief
peb .... last
poz .... primarily
dak .... secondary
fot .... former
mip .... latter
tid .... every
tid .... each
cel.vo .... either
vo .... alternative
tid.cûg .... alternate
mov-cûg .... mutual, one another
cûg .... other
cel.fûl .... neither
kus-fleu .... individual
fleu .... denoting unit or piece
ril.fleu .... discrete unit
pom.fleu .... piece (detached portion)
laz.fleu .... particle
nêz.fleu .... length (long piece)
hôj.fleu .... piece (flat)
plia.hôj.fleu .... layer
siut.hôj.fleu .... slice

hvau.lkô.fleu .... scroll

lub.fleu .... block, mass

plia.fleu .... item

dak.fleu .... dose

sviu .... pair

cim.cel .... both

snou .... plural

mij .... many sorts of

fem-ril .... majority

ris-ril .... minority

plia .... group

nêz.plia .... row, series

brail .... continuous moving line

hôj.plia .... group spread over a surface

lub.plia .... heap, mass

zfê.plia .... bunch, cluster

jzu.plia .... class, order

fal.plia .... rank, grade

jiaz.plia .... class (school)

chêô.plia .... schedule

zfê-gsô.plia .... bundle

lpa.plia .... set

phuê.plia .... array

kêg.plia .... type, kind

pom.plia .... subdivision

iûn-ril .... population

hse-ril .... quorum

jzu-mro-ril .... edition

tliô .... add

czûa .... subtract

mloû .... multiply

poh.mloû .... fourfold, quadruple

sjie	divide
sjie-lbu	quotient
cel-sjie	bisect

2. Quantity

sor.fef	quantity
rûm-laz	maximum
per-laz	minimum
ro-ril	gross
ci-ril	net
vaekô	as much as possible
sor	much
fem	more
rûm	most
an.sor	moderate
fef	little (in quantity)
ris	less
per	least
blop.khau	handful
cim	all
feur-cim	total, sum
mov, cim.mov	whole
iolia	en masse
lên	comprehensive
pom-fiem	proportion, ratio
pom	part
rpû-pom	quota
sen	fragment
lbu-pom	sequel
ôv-cab	extravagant
ôv-sko	redundant

tef ... enough
huv ... confined
nôh ... deficient
cûf ... only
tis ... same
jziû.tis ... monotonous
buv ... uniform
lnu-kuv ... quasi
sê.tis ... different, various
kul ... common
kûs ... equal
kûs-sag ... equivalent
fem-ris ... about (more or less)
jô.fa ... nearby
jô.sêv ... scarcely
rec ... so (to that extent)
rec ... such
im sa hrô ... as follows
sê.ris ... even
fem-rec ... too
mip ... this
fot ... that
sik ... solid (opposed to hollow)
zal ... dense
poc ... hollow
u.poc ... dimple
val-poc ... groove, furrow
fria.creu ... weight
fria ... heavy
creu ... light (in weight)
troi ... strong
troi ... tough

spiû ... weak

dêl ... flimsy

III. Sensory Qualities

1. Light and Sound

lil ... bright

ên.lil ... vivid

an.lil ... dim

jrual ... vague

nûh ... dark

nos ... gloomy

lil, hne-lil ... clear, distinct

dê-lil ... transparent

von ... shady

hev ... colour

troi ... fast (of colour)

mloû-hev ... motley

zel ... white

bih-zel ... grey

poi-bih ... brown

leg-poi-bih ... auburn

bih ... black

bih-dûn ... livid

dûn ... blue

leg-dûn ... violet

dûn-leg ... purple

zov ... green

hiz ... yellow

poi ... orange

leg .... red
pliz .... rosy
vlub-fal .... tone
sluj-buv .... rhythm
vlub.sor .... noisy
jûz .... silent
vliê .... loud
blou .... low (re sound)
jloi .... sharp (re sound)
jroi-jloi .... creaking
jziû .... dull (re sound)

2. Smell, Taste, and Feeling

lûr .... fragrant
hem .... foul (in smell)
hvo.zis .... tasty
hvo.blê .... tasteless
lif .... sweet (in taste)
nos .... bitter
zûr .... salty (in taste)
jom .... sour
bef .... pungent (in taste)
zis .... pleasant to senses
ên.zis .... charming
lif .... softly captivating
hec .... unpleasant to senses
not .... hot
u.not .... lukewarm
lûk .... cold
zoc .... soft
jhus .... plastic

nriô .... hard
nad-nriô .... stiff
griu .... smooth
jroi .... rough
nuap-jroi .... ragged
jroi .... rugged
jroi-dluô .... jagged

IV. Qualities of Objects

1. Judgement

fal .... quality
blêh-fal .... nature (of a thing)
nu-fal .... essence
pan-nu .... intrinsic
kuv, jluz.fa .... real
reu.fa .... extinct
zlôn.fa .... abstract
hôi.fa .... concrete
lva.fa .... positive
nlê.fa .... negative
mul .... condition (state)
jbe-gsô-laz .... crisis
ûpoci .... ad hoc
uput .... respectively
im lêr .... in the long run
dluô-jlô .... by the way, incidentally
ijoh .... vice versa
itcioc .... verbatim
ifu .... in a word, in short

rêh ... manner

hozôo ... *sine qua non*, indispensable condition

ocêgi ... *ceteris paribus*, if other things remain the same

azoh ... *mutatis mutandis*, the necessary changes having been made

man ... intermediate or neutral

sêv ... not

pal ... opposite (in kind)

kul ... ordinary

pa.kul ... unusual

fe-sto ... peculiar

zis-côh ... quaint

vliê ... conspicuous

côh ... rare

pan ... natural

ôv.pan ... supernatural

tên ... suitable

sor ... very

val ... intense

rûm ... extremely

cun ... perfect

cun-cab ... ideal

prû-kôz ... defective

paf-jroi ... crude

cav ... exact

kuv ... true

sik ... genuine

lnu.fa ... ostensible

kêu.fa ... nominal

vûil, o.vûil ... imaginary

pa.kuv ... false

raz ... certain

pan.raz ... of course

lil ... obvious

jô.raz ... probable

fêz ... simple

suz ... easy

nriô, pa.suz ... difficult

bih ... abstruse

nûh ... mysterious

mêj ... glorious

mêj ... majestic

zên ... great

sag, sag-zên ... important

hê ... major

lô ... minor

fôb ... good

pliz ... enchanting

fôb-sag ... fine, excellent

zis ... delicate

lûr ... favourable

zov ... fresh

zûr ... useful and agreeable

tên ... convenient

rud ... bad

hem ... repellent

chui-ban ... sordid

o.kri.ceûl ... funny

o.kri.vce ... deplorable

o.kri.biôm ... admirable

jeûp.rze ... formidable

hfo-zla ... indispensable

jae, lva-sko ... essential

sag.pa ... value

fe-sag ... merit

sag ... valuable

hiz ... precious

glu.sag ... worth doing

bôz, ba-sag ... average

u.sag ... trifling

ban-rud ... base (in value)

paz ... right

kôz ... wrong

pue-kôz ... astray

tuz ... beautiful

zis-tuz ... elegant, graceful

thôuh.ûp ... picturesque

zel, sê.sfuom ... plain, unembellished

kaj ... ugly

vûil-plo ... grotesque

jom-jroi ... awkward

cab ... standard

cab, fe-cab ... orthodox

phuê-cab ... formal

za-cab ... anomalous

pa.cab ... eccentric

kêg ... type

zku-kêg ... brand

sû-plia ... variant

ztê, ztê.keg ... miscellaneous

flua ... example

êh-flua ... precedent

fcô-flua ... sample

phuê ... method

thô-phuê ... procedure

gsô-phuê ... order

phuê-fôb ... neat, tidy

jzû .... disordered
kêg .... general
isô .... in general
pom-chêô .... particular
jzu-côh .... special
chêô .... detail
zal .... flourishing
poc, lbu.blê .... futile, vain
gsô-troi .... tight
gsô-spiû .... loose
jloi .... sharp, cutting
jziû .... blunt
hpi .... quiet
bih-zel .... depressing
siab-biôm.sag .... praiseworthy
stui, rôef-jêh .... dear (costly)
pa.stui .... cheap
fe-sgô .... technical
grêl-troi .... fireproof
khau .... full
pa.khau .... empty
mro.blê .... blank
krauf.blê .... bare
snôi .... wet
vlaul.khau .... waterlogged
u.snôi .... damp
pa.snôi .... dry
vlaul-troi .... waterproof
nriô .... hard (of water)
nriô-hêun .... viscous
pa.chui .... clean
fêz .... pure

chui .... dirty
zca-stui .... fertile, luxuriant
tiûn-tôm .... ripe
pa.thuû .... wild
thuû .... tame
nu-gzauf .... intestine (internal affairs relating to state or country)
za-gzauf .... foreign
gzauf-sû .... international

2. Human Qualities

noê.mul .... manhood
ztê-rze .... half-blooded
vlil .... personal
fêr .... my
sam .... thy
rum .... his, hers, or its
sêf .... our
rôs .... your
fus .... their
fôb-mul .... well
jziû, lie.jziû .... tired
car .... sex
kôr .... male
pêm .... female
mi-paf .... pregnant
tôm .... adult
paf .... immature
nrûn.mul .... fatherhood
zten.mul .... brotherhood
jêh .... tall
ban .... short (in stature)

hiû.zel .... grey-haired
hiû.blê .... bald
coôl-rêh .... gait
bûuj-jô .... intimate
<u>kus</u> .... lonely
hjuez .... original
bûuj-sor .... familiar
pa.bûuj-sor .... strange
<u>mac</u> .... free
bzê .... absolute
<u>sôp</u> .... safe
pa.sôp .... dangerous
stô.blê .... helpless
sla.mac .... leisure
dûn .... profound (knowledge)
vûil, vûil.zla .... imaginative
plal-kut .... holy
plal-sraô .... sin
kut.sraô .... virtue
<u>kut</u> .... moral
kôz-mac .... innocent
<u>sraô</u> .... immoral
u.spiû .... foible
vlair-mul .... dignity
paz-buv .... propriety
jêh-mêj .... sublime
jêh .... noble, lofty
ban, pleuf .... mean
blou .... vulgar
phûun .... solemn
ceid-piûj .... responsible
cav, vêu.cav .... punctual

vliê .... obtrusive
coet-creu .... economical
prôu .... civilized
crêe .... barbaric
bhon .... public
vlil .... private
keû.zên .... famous
lên.o.jci .... popular
kêu.blê .... nameless
kêu-liûz .... anonymous
sla-fal .... qualification
dhô-fôb .... lucky
dhô-rud .... unlucky
o.jci .... dear
stui .... rich
pa.stui .... poor
krauf.blê .... naked

Verbs

I. Universal Action

1. Natural Action

lva .... exist

blêh-jzu .... identify

zlu-lva .... perpetuate

nlê .... do not exist

zu.nlê .... extinguish

pa.lva .... abolish, cancel

prel-siut .... eradicate

vlô .... is

kri.vlô .... possible

lro.vlô .... maybe, perhaps

hlu .... is not

tro.vlô .... impossible

lnu .... seem

zla .... have

blê .... have not

hse .... lack

pa.ro.lu .... exclude

pa.ro.lu .... omit

pa.zla .... deprive

fe.lu .... belong

fe-tbo .... attribute

zvê .... to be present

zvê, hrô-zvê .... appear

zvê-cûg-vuô .... alibi

grê-zvê .... disappear, vanish

fiôf-vrê	abscond
sêûm	put out of sight
jlô	happen
hfo.jlô	inevitable
êh-vêu	premature
êh.jlô	precede (in time)
al.jlô	follow (in time)
vce-jlô	tragedy
ên.vce-jlô	calamity
lto-jluê	predicament
al-mli	posthumous
dhô	chance
fe-dhô	casual
dhô, dhô-jlô	accident
fcô-jlô	omen
draz-dhô	fortune
draz-gsô	fate
zlu	endure
glu	do
so.glu	active
glu-lbu	execute (carry into effect)
piôs-blê	impromptu
zhi-jlô	adventure
lrai.lu	repeat
glu-ciam	practise
pre-seêm	habitual practice
jaz	routine
bauz	addict
jêh-pci	excel
vrê-ôv	surpass
piûj-glu	react
chêô-sla	elaborate

<u>vza</u> .... don't do
rbo-mul .... abeyance
<u>hzô</u> .... cause
<u>lbu</u> .... effect
kri.lbu .... efficient
lbu-zgu .... influence
êz-hrô .... derive
fem-vlô, vlô fem gi .... exceed
czûa-gzô .... surplus
tliô.lu .... increase
czûa.lu .... decrease
zfê-nuê .... span
val.lu .... lengthen, stretch
nôh.lu .... shorten
<u>jza</u> .... spread
ên.jza .... outspread
tho .... spread easily and rapidly
puaf .... pervade
lub-zca .... swell
nuap-vrê .... disperse
sen.cze-stû .... scatter
pa.jza .... pack
ba-vêg .... sag
lub-feur .... shrink
laz-dba .... concentrate
ôv-fiûl .... jut
czil-sjie .... fork, bifurcate
pa.dba .... infinite
<u>dba</u> .... limit
dba-nêz .... boundary
gsô .... settle
tbo-stû .... dispose

<u>bzê</u> .... complete
grê, grê-bzê .... finish
bzê-zku .... complement
tliô-bzê .... supplement
tbo, khau.lu .... fill
mov.lu .... unify
fzi .... situate
zle .... abut
<u>gzô</u> .... remain
piem, lêr.gzô .... linger
msê .... represent
<u>jzu</u> .... mark
jzu-nion .... distinguish
jzu-gsô .... impress
hev-hpu .... stain, discolour
gzô-jzu .... trace, vestige
lto-nuap .... chaos
<u>zgu</u> .... force
zgu-kri .... power
fe-zgu .... authority
toif-zgu .... friction
mru-hsa .... gravitate
ên.zgu .... violent
nu-zgu .... inject
zgu-tbo .... ram
cvo, zgu-za .... eject, expel
za.côof .... emit
lkô-zgu .... squeeze
zgu-nuap .... crush
zgu-nêz .... crumple
<u>vuêl</u> .... shine
en.vuêl .... glare

vuêl-beûl	dazzle
az.vuêl	flash
u.vuêl	glimmer
mloû.vuêl	twinkle
vlic-vuêl	reflect
nûh-vuêl	phosphoresce
kôof-jza	radiate
hue-nuap	radioactive
nuah	burn
nuah-zru	flicker
fe-nuah	smoulder
brôn.lu	smoke
vlaul-cto	parch
ses	sound of splashing water
hêun	blow (wind)
jain, jêh-jain	hover
hêun	flow (water)
cel-pue-hêun	ebb and flow
klû	gush
jzêl-hêun	spurt
poc-hêun	leak
jza-stû	splash
laz.lu	spatter
u.hêun	trickle
vlaul-pca	irrigate
piev	absorb
vlaul-zfê	hydrate
seêm.grêun.lu	continue raining
vlaul-hse	drought
bluên.lu	freeze
zal.lu	coagulate
em.dêl.lu	dilute

luav .... melt
daul .... boil (water)
buên .... evaporate
laz-rpû .... distil
huûl .... wave (water)
u.huûl .... ripple
jaz-vlaul .... whirlpool, eddy
vlaul-fiôv .... plunge
vam-bauz .... dip
vlaul-seêm .... soak
vlû .... imbue
jain .... float
bauz .... sink
blaf.lu .... muddle
vluar.lu .... land

2. Motion and Change

hsa .... move
kri.hsa .... mobile
vlil-hsa .... automatic
môip .... move quietly
fleu-hsa .... gradual
griu-hsa .... glide, slide
al-êh .... to and fro
vrê-hrô .... communicate
huûl-hsa .... fluctuate
vlic-hsa .... recoil
jaz-hsa .... revolve
mloû.jaz-hsa .... revolve round and round
jaz-soun .... orbit
jaz-drô .... rotate

hsa-rpû	overtake
êz.hsa	remove
vuô-hpu	move from place to place
ûp-hsa	transfer
jaz-hsa	circulate
lub-hsa	traffic
vuô-vrê	travel
mac-vrê	wander
hsa-sku	patrol
cgi, cgi-vrê	ride
vlaul-hsa	sail
hêun-vrê	cruise
vrê-nu-slar	embark
pa.hsa	motionless
hsa-vza	inert
vuô-gsô	fixed to one place
vrê	go
vrê	depart
cze	flee
mi-vrê	accompany
vêg-vrê	detour
so.vrê	frequent
zoû.vrê	advance
zgu-hsa	rush
dê.vrê	pass
nu.vrê, vrê nu	enter
za.vrê, vrê za	emerge
lrai.vrê	go back
vlic.vrê	retreat
al.vrê	precede (in place)
êh.vrê	follow (in place)
pa.bauz, hê-vrê	rise

jêh-cze … soar
bauz, lô-vrê … fall
dhô.bauz … accidentally fall
griu-bauz … slip
hrô … come
hrô … arrive, reach
nru.jra … speed, rate
nru … quick
jzêl-nru … sudden
piôs-nru … prompt
nru-creu … nimble
vaekô nru … as fast as possible
em.nru … accelerate
nru-hsa … haste
jra … slow
lêr-tbo … delay
fe-faur … impede
zma … start
lrai.zma … resume
grê … stop
dba-grê … terminus
u.grê … hesitate
nuap … interrupt
mloû.grê … intermittent
grê-frê … adjourn
zfê … join
zle-zfê … contact
ûp-tliô … append
zfê-gsô … bind
jaz.lu … surround
zle-zru … jostle
srô-rial … collide

zgu-frê .... shock
dê-siut .... intersect
dê.vrê .... penetrate
pa.zfê .... separate
vêg.lu .... bend
suz-vêg .... pliant
cel-drô .... fold
drô .... turn
huûl-hpu .... distort, wry
vêg-drô .... twist
jaz-drô .... coil
drô-truôz .... roll
rev.drô .... turn about
cûg, cûg-drô .... reverse
khau.drô .... complete turn
lrai.drô .... re-turn
gsô .... fix
gsô, czuûb.gsô .... tie
gsô-gzô .... stick, adhere
jzêm, fe-gsô .... sticky
jhus .... tenacious
jain-tbo .... hang
pa.gsô .... unfix
zru .... shake
rial-zru .... throb
daul .... agitate
aiz-zru .... earthquake
lpa .... balance
lpa, gûin-lpa .... harmony (of parts)
vzû .... fit
mlûhum .... elastic
htê .... open

fcô, htê-fcô .... expose

meuh-stû .... strip

lkô .... close

lkô .... cover

nu.lkô .... enclose

hpu .... change

suz.hpu .... fickle

seêm .... continue

pa.hpu .... constant

vêu-ciam .... pass time

zca, htê-zca .... develop, evolve

jêh-laz .... climax

zca.pa .... wax and wane

zca .... grow

zma-zca .... sprout

hsa-zfê .... graft

hsa-zca .... transplant

zca-csû .... rear

ztê .... mix

mi.ztê .... intermingle

prel-nuap .... analyse

zma-zku .... found, originate

pca-zma .... pioneer

liôl-sku .... devise

zku .... make

rôûn .... concoct

sdu .... form of parts

gbo-mcu .... counterfeit, forge

zel.lu .... bleach

luam .... repair

paz.lu .... rectify

hues .... improve

sag-pci .... enhance
piôs-hues .... refine
pa.hues .... worsen
bauz .... decline
sag-ris .... depreciate
hues, stô-al .... promote
pa.hues .... demote
rud-jzu .... blemish
lil-cto .... fade
fe-kiuf .... decay, rot
vlaul-cto .... wither
gaif .... destroy
pan-gaif .... natural calamity
nuap-gaif .... ruin
nuap-gaif .... wreck
nuap .... break
sen.nuap .... break in pieces
suz.nuap .... brittle, fragile
ôuv-sjie .... tear
sjie-nuap .... split, crack
nuap.htê .... burst
nuap.htê .... explode
aif-nuap .... grind

II. Actions and Conditions of Living Things

1. Bodily Action

sne .... live
ôv.sne .... survive
lrai.sne .... revive

fôb-mul .... farewell
nuap-vle .... stun
vrouh-hsa .... spasm, convulsion
mli .... die
la.lva .... deceased
zu.mli .... fatal
flo .... healthy
khe-nuap .... disable
kaj-hpu .... deform
slû .... sick
creu.rnû .... ailment
vrôih-slû .... seasick
slû-hev .... pale, wan
rnû .... disease
fria.rnû .... serious disease
rnû-cuem .... contagious, infectious
lên-rnû .... epidemic
tle .... itch
jaz-rnû .... ringworm
leg-cli .... boil
cli-jluz-laz .... pustule
due-laz .... blister
gun-leg .... pimple
nio-laz-plia .... rash
nio-hev-laz .... freckle
khe .... wound
rial-khe .... bruise
nuap-khe .... sprain
ian-stû .... bleed
khe-jzu .... scar
sia-fiôp .... sting
cli .... sore

slû-nuah	inflammation
sriol-nio	leprosy
tle-rnû	scabies
leg-laz	measles
hê-laz-rnû	smallpox
lô-laz-rnû	chicken pox
spiû-ian	anaemia
phi	fever
ûp-plo	delirious
lûk-phi	malaria
sko-blê-zca	excrescence
eul-fiûl	tumour
frûin-vliêl	cancer
plo	giddy
gûi-bli	headache
ueh-rial	sunstroke
cto-hne-rsûh	cataract
tho	cold (the disease)
ûp-tho	influenza
fien-rnû	asthma
cvo	cough
ûp-cvo	hiccup
klû	vomit
vlû.klû	nausea
rilvafvi	tetanus
brem-lub	goitre
dêl-rnû	consumption, tuberculosis
hiz-rnû	jaundice
zcos-bli	stomach ache
zcos-zên-bli	colic
drein-laz-rnû	appendicitis
bliaz-grê	constipation

vlaul-bliaz	diarrhoea
ian-bliaz	dysentery
leg-phi	typhoid
ôuv-klû	cholera
vrouh-bli	rheumatism
pleuf-rnû	plague
car-rnû	syphilis
gziûl-rial	pulse
lreon-luav	digest
rze	bear or produce
vuô-rze	native
pan-rze	indigenous
bêr-rze	abort
tro.rze	barren, sterile
ius-rze	hatch
car-siut	castrate
flo-hsa	exercise
phuê-drô	drill
toif-shu	massage
sje	sport
sje	athletics
ruam-soun	race
gle-ruam	game
jrot-vlêô	football
gêd-spe	chess
fcô	look (appear)
jluê, lie-jluê	attitude
jziû-spiû	languish
drof-hsa	shrug
nôh-hsa	jerk
vêg-hsa	wriggle
fe-zru	shiver

fzi … lie down

ûuc-fzi … nestle

snêul-bauz … bedridden

rbo … sleep

ên.rbo … sound sleep

fe-rbo … torpid

u.rbo … doze

mru.rbo … drowsy

rbo-siab … snore

vrer-htê … yawn

rbo-piûj … hypnosis

sdû … awake

cze … fly

iôm-hsa … flap, flutter

vlaul-coôl … wade

brail-coôl … ford

pdi … swim

vlaul-lô … dive

kiûr, lie.kiur … bathe

cgi … sit

mi.cgi … sit together

ûp-cgi … squat

czo … take

czo-sto … appropriate

zgu-czû … seize

czo-czû … catch

lrai.czo … retract

czo-vrê … take away

tbo … put

dluô-tbo … appose, juxtapose

ba.tbo … interpose

sû.tbo … insert

sku-tbo	set, frame
lrai.tbo	restore
czû	hold
czû	cling
blop-czû	clasp
lie-czû	embrace
rpû-czû	occupy
rial	beat
zu.bauz	fell
blop-cêôm	box
rial	knock, hit
ûp-zle	pat
zoc-rial	tap
blop-rial	slap
rial-tiûn	peck
meuh	pull
pa.meuh	push
zgu-vrê	thrust
rud-hsa	fumble
sme-hsa	gesture
zru-ceud	beckon
glik-fcô	point
vgep-toif	scratch
soun	run
jeûp-soun	stampede
fiôv-soun	gallop
soun-cze	fugitive
soun-czo	chase
fiôv	jump
u.fiôv	skip
fiôv-nru	bounce
drô-fiôv	somersault

<u>coôl</u> .... walk
mlê-coôl .... stroll
zlêu-jzua-coôl .... ramble
pue-cto .... stray
plo-coôl .... walk to and fro irresolutely
rev-bauz .... stumble
fe-zru .... stagger
drô-bauz .... tumble
tbo-jrot .... tread, trample
jrot-jzu .... footprint
cto-coôl .... lame
pet .... sound of footsteps
<u>peôn</u> .... climb
pa.peôn .... descend
<u>kiuv</u> .... creep
jeûp-kiuv .... grovel
<u>moil</u> .... kick
<u>fiûl</u> .... stand
lie-vêg .... stoop
fe-jain-tbo .... droop
vêg.lu .... bow (neck or body)
vric-zfê.lu .... kneel
gûi.zru .... nod
zoû-fri .... countenance
zoû-nêz .... wrinkle
zoû-hsa .... grimace
nio-leg .... blush
jom .... scowl
mloû.vuêl .... wink
hne-dluô .... squint
<u>roih</u> .... weep
<u>fien</u> .... breathe

fien-zru .... pant
dlos-siab .... sneeze
vrer-czû .... hold in mouth
zgu-fien .... gasp
bliûh.lu .... lick
fien-faur .... choke
ceûl .... smile
fe-ceûl .... humour
lên-ceûl .... grin
bef .... sneer
pûen .... kiss
vrer-val .... pout
tiûn .... eat
khau.tiûn .... eat until full
vrer-meuh .... suck
dhûiv-czo .... swallow, gulp
vhoil-siut .... bite
vhoil-toif .... chew
pa.tiûn .... fast, starve
piev .... drink
stû-piev .... carouse
ud-piev .... toast
lrim-piev .... sip
miôz .... sound made by living thing other than human
chuit .... twitter
pfê-miôz .... snarl
hiôp-miôz .... growl
ni .... hum (sound of mosquito)
siab .... human voice
hui .... whistle
ceûl.siab .... laugh
roih.siab .... cry

bli-siab	groan, moan
vlub-fien	sigh
nuap-siab	stammer, stutter
jzu-siab	emphasize
kiaz	shout
jloi.kiaz	yell, scream
blou.siab	murmur, mutter
fien-siab	whisper
lto-siab	grumble
ceud	call
kêu-ceud	roll call
ceud-glu	summon
frê-ceud	greet
roiz	talk
nê.roiz	speech
voiz-vlô	declare
fri-gsô	confirm
nriô-fri	insist
fûl.lu	deny
suêf-fri	contradict
hêun-roiz	chatter
poc-roiz	gossip
kiuf-spe	frivolous
jci.roiz	talkative
cfe.roiz	eloquent
hêun-roiz	fluent
vlil.roiz	soliloquy
dlû-siab	think aloud
sû-roiz	converse
bûuj-roiz	tell
htê-roiz	reveal
lên-roiz	proclaim

czo-roiz	quote
êh-fri	predict, foretell
draz-dhô-fri	fortune-telling
plal-fri	swear
êun, êun-roiz	rumour
ceûl-spe	joke, jest
car.ceûl-spe	obscene jest
fri-vce	lament
stû-roiz	confess
lgi-roiz	confide
jzu-roiz	comment
hpu-drô	prevaricate
khe-roiz	slander
êh-trê	backbite
viaf-roiz	boast
siab-biôm	praise
siab-trê	scold
cto-roiz	dumb
sûig	ask
piûj	reply

2. Action in Regard to Things

sme	mean (re words)
sme-gsô	define
es-zle	relevant
vêg-sme	imply
jaz-fri	circumlocution
sme-niav	ambiguous
fûl-sme	nonsense
fri	express in words
es-fri	mention

chêô-fri .... describe
brail-fri .... narrate
vam-jlô .... news
hne-lil .... explain
lgi-jza .... propagandize
vuô-tbo .... address (as a letter)
jbe-hpu .... revise
nûh-fri .... allude
es-jzu .... refer
czû-fri .... allege
dlû-zvê .... suggest, propose
dluô-fri .... hint
ôv.lu .... exaggerate
nôh.lu .... summarize
rua-hpu .... translate
fcô-jzi .... demonstrate
bûuj-jzu .... sign (expressing meaning)
mro .... write
blop.mro .... handwriting
kêu-mro .... sign (name)
hpu-mro .... transliterate
sfo .... record
thaid-sfo .... tabulate
jloi-jzu .... mark well, *nota bene* (N.B.)
sci-sfo .... account
coet-liôl .... budget
srû .... read
ûp-srû .... recite
mro-roiz .... dictate
cua-siab .... pronounce
mau-srû .... spell
srû-bûuj .... literate

<u>pre</u> ... habituate
ûp-pre ... custom
lva-rêh ... fashion
<u>cfe</u> ... skill
fe-cfe ... expert
jroi ... unskilled
<u>cri</u> ... try
csû-cri ... experiment
jzi, ûp-cri ... test
fe-cri ... strive, struggle
<u>kri</u> ... can
<u>tro</u> ... cannot
pso.pa ... success and failure
<u>pso</u> ... succeed (opposite of to fail)
pa.pso ... fail
<u>prû</u> ... mistake
ên.prû ... blunder
nad.lu ... redress
shu ... recover (return to former condition)
fôb-zku ... make the best of
<u>csû</u> ... manage
fiem-csû ... check
csû-zfê ... organize
phuê-tbo ... arrange
<u>spe</u> ... to play
fe-ruap ... recreation
fiôf-moês ... hide-and-seek
pa.spe ... serious, earnest
<u>sci</u> ... count
<u>rti</u> ... measure
rti ... weigh
<u>sto</u> ... own

sjie.lu ... share

zla-pom ... partake

sko ... need

rpû ... get

lrai.rpû ... recover (get back)

moês, moês.rpû ... find

pa.rpû ... miss

stû ... let go

stû ... pour

cvo, zgu-za ... eject, expel

cze-stû ... throw

fiôp, cze-fiôp ... shoot

nê.cze-fiôp ... fusillade

pci ... gain

lrai.pci ... regain

jzu-côh-pci ... privilege

cto ... lose

meuh ... pick, pluck

feur ... gather

feur ... heap, amass

jzu.plia.lu ... classify

pa.fêz.lu ... complicate

ztê-zfê ... entangle

czûb-zfê ... knot

beûl, plo-ztê ... confuse

mac-jza ... dishevel

pa.pûuk ... unravel

riam ... carry

jlec.riam ... carry in arms

plêm.riam ... carry by vehicle

stô, stô-czû ... support, prop

vrê-rpû ... bring

<u>seêm</u> .... keep
mul-seêm .... maintain
sku, seêm-sku .... watch, guard
seêm-czû .... reserve
seêm, tbo-seêm .... save
czû-tbo .... deposit, pledge
êz.seêm .... avoid
stû .... escape
<u>fiôf</u> .... hide
sku .... screen
fiôf, fiôf-nûh .... secret
beûl-sûig .... riddle
<u>moês</u> .... seek
flêl-cri .... research
moês-bûuj .... explore
bruf-moês .... prospect (for minerals)
jzu-rpû .... aim
moês .... hunt
rpû-piûj .... solve
<u>rûus</u> .... choose
fe-rûus .... prefer
<u>ciam</u> .... use
fe-ciam .... function
rud-ciam .... abuse, misuse
bzê-ciam .... exhaust
<u>kiuf</u> .... waste
khe .... spoil
rze-fûl .... frustrate
<u>piôs</u> .... prepare
piôs-bzê .... ready
liôl .... policy
liôl-rnê .... design

hsa-paz .... adjust
ûp.lu .... assimilate
hpu-fôb .... reform
gsô .... establish
lfe, nriô-lfe .... determine
sôp-gûin .... guarantee
<u>fiem</u> .... compare
fe-gûin .... tally, match
rôef-gûin .... consistent
ûp-fiem .... analogy
moês .... investigate
vluar-rti .... examine carefully in detail
jzu-hne .... inspect
chêô-sûig-jbe .... scrutinise
sag-jbe .... estimate
jbe-siut .... censor
<u>rûif</u> .... adopt
msê .... substitute
<u>fois</u> .... light or set fire
grêl-muir .... quench
ual-htê .... ventilate
ual-jza .... inflate
ual-csû .... air-conditioning
tin .... clink
tôk .... rap
mi-rial .... clap
kôn .... bang (sound of door)
tik .... tick
rin .... ring
<u>kiûr</u> .... wash
kiûr .... purify
toif-kiûr .... scour

creu.kiûr .... rinse
<u>piem</u> .... dwell
vam.piem .... sojourn
hpu-piem .... move house
gzauf-za .... exile
<u>toif</u> .... rub
jloi-toif .... scrape
êz-toif .... wipe
rial-hsa .... sweep
toif-griu .... polish
toif-tbo .... smear
<u>fiôp</u> .... prick
ên.fiôp .... stab
poc-zku .... pierce, bore
<u>siut</u> .... cut
u.siut .... notch
nru-siut .... chop
chûp-siut .... mince, chop
rial-siut .... hew
sjie-siut .... slit
dêl-siut .... slice
sjie-siut .... dissect
fjûb-siut .... mow
fe-siut .... crop
sgêûn-siut .... clip
jav-siut .... trim
siut-jav .... prune
toif-siut .... shave
siut, siut.zku .... carve
nêz-siut .... engrave
<u>pûuk</u> .... sew
fe-pûuk .... stitch

thaid-zfê .... knit
czuûb-zku .... spin
sdôus-zku .... weave
zgu-fzê .... weld
roic .... wear
hpu-fcô .... disguise
coet .... spend
rpû-suêt .... cost
cofse .... cost of living
kiuf-coet .... prodigal
coet-siut .... retrench

III. Mental Action

1. Sensation and Thought

vle .... sensation
vle, sdû-bûuj .... conscious
pa.vle .... swoon, faint
cto-vle .... paralyse
hne .... see
ên.hne .... gaze, stare
u.hne .... glimpse
az.hne .... glance
fiôf-hne .... peep
glif-drô .... ogle
vlic-hne .... retrospect
êh-hne .... foresee
hne-bûuj .... witness
glif-troi .... eyesight
cto-hne .... blind

hli .... hear

dluô-hli .... overhear, eavesdrop

beo-troi .... hearing

cto-hli .... deaf

nlo .... smell

hvo .... taste

hvo-nriô .... fastidious

vlû .... feel (physically)

grê-vlû .... numb

zle .... touch

zle-lto .... tickle

zle-hsa .... grope

gle .... pleasure

stui-gle .... luxury

ruap, zu.gle .... amuse

gle-kiuf .... dissipated

bli .... pain

bli .... suffer

chaêv-bli .... torture

zhi .... thrill

vlû-fiôp .... tingle

car.zri .... lust

stû-spe .... wanton

car-vza .... chaste

uem.zri .... appetite

uem-jro .... greedy

jlo .... hunger

uem-hse .... famine

vlaul-jlo .... thirst

mjê-znû .... genius

pan-kri .... talent

kul-dlû .... common sense

kri ..... ability
jza-znû ..... versatile
vlil-fal ..... idiosyncrasy
dlû ..... think
nzo-dlû ..... deliberate
dlû-ciam ..... consider
nriô-dlû ..... contemplate
dlû-fcô ..... theorize
dlû-gsô ..... obsess
jbe-lgi ..... opinion
guz ..... point of view
hjuez, nzo-hsa ..... motive
znû ..... wise
lil ..... intelligent
fôb-dlû ..... sensible, judicious
glu-znû ..... clever
vêg-znû ..... cunning
ceûl-znû ..... wit
lbe ..... foolish
bûuj-hzi ..... intuition
hzi ..... instinct
lgi ..... believe
lgi, fe-lgi ..... trust
hzi-lgi ..... faith
lbu-lgi ..... convince
suz.lgi ..... credulous
vrih-lgi ..... tradition
nûh-lgi ..... superstition
êh-dlû ..... prejudice
niav ..... suspect
nzo ..... reason
nzo-rpû ..... deduce, infer

vle-nzo	induction
pa.nzo	absurd
vzû	understand
kri.vzû	understanding
fiôv-bûuj	suddenly realize
jloi	quick to understand
vsud-maûs	receptive (to ideas)
vsud-zvê	presence of mind
jbe	to judge
jbe-fri	criticize
vzû-jci	appreciate
jbe-sfu	approve
fe-trê	condemn
jom	captious
moês-trê	find fault
jzi	prove
jbe-gsô	decide
paz-fôb	upright
pa.gbo	honest
gbo	deceive
roiz-gbo	lie
spe-gbo	hoax
jzû	mad
aot-jzû	drunk
liôl	plan
pa.liôl	haphazard
lgi-raz	confident
nriô-lfe	obstinate
kôz-troi	perverse
czo-dlû	suppose
heun	guess
niav	doubt

flêl-niav ... sceptical
vûil ... imagine
vûil-mêj ... romantic
gbo-hne ... hallucinate
niûh ... dream
jeûp-niûh ... nightmare
lien ... remember
pa.lien ... forget
nion ... recognise
hpu-dlû ... caprice, whim
vsud-hsa ... impulse
beûl ... perplex
lto-beûl ... bother
rseut-lto ... fuss
beûl-lto ... disturb
gûin ... agree
cim-gûin ... unanimous
gûin ... promise
giêf-gûin ... vow
rev-rev ... compromise
gûin-glu ... comply, conform
jiaz ... learn
frê-bûuj ... experience
bûuj ... know
cim.bûuj ... omniscient
êh-piôs ... anticipate
liûz ... don’t know
lil-czu ... culture
jiaz-zêu ... learned

2. Will and Emotion

lfe	will
lfe-zri	willing
vlil.lfe	voluntary
fem-lfe	rather
lfe.pa	*nolens volens*, without any choice
ib	purpose, aim
vsud-raz	resolute
zrôp	firm
stû-jain	relax
fois, hêun-lbu	inspire
hêun-hsa	encourage
hse	want
maûs-czo	accept
zri.vlô	would-be
gsô-hfo	peremptory
vri	do not want
vri-stû	renounce, give up
pa.hse	refuse, reject
lro	may
hfo	must
paz.hfo	ought, should
glu-hfo	duty, obligation
nrû	obey
vsud-fal	character, disposition
vsud-mul	temper
sraô-drû	scruple
bre	emotion
bre-mul	mood
leg, ên.bre	passion
dêl	sensitive

zal .... insensitive
<u>zri</u> .... wish
jlo .... yearn
kôz-hse .... covet
stû .... indulge
chauk-jro .... avaricious
coet-bli .... miserly
mru .... incline
mru-hsa .... bias, tendency
tû-jbe .... partial
mru-seêm .... conservative
<u>jfi</u> .... hope
jfi-hrô .... optimistic
jfi-sma .... expect
<u>jro</u> .... eager
jro .... enthusiastic
bûuj-jro .... curious, inquisitive
pa.jro .... reluctant
pa.jro .... dispirit
jêh, pso-hse .... ambitious
<u>zmo</u> .... contented
fe-zmo .... satisfy
<u>drû</u> .... care (anxiety)
bûuj-drû .... careful, heedful
drû-znû .... prudent
jeûp-drû .... cautious
niav-drû .... beware
fiôv-glu .... rash
vsud-stû .... reckless
liûz-drû .... careless
<u>zsû</u> .... happy
vliê-zsû .... merry

spe-gle .... fun
pso-zsû .... triumph
u.zsû .... comfortable
vce .... sad
roic-vce .... mourn
trê-bli .... remorse
vce-kôz .... repent
bre-kôz .... regret
pa.hpi .... excited
hpi .... calm
hpi-zlu .... patient
lto .... trouble
mloû-lto .... harass
lkû .... shame
u.lkû .... shy
car.lkû .... shame concerning sexual matters
zpe .... selfish
pci-mru .... interest
vsud-srô .... attention
gziûl-gzô .... devote
mi-bre .... sympathy
bke .... indifferent
fe-bke .... ignore
bke-stû .... neglect
bhon .... sociable
za-rêh .... aloof
jci .... love
ên.jci .... adore
lbe.jci .... dote
u.jci .... like
jci.stô .... helpful
cun-cab.jci .... idealism (devotion to ideals)

gzauf-jci .... patriotic
car.jci .... sexual love
nrûn.zrel.jci .... parental love
zlog.jzez.jci .... filial love
zto .... hate
ên.zto .... loathe, disgust
zkû .... kind
lûr .... benevolent
cuem-fôb .... well-meaning
zri-fôb .... bless
cuem-zkû .... generous
fe-zkû .... charity
zoc.lu .... relent
iûr .... brutal
hem .... malicious
zri-rud .... curse
tle-cêôm .... aggressive
nriô-zpe .... callous
nriô .... unfeeling, harsh
lûur .... gentle
zoc-zkû .... lenient
cua-lûur .... polite
nriô-lûk .... severe, grim
troi-fria .... strict
nriô .... stern, austere
oic .... fierce
not .... vehement
kôz-nriô .... cantankerous
roiz-jroi .... rude
nriô-nru .... brusque
iep .... surly
hiêm .... just (equitable)

viaf .... conceited

viaf-rêh .... proud

pa.viaf .... humble, modest

thuû .... submissive

nius .... surprise

nius, nius-dlû .... wonder

lgi-kuv .... loyal, faithful

biôm .... admire

rpê-biôm .... flatter

giêf .... worship, (revere)

fe-biôm .... honour, respect

grib-zkû .... favour

creu.lu .... hold in slight regard

viûr .... pity

hiôp .... angry

ên.hiôp .... fury

nos .... acrimonious

dlû-khe .... resent

u.hiôp .... annoy

bre-cru .... grateful

tsu-stû .... forgive, pardon

diuk .... revenge

jeûp .... fear

jeûp-nius .... startle

hzô-jeûp .... alarm

jeûp.blê .... brave

pa.jeûp .... dare

giûk .... jealous

ûp-giûk .... envy

IV. Social Action

1. Work

sla	work
ên.sla	toil
lie-sla	labour
zgu-sla	forced labour
u.sla	light work
sla	occupation
fe-sla	job, post
kûz-rze	masterpiece
sla, sla-lbu	operate
zfê-stô	cooperate
czo-glu	undertake
lbu	fulfil
sla-liôl	project
jzu-sla	enterprise
zfê-glu	enlist, enrol
czû-sla	occupy office or post
sla-vrê	career
siut-stû	retire
sla-stû	resign
plia-grê	strike (labour)
bef	tensely active
so.sla	busy
jloi	energetic
pa.sla	rest
sê.sla	idle
pa.mlê	diligent
mlê	lazy
gle-glu	hobby

eiz.lu .... serve
mjê .... create
ûp-mro .... compose
feur-mro .... compile
mro-piôs .... edit
jzu-mro .... print
mcu-mro .... copy
jza-rza .... publish
jza-rza-paz .... copyright
rnê .... draw or paint
rnê-fri .... illustrate
hpu-ûp .... caricature
nêz-fcô .... graph
jav-rnê .... outline, draft
fcô-ûp-kuv .... perspective
flô .... play music
plaul-zku .... sculpture
ckô-moês .... detect crime
rlu .... teach
rlu-roiz .... lecture
plal-roiz .... sermon
uûk-csû .... treat (medically)
shu .... cure
shu-fri .... prescribe
drû-sku .... nurse
rze-sma .... midwifery
tla .... act (in theatrical performance)
thô-tla .... work as actor professionally
plê .... sing
chê .... dance
klô .... magic
cfe-nru .... legerdemain

pca-csû — pilot
vlaul-riam — ferry
sla-hsa — drive, steer
clu-rze — industry (economic activity)
czaf-zku — manufacture
thô — business
kus-clu — monopoly
chauk-nuap — bankrupt
clu — trade
khu — buy
pci-khu — bargain
rza — sell
ên.rza — wholesale
u.rza — retail
lô-rza — undersell
rial-rza — auction
rza-seêm — stock (keep goods)
krauf-kiûr — launder
mjê — invent
sgô — engineering
vluar-rti — survey
sdu — build
zvôt-gsô — gild
czu — till (cultivate)
snil-tbo — sow
siut-czo — reap
chûp-feur — harvest
pauh — dig
czuûb-rpû — angle (for fish)
sla-jza — ferment
rôûn — to cook
nuah-rôûn — roast

gai.rôûn .... fry
uêj.rôûn .... steam
lkô-daul .... stew
due-seêm .... pickle
pa.rôûn .... raw

2. Actions Toward People

rêh.lu .... behave
ruap .... treat (behave towards)
vzû-csû .... tact
jêh-zkû .... condescend
glu-nion .... salute
pleuf-vêg .... cringe
zsû-maûs .... welcome
cab-giêf .... ceremony
coet-fcô .... pomp
vuêl-jzu .... celebrate
cietûem .... funeral
<u>sma</u> .... wait
<u>frê</u> .... meet
vrê-hne .... visit
plia-mru .... gregarious
gle-feur .... social gathering
frê-sûig .... interview
zvê, czo-bûuj .... introduce
sû-cuem .... contribute
mi-liôl .... conspire
za.lu .... dismiss
sûig-jbe .... examine (by questioning)
kêu-rûus .... nominate
ril-rûus .... vote

lên-rûus .... elect
rûus-zku .... appoint
msê .... deputize
tla .... act in lieu
srô .... involve
es-ztê .... interfere
mru .... attract
klô-mru .... glamorous
lên-bûuj .... advertise
zvê-fôb .... recommend
biôm-lbu-zgu .... prestige
sfu .... allow
fri-zla .... acknowledge
sto .... admit
cuem-bûuj .... inform
pra-hse .... require
pra .... request
nriô-pra .... demand
fri-sto .... claim
moês-sûig .... apply
stô-roiz .... plead
ûp-hpi .... soothe
mru-pra .... cajole, coax
hzô-lgi .... persuade
mru .... tempt
jfi-cri .... entice
glu-ceud .... provoke
fois .... incite
sdû .... rouse
toif .... tease
csa .... advise
zgu-csa .... urge

zgu-pra	command
mloû-tbo	inculcate
csa-rlu	preach
csa-sûig	consult
zu.jeûp	scare
csa-pra	warn
fri-khe	threaten
fri-vza	forbid, prohibit
fri-biôm	compliment
fri-zsu	congratulate
fcô-biôm	applaud
bef	sarcastic
trê	blame
fri-vce	complain
poc-suêf	cavil
trê-fri	accuse
hiôp-lto	offend
ceûl-spe	mock, ridicule
fri-rud	insult
roiz-liôl	negotiate
zu.gûin	reconcile
rial-pfê	fight
rôef.rial-pfê	fight one another
pfê	quarrel
moês-jci	woo
krô	beg
ên.krô	implore
mro-pra	petition
krô, bre-sûig	appeal
giêf-krô	pray
giêf-cuem	sacrifice
cru	thank

tsu ... excuse
fri-kôz ... apologize
sca ... message
pruv.lu ... correspond
cûg-fri ... report
roiz-htê ... frank, blunt
rpê ... pretend
vêg-cfe ... trick
gbo-liôl ... wile
gbo-mru ... seduce
drûd-cuem ... betray
fcô ... show
fe-fcô ... indicate
mru-fcô ... pageant, spectacle
fcô-vuêl ... ostentatious
fcô-glu ... stunt
mloû.lu ... pool (re resources)
stô ... help
lô-stô ... subserve
sôp.lu ... rescue
sôp.seêm ... preserve
ciam ... benefit
pci-cuem ... avail
stô-tliô ... accessory
czûa-stô ... relieve
piem, stô-sko ... rely, depend
mcu ... imitate
sku ... protect
jci-sku ... cherish
drû-cûg ... foster
stô-zca ... nourish
zfê-vrê ... escort, see off

pca	to lead
pue-pca	guide
phuê-tpê	discipline
tpê	govern
tpê-stû	abdicate
chêb-czû	arrest
jbe	trial (in court)
chêb-moês	sue
chêb-siut	outlaw
gzauf-zgu	banish
zvê-tbo	bail
chauk-bli	fine (impose money penalty)
plaz.lu	nationalize
plaz-czo	confiscate
zfê	attach
zgu-czû	usurp
prel-hpu	revolutionize
nriô-suêf	revolt
tpê-suêf	rebel
lto-suêf	riot
ckô	crime
ckô-jzu	guilty
trê-bli-cto	forfeit
gaif-trê	acquit
faur	prevent
ûp-grê	curfew (restriction)
grê-siab	gag
ruam	compete
jzi-ruam	argue
czû-ruam	wrestle
rial-liôl	stratagem
cêôm-sma	ambush

nûh-zvê .... spy
<u>suêf</u> .... oppose
fe-suêf .... resist
fri-suêf .... protest
vlic.zgu .... repulse
ceud-puêr .... challenge
lô.lu .... submit
mêus-gûin .... engage (re marriage)
<u>mêus</u> .... marry
pa.mêus .... divorce
car.lu .... sexual intercourse
car-môip .... adultery
car-zgu .... rape
car-cûg .... heterosexual
car-tis .... homosexual
ceud-piôs .... mobilise
<u>puêr</u> .... war
nu-gzauf puêr .... civil war
<u>cêôm</u> .... attack
fe-cêôm .... invade
zto-lto .... persecute
nius.cêôm .... surprise attack
cêôm-lkô .... siege
jzêl-cêôm .... raid
ôv-hsa .... encroach
kôz-hrô .... trespass
ûp-khe .... injure, harm
zgu-bauz .... oppress
trê-bli .... punish
rud-jzu .... stigma
bhon-siut .... ostracize
kêu.rud.lu .... libel

sku .... defend
gzauf-nu .... immigrate, import
gzauf-za .... emigrate, export
puaf .... conquer
druin.lu .... overwhelm
lô-tbo .... subdue
gsô-lkô .... repress
kut-gsô .... oblige
grê-seêm .... detain
tpê .... control
cuem-cto .... surrender
tuês .... prey
zgu-czo .... kidnap
muir .... kill
hia-muir .... homicide
ôuv-muir .... massacre
sraô-muir .... murder
fien-gaif .... strangle
jbe-muir .... execute
vlil.muir .... suicide
ôuv-khe .... outrage
lkû-jlô .... scandal
sêûm .... bury
tliô-zfê .... federate
grib-zfê .... ally
rôef .... exchange
maûs .... receive
cuem .... give
sjie-cuem .... distribute
piôs-cuem .... offer
za-cuem .... issue
fe-stû .... deliver

tbo-cuem.. commit
fe-frê-cuem..equip
frê-cuem.. supply
lrai.cuem .... give back
gzô-cuem.. bequeath
rpû-gzô.. inherit
kôof..send
tuûs ....invite
ruap ....entertain
ruap, zu.gle..amuse
jraim-ruap .... picnic
stû-ruap..pamper
roiz-jziû..bore
rpû, chauk.pci ....earn
suêt .... pay
sû-suêt.. subscribe
lrai.suêt ....requite
lpa-suêt .... compensate
suêt-ciam.. hire, rent
tuês-suêt.. ransom
sla-ciam.. employ
suêt, sla-suêt .... salary, wages
cuem-ruap..reward, give prize
pa.suêt.. owe
pauk..loan
êz.pauk.. borrow
hôi-pauk.. pawn
ud.pauk..lend
saic .... gamble
ûp-saic..bet
czo-saic.. lottery
môip ....steal

vrôih-môip ... pirate
cuit ... tax
clu-cuit ... duty
vluar-sjie ... agrarian
zku-raz ... insure
chauk-csû ... bribe

Nouns

I. Universe

1. Non-Material Objects

lua ... The First Cause
vaê ... universe
pan.blêh ... nature
nuê ... space
fûl-hue-nuê ... vacuum
czo-nuê ... space taken
nuap-nuê ... interval (of space)
gu, gu.jô ... distance
vuô ... place
az.vuô ... locality
ual ... environment
pan.thêt ... habitat
jroz.uô ... neighbourhood
ô.ud ... destination
ûuc ... refuge
jci-vuô ... resort
glaif ... abandoned place
jzuis ... scene

vrôih .... continuous expanse

poc, poc.uô .... hole

czû-poc .... socket

zfê.uô .... joint, junction

vrer, nu.vrê.uô .... entrance

za.vrê.uô .... exit

hau .... assumed world

zsû-hau .... heaven

bli-hau .... hell

vêu .... time

do .... period

gsô-vêu .... term

nuap-vêu .... interval (of time)

ba-vêu .... interim

czo-vêu .... time taken

az.vêu .... instant, moment

hlan .... date

gas.vê .... futurity

gu.gas.vê .... distant future

nôf.has .... age

draz.vê .... lifetime

heu.vê .... boyhood

fruc.vê .... school time

vliêc.vê .... reign

nôu .... daytime

êh nôu.ba .... *ante meridiem*, a.m.

zôa .... morning

zma.zôa .... dawn

nôu.ba .... noon

al nôu.ba .... *post meridiem*, p.m.

bua .... afternoon

guê .... night

dau .... yesterday
dau.guê .... last night
jêu .... today
jêu.guê .... tonight
nlôl .... tomorrow
nlôl.guê .... next night
lô.pom.vlul .... second (of time)
hê.pom.vlul .... minute (of time)
vlul .... hour
hlan .... day
ghal-jzu .... anniversary
mac-hlan .... holiday
jzu-hlan .... festival
tid.hlan .... daily
vnên-jluz .... week
hlan-a .... Monday
vnên .... month
hnuv .... season
rie.vê .... fruit season
hnuv-a .... spring
hnuv-e .... summer
hnuv-ê .... autumn
hnuv-i .... winter
ghal .... year
zma.ghal .... New Year
tid.ghal .... annual
tid.cel.ghal .... biennial
mij.ghal.ia .... century
vêu-slôn .... cycle
ghal-nêz .... era
blêh .... any object or thing
ar .... anything

fleu.blêh .... something
fûl.blêh .... nothing
vle.blêh .... phenomenon
pêa .... feature, characteristic
zoû .... aspect
zoû-hev .... complexion
zfê-blêh .... associated thing
ztê-jzab .... mixture
priêk .... any irritating thing
ne cûg .... and the rest, etc.
kuv.blêh .... fact
dlû-vlil .... subject
dlû-blêh .... object (antonym of of subject)
lif.nos .... fortune and misfortune
tluat .... protecting thing
fjûb-chiûs .... secret danger
lbu-blêh .... means
cêi .... means of solving a difficulty
sgon .... main part
lai .... component
pêa .... subsidiary device
jzu-blêh .... target
mi-jlô .... circumstances
vo-nriô .... dilemma
hsa-glu .... incentive
hôj .... surface
gûi .... top
jrot .... bottom
<u>zlôn</u> .... abstract object
ûp-blêh .... image
kêu .... reputation
rnû-jzu .... symptom

ô.jlô	event
jlô	affair
phuê, jlô-nêz	process
ô.êz	origin
pca-laz	clue
pci	sake, behalf
mi	company (presence in association)
coôl.eu	step (in walking)
glun	sky
grêun-czuûb	rainbow
glun-aiz-nêz	horizon
glun-mul	climate
ual-mul	weather
huûl-zgu	radiation
vzôn	electricity
jzêl	thunder or lightning
hmav	light
nê.hmav	ray
dê-hmav	X-ray
ôv-hmav	twilight
hmav-cto	eclipse
hev.ia	spectrum
aiz-laz	pole
aiz-ba-jaz	equator
lên-aiz-nêz	latitude
val-aiz-nêz	longitude
grêl	fire
not.lûk	heat
not.lûk	temperature
brôn	smoke
vlub	sound
vliê-lto	clamour

lrai-vlub .... echo
jluz .... real thing
vaê.jluz .... noumenon
jzab .... substance
thin-faê .... grain (of wood)
hrôz .... assumed thing
gbo-thôuh .... mirage
iêt-hrôz .... phoenix
chiûs-hrôz .... dragon
zên-hrôz .... monster
vsud .... mind
suô .... faculty (bodily or mental)
vsud.suô .... mental faculty
ô.dlû .... idea
suô.lien .... memory
suô.vûil .... imagination (faculty)
glu.vûil .... imagination (act)
ceûl-suô .... sense of humour
suô.kut .... conscience
hue.suô .... sense (faculty)
suô.nlo .... smell (sense)
ô.nlo .... smell (odour)
draz .... life
htug .... assumed person
tpê-htug .... god
kut-htug .... angel
sraô-htug .... devil
vsud-htug .... spirit
mli-htug .... ghost
ûp-vsud .... soul
klô-htug .... fairy
jêh-htug .... giant

jeûp-htug .... ogre
oic-flier-htug .... werewolf

2. Matter

hue .... matter
ba-jzab .... nucleus
jain-hue .... scum
nuah-hue .... fuel
grêl-gzô .... embers
grêl-chûp .... spark
lai .... element (chemical)
creu-luû .... helium
leg-luû .... neon
hiz-hmav .... sodium
zel-nuah .... magnesium
creu-glup .... aluminium
buû-jluz .... silicon
nûh-hmav .... phosphorus
zoc-glup .... potassium
jzêm-lai .... calcium
tuz-glup .... chromium
nriô-suz-nuap .... manganese
dûn-uêr-lai .... cobalt
ûp-jzêk .... nickel
fluam-lai .... arsenic
leg-due .... bromine
suz-nuap-lai .... antimony
leg-dûn-lai .... iodine
jêh-luav-laz .... tungsten
sag-fria .... platinum
hêun-jzêk .... mercury

zel-dêl-glup .... bismuth
vlil-nuap-lai .... radium
fria-lai .... uranium
zfê-hue .... compound (chemical)
sujôj .... alkali
jôzue .... salt (ionic compound)
racip .... hydrocarbon
zûfue .... chloride
cerahi .... sulphuretted hydrogen
lûporazû .... sal ammoniac
haracikoje .... sodium bicarbonate
cehacikoje .... sodium carbonate
hajera .... sodium hydroxide
zahipoje .... magnesium sulphate
zucuhijef .... alum
buceje .... silica
zulûkoje .... saltpetre
rôhipoje .... copperas (ferrous sulphate)
vêi .... atom
hue-laz .... molecule
hôi .... concrete object
dlos .... protuberance, knob
gzô.ôi .... remains
jain-jzu .... buoy
nio .... covering
za.ôi .... wrapper
rze.ôi .... product
cgi.ôi .... seat
poc.czû.ôi .... sheath
czû.ôi .... thing held
czû.ôi .... contents
sto.ôi .... property, assets

riam.ôi .... load

kiuf.ôi .... refuse, rubbish

hne.ôi .... sight

lien.ôi .... souvenir

rseut .... nuisance

clu.ôi .... goods

fe-faur.ôi .... obstacle

ruam.ôi .... prize

cuem.ôi .... gift

seêm.cuem.ôi .... keepsake

hkaip .... source of supply

pa.suêt.ôi .... debt, liability

môip.ôi .... stolen goods

puêr-tuês .... booty

nui .... lifeless object

dêl-nio .... film

aif .... powder

nê.nui .... bar, rod

jaz, sik-jaz .... disk

poc-jaz .... ring, hoop

bôz-gsô .... band (flat strip)

vlêô.ôi .... ball

hvau.ôi .... cylinder

jom.ôi .... acid

sag.ôi .... treasure

chui.ôi .... dirt

stui.ôi .... wealth

luû .... gas

rud-za-fien .... miasma

muir-luû .... poison gas

creu-lai .... hydrogen

ual-luû .... nitrogen

jae .... oxygen
sû-jae .... ozone
zov-luû .... chlorine
cipora .... methane
lûkora .... ammonia
ciceje .... carbon dioxide
due .... liquid substance
poc-due .... bubble
ceraceje .... hydrogen peroxide
picikerajera .... carbolic acid
ceracikoje .... carbonic acid
ralûkoje .... nitric acid
cerahipoje .... sulphuric acid
cirakozû .... chloroform
razû .... hydrocholic acid
gai .... oil
raciz .... petroleum
raciz-jluz .... kerosene
hsa-gai .... petrol
rêv.bôi .... gel
fleu.rev.bôi .... clot
bih-jzêm .... asphalt
bôi .... solid substance
chûn-lai .... carbon
bih-brat .... blacklead
hiz-lai .... sulphur
focitera .... naphthalene
jui .... stone
oi.jui .... rock
buû .... sand
vlêr .... dust
az.vlêr .... mote

<u>lhôm</u> .... earth or soil
sû-lhôm .... loam
lhôm-uem .... manure, fertilizer
<u>blaf</u> .... mud
vlaul-hue .... sediment
<u>jhus</u> .... clay
jhus-zrôp .... ochre
zrôp-jui .... granite
jzêm.jui .... limestone
blaiv-jzêm .... chalk
griu-jzêm-jui .... marble
<u>jzêm</u> .... lime
<u>hmaf</u> .... slate
<u>zrar</u> .... jewel (precious stone)
<u>jsôm</u> .... diamond
iuv-zrar .... opal
dûn-zrar .... sapphire
leg-dûn-zrar .... amethyst
rsûh-zrar .... emerald
zov-sfuom-jui .... jade
leg-zrar .... ruby
<u>bruf</u> .... mineral
glup-bruf .... ore
lil-buv-jui .... crystal
buû-bruf .... quartz
<u>drês</u> .... tin
drês-brat .... pewter
<u>blac</u> .... salt (sodium chloride)
<u>glup</u> .... metal
nê.glup .... wire
ztê-glup .... alloy
glup-jzêm .... solder

zvôt	gold
jzêk	silver
vmac	copper
vmac-drês	bronze
vmac-vtuk	brass
zrôp	iron
vlôi-zrôp	magnet
zrôp-zca	rust
zoc-zrôp	wrought iron
troi-zrôp	steel
nriô-zrôp	cast iron
brat	lead (the metal)
vtuk	zinc

3. Air and Water

ual	air
fien-ual	breath
dak-ual	whiff
êun	wind (moving air)
ôuv	storm
a.êun	breeze
uêj	steam
vlaul	water
ual-vlaul	foam
bluên	ice
blêa-bluên	icicle
jrual	cloud
vluar-jrual	mist
grêun	rain
a.grêun	drizzle
blaiv-grêun	sleet

blaiv .... snow
bluê-grêun .... hail
guê-vlaul .... dew
guê-bluên .... frost
vrôih .... sea
nu-za-vlaul .... tide
oi.vrôih .... ocean
vrer-vrôih .... bay
jlec-vrôih .... gulf
brik-vrôih .... cove
brem-vrôih .... strait
brail .... river
hjuez .... source (of river)
hia.zku.brail .... canal
vlaul-pue .... channel
soun-vlaul .... current
troi-hêun .... torrent
fiôv-brail .... waterfall
druin .... flood
jruûn .... lake
grôiv .... pool, pond
a.grôiv .... puddle
hjuez .... spring (water)
cze-hjuez .... geyser
vraid .... well (water)
vlaul.uô .... reservoir

4. Land

êol-jrual .... nebula
êol-brail .... Milky Way
êol.ia .... constellation

fi.êol .... heavenly body
êol .... star
euf-êol .... comet
hêun-êol .... meteor
ueh .... sun
hsa.êol .... planet
mi-hsa-êol .... satellite
ôin .... moon
vêg.ôin .... crescent
aiz .... earth (the planet)
uûd .... world
vluar .... land
kiuf.vluar .... wasteland
brail.dluô.vluar .... bank (river)
brail.vluar .... river bed
vluar-siut .... trench
vluar-poc .... pit
sma-pco .... pitfall
vluar-pêa .... topography
not-jaz .... tropics
jluêm .... region
oi.jluêm .... continent
gzauf .... country
oi.gzauf .... empire
lruic-gzauf .... colony
sgon-vluar .... mainland
nu-vluar .... inland
vrôih.dluô.vluar .... shore
jô-nrôus .... peninsula
vluar-laz .... cape
brem-vluar .... isthmus
nrôus.ia .... archipelago

nrôus .... island
vlair .... hill
nad-vlair .... cliff
ôv-fiûl-nêz .... ridge
vlair-laz .... peak
pa.vlair .... valley
vluar-vrer .... cave
grêl-vlair .... volcano
luav-jui .... lava
poc-luav-jui .... pumice
a.vlair .... mound
ôv-fiûl-blêh .... hump
bluim .... plain (level tract of land)
htê-hôj .... open space
jêh-bluim .... plateau
glaif .... desert
glaif-druap .... oasis
jzuis .... landscape
vlic-vluar .... background
jraim .... countryside
druap .... field
rkec.druap .... rice field
due-vluar .... swamp
grêut .... forest
tûu-uô .... wood (wooded country)
lruic .... plantation
rie.lruic .... orchard
hkaip .... mine (of minerals)

II. Life

1. Uneatable Plant Life

sia........living thing
sia.ia........species
ciam.sia........parasite
sia.czuûb........fibre
reu........extinct thing
gzô-reu........fossil
piô........any vegetable life
zca-lô........undergrowth
tûu.ia........grove
tûu-trêf........hedge
tûu........tree or plant
hê.tûu........tree
lô.tûu........plant
thin-tûu........shrub
snil........seed
rvoh........thorn
phûl........juice
phûl-jluz........resin
hiz-phûl-jluz........amber
jhus-phûl........gum
kson-gai........turpentine
flûgêt........camphor
tûu.nio........bark
bef-nio........cinnamon
ûp-bef-nio........cassia
thin........wood
lub.thin........block of wood
hôj.thin........board, plank

dêl-thin	veneer
dêl-thin	lath
nê.thin	stick, pole
az.thin	splinter
thin-vlêr	sawdust
grêl-thin	firewood
ûp-chûn	charcoal
lûr-thin	sandalwood
chûn-thin	ebony
chûn	coal
chûn-jluz	tar
khov	ashes
ûp-khov	soot
sgon	trunk
sgon-gzô	stump
rseut-sgon	stalk, stem
hsa-sgon	cane
nu-lifûe	pith, marrow
czil	branch
rseut-czil	twig
peôn-voi	tendril
rsûh	leaf
prel	root
plif-prel	beetroot
bef-prel	ginger
svaup-rsûh	palm tree
kiuv-tûu	creeper
kson	pine (tree)
jui-tûu	teak
zrôp-tûu	oak
prel-czil	banyan
blaf-tûu	mangrove

czuûb-tûu .... hemp
smuas. tûu .... flax
truar-tûu .... mulberry
krev .... bamboo
krev-zma-zca .... bamboo shoot
val-sgon-tûu .... rattan
plif-krev .... sugarcane
pler.tûu .... vine
lûr.lrim .... mint
bef-lûr .... peppermint (plant)
fiôp-tûu .... nettle
kruod-tûu .... thistle
rvoh-thin-tûu .... bramble
nos-tûu .... wormwood
rze-leg .... madder
vlaul-sgon .... cactus
huûl-tûu .... willow
thuas-tûu .... poppy
jain-rhez .... lotus
spol.ia .... bouquet
spol-jaz .... garland
spol .... flower
vam-zca .... bud
spol.eu .... petal
spol-kôr .... stamen
spol-pêm .... pistil
spol-hiz .... saffron
spol-kraug .... calyx
spol-kraug.eu .... sepal
rhez .... lily
zvôt-spol .... chrysanthemum
vlêô-mêj-spol .... peony

pliz	rose
sfuom-vlêô-spol	hydrangea
fi.fjûb	herb
pleuf-fjûb	weed
fjûb	grass
siut-fjûb	hay
ûp-fjûb	rush
vlaul-fjûb	reed
rmed	moss
vlêr-rmed	mould
sla-piô	yeast

2. Eatable Plant Life

flo-jzab	vitamin
chûp-hue	starch
rie	fruit
rie-nio	peel
rie-zoc	pulp
rie-pom	segment of fruit
foi	nut
foi-vliêl	kernel
lûr-foi	nutmeg
rûo	coconut
vluar-foi	groundnut
poi-bih-foi	chestnut
sriol-rie	pineapple
glik-rie	banana
siû	apple
ûp-siû	pear
ûif-poi	pomelo
poi	orange

sor-snil ... pomegranate
hiû-rie ... rambutan
pliz-rie ... peach
kiû ... lemon
val-jaz-foi ... almond
ius-rie ... olive
pler ... grape
cto-phûl-pler ... raisin
chim ... berry
plif ... sugar
thûs ... tea
fdem ... coffee
tûu-aif ... cocoa
tzif ... vegetable (eatable)
smer ... gourd
phûl-smer ... melon
vlaul-smer ... watermelon
sû-smer ... cucumber
sriol-rsûh ... asparagus
rfom ... cabbage
iuv-phûl-tzif ... lettuce
sû-rfom ... cauliflower
ûp-crif ... yam
crif ... potato
siû-prel ... turnip
blêa-prel ... carrot
zoc-siû ... tomato
tres-tzif ... leek
tres ... onion
ûp-tres ... garlic
fi.spom ... fungus
spom ... mushroom

fi.rcûf .... pulse
<u>rcûf</u> .... bean
zvôt-rcûf .... soya bean
ûp-rcûf .... pea
fi.flec .... spice
bef-tzif .... chilli
<u>flec</u> .... pepper
<u>chûp</u> .... cereal
chûp-nio .... chaff
chûp-sgon .... straw
<u>phit</u> .... maize
<u>rjok</u> .... barley
<u>fsep</u> .... oats
<u>trot</u> .... wheat
<u>rkec</u> .... rice
nio.rkec .... paddy
nio.blê.rkec .... hulled rice

3. Creatures of Air and Sea

<u>iar</u> .... creature (excluding humans)
iêt-hê .... crest (of bird)
<u>iôm</u> .... wing
hiû, rsûh-hiû .... feather
truar-hiû .... down
<u>euf</u> .... tail
vrouh-lreon .... gizzard
<u>ius</u> .... egg
zrôp-nio .... shell
ius-zel .... albumen
ius-hiz .... yolk
<u>ûuc</u> .... nest

iêt .... bird
ûif-iêt .... ostrich
jivoi .... heron
leg-vric .... stork
val-vric .... crane
phêuz-vrer .... pelican
czo-sgiel .... cormorant
sgiel-euk .... osprey
euk .... eagle
ûp-euk .... hawk
hem-vliêl .... vulture
svaup-iêt .... peacock
fnoôl .... crow (bird)
rseut-fnoôl .... jackdaw
chûn-iêt .... blackbird
chiul .... bat
phûun .... owl
tziôl .... pigeon
tziôl-uô .... dovecot
mrean .... parrot
sû-mrean .... cockatoo
suz-ûuc .... cuckoo
ûp-fnoôl .... magpie
flêz-iêt .... thrush
zvôt-iêt .... oriole
guê-iêt .... nightingale
priôh .... swallow (bird)
frual-iêt .... skylark
ftûuv .... sparrow
kzoêp-iêt .... hummingbird
ploil .... goose
leg-chiûv .... turkey

thien .... duck
ûp-thien .... swan
chiûv .... common domestic fowl
iêt-reu .... pterodactyl
sgiel .... fish
fien-voi .... gill
iôm .... fin
sriol .... scale (fish)
tuês-sgiel .... shark
hvau-sgiel .... eel
zvôt-sgiel .... goldfish
jzêk-sgiel .... silverfish
zoc-lie .... jellyfish
znaisib .... shellfish
fi.frûin .... crustacean
frûin .... crab
frûin-troih .... lobster
troih .... shrimp or prawn
tev-jlec .... octopus
ftiûn .... cuttlefish
mov-zrôp-nio .... univalve
cel-zrôp-nio .... bivalve
ûp-cheud .... mother-of-pearl
phoôz .... oyster
cheud .... pearl
phoôz.uô .... oyster bed
thiez .... clam
vrôih-jzêm .... coral
priog .... sea animal
nrôus-priog .... whale
ûif-priog .... walrus
srûuf-priog .... porpoise

vrôih-phiom .... otter
vrôih-flier .... seal
priog-reu .... ichthyosaur

4. Creatures of the Land

iûr .... animal
pa.thuû.iûr .... wild animal
thuû.iûr .... domestic animal
ztê-iar .... mongrel
zma-sia .... embryo
oim .... horn
zal-iûr-hiû .... fur
iûr.uô .... den
dlos-oim .... rhinoceros
ûif .... elephant
ûif.vhoil .... tusk, ivory
val-brem .... giraffe
gûi-oic .... lion
oic .... tiger
laz-oic .... leopard
iep .... bear (animal)
ceûl-siab-flier .... hyena
oic-flier .... wolf
ûp-flier .... jackal
iot .... deer
ûp-eûk .... ape
hia-eûk .... orangutang
oic-eûk .... gorilla
eûk .... monkey
khier .... fox
fiôf-tuês-iar .... weasel

sjie-lrim-iûr	hare
pauh-iar	rabbit
pauh-guê-iûr	badger
tûu-pleuf	squirrel
pleuf	rat
ûp-pleuf	mouse
glaif-iûr	camel
czûus	horse
fôb.fal.czûus	steed
rud.mul.czûus	jade, nag (horse)
rud.rêh.czûus	vicious horse
rseut-czûus	pony
ztê-czûus	mule
ûp-czûus	donkey
nêz-czûus	zebra
friêm	ox
srûuf	pig
srûuf.dlos	snout
rvoh-srûuf	hedgehog
criôm	goat
ûp-criôm	sheep
ûp-criôm.hiû	wool
flier	dog
phiom	cat
rze.vam.phiom	newborn kitten
ûif-reu	mammoth
fi.chiûs	reptile
chiûs	snake
nuap-chiûs	python, boa
fluam-chiûs	viper, adder
crum-chiûs	cobra
vric-chiûs	crocodile

<u>sboif</u> .... lizard
hpu-hev .... chameleon
<u>smior</u> .... tortoise
ûp-smior .... turtle
<u>fries</u> .... frog
of-fries .... tadpole
ûp-fries .... toad
chiûs-reu .... plesiosaur
<u>priûm</u> .... snail
<u>trief</u> .... spider
trief-thaid .... web
fiôp-troih .... scorpion
hvau-sor-vric .... millipede
sor-vric-iar .... centipede
krois.ia .... swarm
<u>krois</u> .... insect
gaif.krois .... destructive insect
vza-krois .... pupa, chrysalis
zma-krois .... larva, grub
krois-hvau .... cocoon
<u>fpies</u> .... grasshopper
gaif-krois .... locust
vliê-krois .... cicada
nrio-iôm .... beetle
<u>kleuc</u> .... butterfly
of-kleuc .... caterpillar
val-euf-krois .... dragonfly
<u>chiat</u> .... cockroach
<u>phiôk</u> .... cricket (insect)
<u>kzoêp</u> .... bee
kzoêp.uô .... honeycomb
kzoêp-jzêm .... wax

kzoêp-plif .... honey
kzoêp-phêuz .... beehive
ûp-kzoêp .... wasp
guê-krois .... moth
hmav-krois .... firefly, glow worm
<u>rseut</u> .... fly (insect)
of-rseut .... maggot
friêm-rseut .... gadfly
ian-rseut .... gnat
ian-krois .... flea
hiû-krois .... louse
snêul-krois .... bug
<u>priêk</u> .... mosquito
jzêk-krois .... silverfish
<u>thûic</u> .... ant
<u>smiûp</u> .... worm
lhôm-smiûp .... earthworm
ian-smiûp .... leech
<u>proic</u> .... germ

III. Human Beings

1. Relationship

hia.i .... humankind
plia.hia .... crowd
kol.ia .... trio
<u>hia</u> .... human being
sne.hia .... live person
rec-fleu .... so-and-so
ban.û .... dwarf

lub-vlic	hunchback
mil.ghal.û	centenarian
car-cto-noê	eunuch
zma-hia	savage
hia.tiûn.io	cannibal
mli.hia	dead person
fûl.hia	nobody
noê	man
viô	woman
heu	boy
vnên-rze	baby
liu	girl
car-vza-liu	virgin
nûu	I
jea	thou
boa	he, she, or it
diô	we
zeu	you
gou	they
vlil	self
sehi	race
luisehi	Mongolian
dêisehi	Caucasian
zusehi	Negroid
bhon	society or community
gzauf-hia	nation, people
hia.ia	party, organization
dba-plia	clique
plaz-bhon	party (political)
sla-bhon	trade union
gle-bhon	club
sma-nêz	queue

vrê.plia .... caravan

hli.io.ia .... audience

sê.mêus.io .... bachelor

mêus.noê .... bridegroom

mêus.viô .... bride

ôr.mêus.io .... married man

em.nôf.û .... elder, senior

ri.nôf.û .... junior

oi.jlûv .... clan

jlûv .... family

hbel.jzon .... relative (any kind)

hbel .... blood relative

jzon .... relative by marriage

nrel .... generation

vrih .... ancestor

hron .... relative apart by one more generation

hron.nrûn .... grandfather

nrûn .... father

zrel .... mother

broh .... uncle

gren .... aunt

drin .... husband

drûuk.drin .... actress's husband

zriv .... wife

drûuk.zriv .... actor's wife

seêm-viô .... mistress, concubine

siut-mêus.viô .... widow

mi-rze .... twin

zten .... brother

rev.zten .... half brother

jzon.zten .... brother-in-law

vlez .... sister

blib	male cousin
jlûd	female cousin
zlog	son
lrai zlog	stepson
rûif.zlog	adopted son
sviu-blê	orphan
jzez	daughter
jzod	nephew
vriz	niece
lrob	descendant
jroz-hia	fellow human
gzauf-jroz	compatriot
mai-jroz	fellow citizen
jroz	neighbour
jroz-grib	fellow, mate
fruc-jroz	schoolfellow
sla-jroz	colleague
ôêp-jroz	one at same table
grib	friend
sû-grib	comrade
mi.û	companion
liûz.e	stranger
ruap.io	host
ruap.e	guest
ruam.io	rival
drûd	enemy

2. External Parts of Body

lie	body
mli.lie	corpse
voi	organ (internal or external)

nio .... skin
gûi.nio .... scalp
vêi-poc .... pore
lie-vlaul .... sweat
cli-sriol .... scab
nio-laz .... mole
hiû .... hair
gûi .... head
beo .... ear
zoû .... face
vlûr .... forehead
jô-vlûr .... temple
blem .... eyebrow
glif .... eye
glif.hiû .... eyelash
glif-vlêô .... eyeball
glif-ba .... pupil
dlos .... nose
dlos-poc .... nostril
jzef .... cheek
vrer .... mouth
lrim .... lip
nrûs .... beard
zrir .... chin
brem .... neck
brem.al .... throat
brem.êh .... nape
drof .... shoulder
grûs .... chest
hpim .... nipple
lie-ba .... waist
zcos .... belly

zcos-laz ... navel
vlic ... back
vric-zma ... hip
lô-zcos ... pelvis
zcos-vric-nêz ... groin
nlep ... buttock
nlep-poc ... anus
hlût ... sexual organ
ôr.hlût ... penis
kôr-phêuz ... scrotum
kôr-vlêô ... testicle
ê.hlût ... vulva
jlec ... arm
jlec-nuê ... armpit
jlec-zfê ... elbow
blop-zfê ... wrist
blop ... hand
blop-al ... palm
lkô-blop ... fist
glik ... finger
poz.glik ... thumb
glick-jui ... knuckle
vgep ... nail (finger and toe)
vric ... leg
hê-vric ... thigh
cgi-vric ... lap
vric-zfê ... knee
lô-vric ... leg below knee
lô-vric-al ... shin
vric-zal ... calf
jrot-zfê ... ankle
jrot ... foot

jrot-êh .... heel
jrot-lô .... sole
brik .... toe
poz.brik .... big toe
brik.laz .... tiptoe

3. Internal Parts of Body

lifûe .... tissue
eul .... cell
voi-nio .... membrane
dlos-due .... mucus
sjie-voi-nio .... diaphragm
due-voi .... gland
phûl .... secretion
cli-jluz .... pus
ian-czuûb .... blood vessel
êz-ian-czuûb .... artery
ud-ian-czuûb .... vein
ian .... blood
iuv .... milk
ouz .... nerve
vliêl .... flesh
jliun .... fat (the substance)
vrouh .... muscle
zfê-vrouh .... sinew, tendon
of-brian .... cartilage
brian .... bone
brian.i .... skeleton
gûi.brian .... skull
vrer-brian .... jaw
vlic.brian .... spine

grûs-brian	rib
dreuv	brain
glif.due	tear
beo-rze	earwax
vrer-crum	palate
vhoil-vliêl	gum
vhoil	tooth
bliûh	tongue
gloin	saliva
dhûiv	gullet
cvo-phûl	phlegm
fien-dhûiv	windpipe
zcos-voi	viscera
lbion	lung
gziûl	heart
lreon	stomach
lbu-ian-voi	spleen
jô-lreon	pancreas
jriol	liver
jriol-due	bile
drein	intestine
drein-luû	flatus
bliaz	faeces
vriôb	kidney
glied	bladder
broig	urine
kôr-due	semen
ius-voi	ovary
rze-voi	womb

4. Occupation

<u>ûil</u>	one characterized by a certain quality
znû.û	sage
cun-cab.û	idealist
lnu-znû.û	wiseacre
fûl.flêl.û	ignoramus
ûp-czûus	fool
kut.û	saint
lgi.mli	martyr
pa.jeûp.û	hero
sraô.û	villain
khe.spiû	bully
jeûp.û	coward
tuês-hia	bandit
zgu.môip.io	robber
lie.môip.io	pickpocket
kus.û	hermit
thêt.blê.û	vagabond
sdut.û	prisoner
iûn	member (group or society)
ba.û	middleman
plaz.û	citizen
ba-plia-hia	bourgeois
tzif.tiûn.io	vegetarian
jô.fiûl.io	bystander
plêm.cgi.io	passenger
sto.io	owner
mcu-flua	model, pattern
khu.io	customer, client
czo-czû.e	hostage
oih.i	elite

oih .... person above ordinary grade

kêu.zên.û .... celebrity

gûi, kûz.û .... chief

bhon-oih .... aristocrat

puaf.io .... champion

iûh .... respectable man or Mister

oin .... respectable woman or Madam

rza-viô .... prostitute

iûn .... inhabitant

hjuez-iûn .... aborigines

srêm-iûn .... inmate

vrê-nêz .... procession

êh.jlô.io .... predecessor

êh.vrê.io .... follower

bleus .... disciple

siut-hpu.io .... renegade

hê.û .... superior

lô.û .... inferior

iov .... master

ûp-euf .... retinue, suite

eiz .... servant

zgu-eiz .... slave

iob .... doer

mro.io .... writer

msê.io .... agent

csû-kûz .... chairman

piôs-iûn .... secretary

zku.io .... maker

eûd .... receiver

suêt.e .... payee

nliôr .... founder

bleus .... believer

pci.zdoaf	graduate
zdoaf	student
vluar.sto.io	landowner
srêm.gûi	landlord
srêm.ciam.io	tenant
vriam.ia	staff, personnel
vriam	worker (one who works)
zfê-thô.io	partner
stô.vriam	assistant
gle-vriam	amateur
gbo-zla	quack, charlatan
sêv-vriam	layman, civilian
jriêf	one practising intellectual art
prôh.jaz	literary circle
driôs	author
mro-piôs.io	editor
jiaz.û	scholar
hlier	philosopher
hue.be	materialist
bloim	scientist
crul.flêl.û	connoisseur
glûis	literator
jziem	poet
fkal.driôs	novelist
cûg-fri.vriam	reporter
hfios	painter (one who paints pictures)
plaul.jriêf	sculptor
mro-droim	composer
droim.ia	band, orchestra
droim	musician
srêm.jriêf	architect
griûs	priest

<u>vliêc</u> .... ruler (of country)
vliêc-nêz .... dynasty
rze.vliêc .... monarch
zgu-vliêc .... dictator
zgu-bauz-vliêc .... tyrant
rûus-vliêc .... president
msê.rûus-vliêc .... vice president
jôm-rûus-vliêc .... ex-president
rêe.kûz .... governor
mai.kûz .... mayor
<u>bloêp</u> .... politician
plaz-msê-dliôt .... ambassador
tpê-gûi .... prime minister
tpê-zlec .... minister (government)
<u>dliôt</u> .... official (government)
plia-jlec .... official (private organization)
<u>gliuk</u> .... police officer
ckô.moês.io .... detective
sdut.seêm.io .... jailer
lziap.ia-mo .... army
lziap.ia .... troop
<u>lziap</u> .... soldier
sku-lziap .... sentry
vam.lziap .... recruit
oi.lziap .... officer
oi.lziap-a .... general
<u>jzûut</u> .... teacher
<u>vreuc</u> .... clerk
chauk-sfo-vreuc .... bookkeeper
seêm-srêm.vriam .... storekeeper
<u>jriap</u> .... doctor (medical)
blop-jriap .... surgeon

drû-sku.vriam	nurse
briêt	athlete
briêt-drûuk	acrobat
drûuk	actor
plê.ia	chorus
plê.io	singer
tla-lbe	clown
klô.io	wizard
zpiat	pilot
vlioc	sailor
oi.vlioc-a	admiral
slar.kûz	captain
jleûp	driver
csû.io	manager
ba-gloit	broker
gûin-gloit	contractor
gloit	merchant or trader
vliêl.gloit	meat seller
srêm-sko-gloit	grocer
krat.vriam	shop assistant
bloek	labourer
riam.bloek	porter
sma.vriam	waiter
nziop	engineer (the professional person)
sdu.nziop	civil engineer
vzôn.nziop	electrical engineer
czaf.nziop	mechanical engineer
zboec	mechanic (engineering and allied trades)
hriûp	craftsperson
zvôt.hriûp	goldsmith
zrôp.zboec	blacksmith
thin-hriûp	carpenter

jraim.û .... peasant
zmeop .... farmer
friêm.seêm.io .... cowherd
iûr.muir.vriam .... butcher
broit .... cook
aif-jluz.broit .... baker
griûk .... tailor
snuim.luam.io .... cobbler
hiû.siut.vriam .... barber
grêl.û.ia .... fire brigade

IV. Human Products

1. Abstract Products

rua .... language
rua-sjie .... dialect
mro-rêh .... style
rua-rêh .... diction
fcô-rua .... bombast
nru-mro .... shorthand
vlub-thaid .... metre
faê .... grammar
nad-roiz-puô .... direct speech
vêg-roiz-puô .... indirect speech
cab-fri .... idiom
vêg-fri .... figure of speech
fiem-kaê .... metaphor
tis-zma-vlub .... alliteration
tis-grê-vlub .... rhyme
sûig-cua .... interrogatory term (Luif)

bre-cua ... exclamatory term (Luif)
suô ... part of speech
poz-suô ... original part of speech (Luif)
hpu-suô ... transformed part of speech (Luif)
iov-cua ... principal word (Luif)
eiz-cua ... subordinate word (Luif)
blêh-suô ... noun
iob-cua ... subject
eûd-cua ... object
ceud-blêh-suô ... vocative noun (Luif)
hne-lil-blêh-suô ... explanatory noun (Luif)
dluô-blêh-suô ... appositional noun
sto-blêh-suô ... possessive noun (Luif)
kêu-blêh-suô ... name noun (Luif)
vlil-blêh-suô ... self-noun (Luif)
cua-hia ... person (re words)
fal-suô ... qualifier (Luif)
blêh-fal-suô ... object qualifier (Luif)
glu-suô ... verb
zfê-suô ... connective (Luif)
mau.i ... alphabet
mau ... letter of alphabet
poz-mau ... initial
lkô-mau-plia ... consonant group (Luif)
sviu-lkô-mau ... double consonant (Luif)
lkô-mau ... consonant
htê-mau-plia ... vowel group (Luif)
sviu-htê-mau ... diphthong
htê-mau ... vowel
rôu ... figure (numerical symbol)
foz-phuê ... decimal system
pêa ... punctuation mark

nôh-pêa .... comma
val-pêa .... full stop, period (punctuation)
bre-pêa .... exclamation mark
pra-pêa .... request mark (Luif)
sûig-pêa .... question mark
nuap-pêa .... dash
roiz-pêa .... speech mark (Luif)
zgu-pêa .... emphasis mark (Luif)
zfê-pêa .... hyphen
keû-pêa .... name mark (Luif)
foz-sen-tau .... deciamal mark (Luif)
sjie-sen-tau .... vulgar fraction mark (Luif)
cua.i .... vocabulary
cua-sjie .... vocabulary division (Luif)
suô-cua-sjie .... part-of-speech division (Luif)
hê-cua-sjie .... major vocabulary division (Luif)
lô-cua-sjie .... minor vocabulary division (Luif)
kêu-thaid .... nomenclature, terminology
<u>cua</u> .... word
cua-pom .... syllable
vlub-cua .... onomatopoeia
prel-cua .... basic word (Luif)
ztê-cua .... composite word (Luif)
lbu-cua .... resultant word (Luif)
zfê-cua .... compound word
czuûb-cua .... serial word (Luif)
tliô-cua .... synthetic word (Luif)
poz-sme .... primary meaning (Luif)
dak-sme .... secondary meanond (Luif)
hli-cua .... hearsay
<u>kaê</u> .... phrase
zfê-kaê .... aggregated phrase (Luif)

jza-kaê .... expanded phrase (Luif)
gzô-kaê .... miscellaneous phrase (Luif)
tuê-pom .... clause
tliô-tuê-pom .... additional clause (Luif)
tuê .... sentence
fêz-tuê .... simple sentence
ztê-tuê .... complex sentence
fri-tuê .... statement sentence (Luif)
sûig-tuê .... interrogative sentence (Luif)
pra-tuê .... request sentence (Luif)
bre-tuê .... exclamatory sentence (Luif)
tuê-puô .... paragraph
kraut-puô .... chapter
puô .... written passage
buv-puô .... regular passage (Luif)
gsô-cua .... text
sû-puô .... note
lien-puô .... memorandum
bûuj-puô .... notice
mro-fleu .... exercise (school)
mru-cua .... slogan
zma-cua .... preface
tliô-mro .... postscript
tau .... symbol
clu-tau .... trademark
kêu .... name
cûg.kêu .... alias
spe-kêu .... nickname
jlûv.kêu .... surname
fkal-kêu .... pseudonym
kêu, ûp-kêu .... title
chêô-fri-kêu .... descriptive title

ô.es	matter (subject engaging attention)
flêl-blêh	subject matter
roiz-blêh	theme
flua-jlô	case
hôj	scope
gûi-laz	gist
mau	rudiments
cuem-kuv	data
rlu.eu	lesson
ô.gûin	bond, contract
puô-og	proviso
sûig-blêh	problem
htê-kruod	solution (of problem)
flêl-fri	formula
jzi-flêl	theorem
slôn-mau	principle
cab	rule
rêh-chêb	etiquette
rlu-tuê	maxim
flêl-tuê	proverb
flêl	knowledge
kraut-flêl	learning, scholarship
slôn	system of ideas
faê	set of rules
ûp-slôn	code
liôl-uam	programme
glu-blêh	agenda
fleu-puô	list (of things)
feur-sfo	index
ril-kuv	statistics
uem-fleu-puô	menu
flêl-czil	subject (of study)

snuv	philosophy
vaê-snuv	metaphysics
hue.sô	materialism
tuz-flêl	aesthetics
nzo-flêl	logic
kut-snuv	ethics
plal	religion
leliv	pantheism
lesotêh	polytheism
lemtêh	monotheism
fûfel	agnosticism
neufla	scepticism
nêftêh	atheism
thêh	science
khôn	mathematics
sci-khôn	arithmetic
mau-khôn	algebra
jav-khôn	geometry
zêj-khôn	trigonometry
gun-khôn	calculus
phun	physics
chav	astronomy
êol-crul	astrology
fbun	chemistry
czal	geology or geography
hôj.czal	geography
jzab.czal	geology
czôn	biology
mrêl	psychology
vsud.rnû.flêl	psychiatry
srah	social science or philosophy
bhon-srah	sociology

rze-srah	economics
fi.smôn	story
fi.smôn.eu	episode
plaul	character (in book)
kûz-plaul	hero
smôn	history
smôn-hrôz	legend, myth
draz-smôn	biography
nôf-blêh-thêh	archaeology
crul	art (fine art)
crul.eu	work of art
prôh	literature
jêh-kraut	classic
kran	prose
roiz-crul	oratory
trun	essay (type of literary composition)
pal-biôm-prôh	satire
pruv	letter (missive)
fkal	fiction
a.fkal	short story
stôh	poetry
flêz-stôh	lyric
skun	drama
zsû-skun	comedy
flêz	song
sluj	music
srêm-crul	architecture
blop-crul	palmistry
gloit.sla	trading
hriûp.sla	craftsmanship
hriûp-crul	art (practical art)
ô.czu	agriculture

plal-bhon........ religious organization
plaz........ state (political community)
bhon-plaz........ republic
iûn-plaz........ democracy
oih-plaz........ aristocracy
mov-vliêc-plaz........ autocracy
rze-vliêc-plaz........ monarchy
griûs-plaz........ theocracy
fûl-tpê........ anarchy
plaz-rêh........ constitution
plaz-blêh........ politics
tpê-voi........ government
tpê-lruic........ council
chêb-lruic........ legislative council
csa-lruic........ advisory council
glu-lruic........ executive council
csû-lruic........ committee
plaz-chaêv........ civil service
lai........ department
plaz-lai........ ministry
puêr-csû........ strategy
druap-hsa........ tactics
puêr.eu........ battle
chêb........ law
rtam........ scale (of degrees)
peôn-jzu........ degree, grade
fi.thôd........ unit (quantity serving as standard of measurement)
thôd........ unit of length
khug........ unit of area
sbaz........ unit of volume
frôj........ unit of weight
krêd........ unit of money

hsa-liôl	itinerary
seêm-flo	hygiene
faê	structure (organization)
ô.frê	conference
mov-drin-zriv	monogamy
snou-drin-zriv	polygamy
fe-chauk	finance

2. Towns

rêe	district or division of country
hê.rêe	province
lô.rêe	district
mai	town
mai.dluô	suburbs
oi.mai	city
a.mai	village
tpê.mai	capital
zrôp-vuô	fort, stronghold
rui.mai	port
rui	harbour
suo	farm
iêt-jeûp	scarecrow
gle-lruic	park
fuû	garden
iar.seêm.uô	zoo
sêûm-poc.uô	cemetery
sêûm-poc	grave
jui.uô	quarry
seêm-vuô	depot
tuû.uô	airport
slar.uô	dock

srêm.uô ... site
pue ... road
srêm-pue ... street
pue-guz ... crossroad
em.nôh.pue ... shortcut
a.pue ... lane, path
coôl-pue ... footpath, pavement
vlair-pue ... pass (mountain)
lô-vluar-pue ... tunnel
zrôp-pue ... railway
sdu-ôi ... structure (engineering)
tû-lien ... monument
zku-hjuez ... fountain
grê-vlaul ... dam
grê.ôi, trêf ... barrier
dba-trêf ... fence
cêi ... bridge
stô-cêi ... abutment
prel, stô-nui ... foundation, base
ud-vrôih-cêi ... pier, jetty
vluar-glu-skêf ... wharf
fi.plêm ... vehicle (all types)
drô-truôz ... wheel
ba-nad ... spoke
truôz-kruod ... axle
truôz-ba ... hub
phûl-jaz ... tyre, tire (rubber)
grê-plêm ... brake
tuû ... airplane
sôp-tluat ... parachute
cze-hvau ... rocket
slar.ia ... navy

slar.ia	fleet
slar	ship
sla-hsa-nui	propeller
sla-hsa.aê	helm, rudder
slar-sgon	mast
hsa-sdôus	sail
stô-hue	ballast
grê-slar	anchor
vrôih-stô	lifebuoy
uêj.slar	steamship
puêr.slar	warship
a.slar	boat
hsa-slar	oar
jain-bôz	raft
lô-vlaul-slar	submarine
plêm	vehicle (carriage)
nê.plêm	train
bhon-plêm	bus
clu-plêm	lorry, truck
czaf-plêm	motorcar
suêt-plêm	taxi
lpa-plêm	motorcycle
vric-plêm	bicycle
jroi-plêm	cart
blop-plêm	handcart
phêuz-plêm	wheelbarrow
chuf	instrument of war
khe.aê	weapon
puêr-hue	ammunition
phôs	gun
stû-phôs	trigger
phôs-vlêr	gunpowder

phôs-vlêô .... bullet
oi.phôs .... cannon
vlêô-chuf .... bomb
fiôf-nuap-chuf .... mine (explosive)
lô-vrôih-chuf .... torpedo
vêg-chuf .... bow
cze-chuf .... arrow
laz-chuf .... spear
phaiv-chuf .... sword
fiôp-chuf .... dagger
phôs-phaiv .... bayonet
bli.aê .... instrument of torture
sgam .... communicating instrument
hne-sgam .... television
nuê-sgam .... radio
sca-sgam .... telegraph
roiz-sgam .... telephone
czaf .... machine
vlil-hsa-czaf .... automaton
czaf .... engine
hsa-czaf .... motor
zku-vzôn .... dynamo
aif-nuap-czaf .... mill
jav-czaf .... lathe
jzu-mro-czaf .... printing press
due-czaf .... pump
hsa-hvau .... piston
meuh-drô-truôz .... pulley, windlass
mlûhum-glup .... spring
drô-kruod .... pivot
srêm .... house
vliêc.srêm .... palace

oi.srêm .... mansion
a.srêm .... hut
sgon-srêm .... tower
creu-srêm .... pavilion
jroi-srêm .... shed
jroi-piem .... camp
nriô-sdôus-srêm .... tent
lkô-nuê .... court (enclosed space)
htê-skêf .... terrace
sfas .... room
dluô-skêf .... veranda, balcony
sfas-pue .... corridor
ud-krôf .... porch
oi.sfas .... hall
cgi.sfas .... parlour, living room
rbo.sfas .... bedroom
lie.kiûr.sfas .... bathroom
rôûn.sfas .... kitchen
bliaz.sfas .... latrine
vluar-sfas .... cellar
thô.sfas .... office
crum .... roof
crum-fjûb .... thatch
crum-jhus .... tile
crum.dluô .... eaves
stô-crum .... truss
vêg-crum .... vault
sku-sfas .... ceiling
vêg-sdu .... arch
trêf .... wall
trêf-poc .... niche
sû-trêf .... parapet

grê-prus ... railings
peôn-thaid ... scaffolding
krôf ... door
fe-krôf ... threshold
zfê-krôf ... hinge
gsô-krôf ... bolt
tras ... window
fe-tras ... sill
prus ... beam or post
fzi.prus ... beam
êfpec ... rafter
htê-prus ... lintel
fiûl.prus ... post
rtam ... stairs
ûp-rtam ... ladder
rtam.eu ... step (stairs)
skêf ... storey
skêf ... floor
jêh-skêf ... platform, stage
flêc ... oven
oi.flêc ... furnace, kiln
ûp-flêc ... stove
brôn-slôp ... chimney
fi.slôp ... tube
slop ... pipe (tube for fluids)
due-htê ... tap
plat ... drain (channel for refuse water)
lhôm-plat ... ditch
bliaz-slôp ... sewer
broig-khuêj ... urinal
thêt ... home
thêt ... private dwelling

vam-thêt .... hostel

ûuc-srêm .... lodging house

grê-srêm .... hotel

sku.uô .... shelter

sku.uô .... asylum

chôk .... temple or place of religious worship

rgêp .... office (public)

thô.srêm .... office (private)

tpê-vuô .... headquarters

pruv.rgêp .... post office

jbe-rgêp .... court (of justice)

chauk.seêm.uô .... treasury

chauk-rgêp .... bank

sdut .... prison

kraut-srêm .... library

fcô-hôi-srêm .... museum

sgiel.uô .... aquarium

fruc .... school

oi.fruc .... university

vrôih-hmav .... lighthouse

mrak .... hospital

prêc .... station (building like police station)

iûr.muir.uô .... abattoir

trôp .... market

mi-thô .... company, firm

plêm.uô .... garage

chûp.srêm .... granary

seêm-srêm .... storehouse

chuf.seêm.srêm .... arsenal

czûus.srêm .... stable

srûuf.uô .... pigsty

krat .... shop

aot.krat .... wine seller's shop
aif-jluz.krat .... bakery
spuc .... factory
luav-spuc .... foundry
thin.siut.spuc .... sawmill
tiûn-srêm .... restaurant
thûs-srêm .... teahouse
fdem-srêm .... café
aot-srêm .... bar, pub
stêk .... theatre
thôuh-stêk .... cinema
saic.srêm .... casino
car.srêm .... brothel

3. Household Goods

uêr .... paint (the substance)
uêr-vuêl .... varnish
vuêl-crêus .... enamel
hev-jzab .... dye
tûu-dûn .... indigo
gso-blêh .... glue
nriô-phûl .... rubber
nûmhi .... vulcanite
uam .... paper
smuat-uam .... blotting paper
nriô-uam .... cardboard
drês-rsûh .... tinfoil
gsô-jzêm .... cement
jzêm-buû .... plaster
sdu-ztê .... concrete
sdu-jhus .... brick

jhus-jzab .... plastic

auf .... glass

hpu-auf .... lens

luav-glup .... fuse

thaid .... frame

ûp-crum .... hood

fi.ôêp .... furniture

êus .... cupboard

fcô-êus .... cabinet

krauf.uô .... wardrobe

gsô-thin .... shelf

uac .... drawer (the receptacle)

ôêp .... table

mro-ôêp .... desk

clu-ôêp .... counter

ôut .... chair

zrar-ôut .... throne

vlic-vlê-ôut .... stool

val-ôut .... sofa

sû-ôut .... bench

zru-nui .... swing

snêul .... bed

zma-snêul .... cradle

svuan .... lamp

vzôn.svuan .... electric light

vzôn-auf .... electric bulb

riam-hmav .... torch

jzu-hmav .... beacon

hmav-phêuz .... lantern

kzoêp-jzêm-hmav .... candle

svuan-czuûb .... wick

zku-grêl .... match

nuah-khuêj	brazier
plaul	statue
giêf-plaul	idol
jzu.ôi	seal
jzu-glup	medal
roic-tau	badge
tau-thôud	emblem
bûuj-jzu-hôj	signboard
thôuh	picture
hia-thôuh	portrait
ceûl-thôuh	cartoon
fbun-thôuh	photograph
thôuh-skun	cinema picture, movie
khuên	flag
czûus.cgi.ôi	saddle
pca-czuûb	rein
chaêv	instrument
sbaun	handle
zgu-sgon	lever
ûp-ftuav	wedge
huûl-jui	pendulum
glup-czuûb	chain
glup-czuûb.eu	link
ckô-zrôp	handcuffs, fetters
sruêl	a brush
hsa-vlêr	duster
skêf-sruêl	broom
lkô-truôz	lock
htê-kruod	key
czo-czû.aê	trap
rial-czuûb	whip
czû-thin	baton

tû-coôl ... walking stick

siut-lub ... chopping block

shail-zrôp ... anvil

jloi.lu.jui ... whetstone

czu.aê ... plough

kraun ... spade

pauh.aê ... hoe

ûp-kraun ... shovel

vhoil.lu.aê ... rake

fjûb-siut.aê ... scythe

ftuav ... axe

vluar-ftuav ... pickaxe

siut-nui ... chisel

poc-zku.aê ... drill

fiôp.aê ... awl

nu-zgu.aê ... syringe

shail ... hammer

meuh.aê ... pincers

czû.siut.aê ... pliers

a.meuh.aê ... tweezers

czû.aê ... tongs

drô.aê ... spanner, wrench

tluin ... saw (tool)

griu-zrôp ... iron (for clothing)

jzêm-buû.lu.aê ... trowel

griu.lu.aê ... plane

bôz.lu.aê ... file

phaiv ... knife

phaiv-jluz ... blade

a.phaiv ... penknife

sgêûn ... scissors

hêun.aê ... bellows

mru-vlêr ... vacuum cleaner
mro-czaf ... typewriter
fbun-thôuh-phêuz ... camera
nêz.zku.aê ... ruler
jaz.rnê.aê ... compasses
czuel ... measuring instrument
lpa.aê ... balance, device for weighing
sci.aê ... calculator
sci-thaid ... abacus
mrail ... recording meter
vlôi-mrail ... compass
ual-mrail ... barometer
not-mrail ... thermometer
êun.cfô.aê ... vane
kruin ... clock
a.kruin ... watch
truûv ... magnifying glass
gu.truûv ... telescope
jô.truûv ... microscope
vliê.lu.aê ... microphone
spuin ... bell
jloi.lu.aê ... whistle
fluaz ... basket
ûp-fluaz ... sieve
hêun-kiûr ... filter
fi.phêuz ... holding article, receptacle
phêuz ... bag or box
vrê-phêuz ... luggage
iar-sdut ... cage
sêûm-thin ... coffin
poc.ôi ... vessel
drês.poc.ôi ... tin

khuêj	basin
jêh-khuêj	bucket, pail
oi.khuêj	tank
due-phêuz	cask
ûp-khuêj	tub
hvau-khuêj	jar
sbaun-khuêj	jug
spol.czû.ôi	vase
thaub	bottle
stû-blêa	funnel
za-slôp	nozzle
thûs.poc.ôi	teapot
fdem.poc.ôi	coffeepot
due-vrer	spout
lkô.ôi	lid, cover
jhus.poc.ôi	crockery
chôud	cooking vessel
rôûn-pluiz	ladle
bôz-chôud	pan
vlêô-chôud	pot
oi.rmuêz	cauldron
rmuêz	kettle
uêj-phêuz	boiler
riam-truôz	tray
ûp-truôz	dish
truôz	plate
kraug-truôz	saucer
jaz-poc	bowl
kraug	cup
auf.kraug	glass, tumbler
pluiz	spoon
glik-sbaun	fork

uem-sviu .... chopsticks
fiôf-sdôu .... curtain
ôêp-sdôus .... tablecloth
thaid .... a net
priêk-thaid .... mosquito netting
skêf-sdôus .... carpet
ûp-sdôus .... mat
nriô-thaid .... trellis, lattice
zrôp-thaid .... grating, gridiron
oi.czuûb .... rope
czuûb .... a string
nuê-czuûb .... loop
a.czuûb .... thread
lkô.ôi .... stopper, cork
grê-poc .... plug
grê-vrer .... muzzle
czuûb-hvau .... screw
ûp-kruod .... peg
gsô-kruod .... nail
kruod .... a pin
pûuk.aê .... needle
sku-glik .... thimble
vêg.ôi .... hook
mru-sgiel .... bait

4. Personal Articles

uem .... food
uem.eu .... viand
dak-uem .... meal
dak-uem.eu .... course (of meal)
zôa-uem .... breakfast

ba-uem .... lunch
guê-uem .... dinner
zam-uem .... supper
stui-uem .... feast
mi-rkec .... food eaten with rice
zûr.zis.uem .... salty delicacy
creu-uem .... refreshments
sêv-rôûn-tzif .... salad
zoc-giu .... jelly
chûp-vliêl .... mincemeat
bef-hiz .... curry
<u>aif</u> .... flour
aif-jluz .... bread
czuûf-aif .... noodle
rôûn.rkec .... cooked rice
due-rkec .... congee
daul.ius .... boiled egg
rsûh-ius .... omelette
friêm.vliêl .... beef
srûuf.vliêl .... pork
blac-vric .... ham
blac-srûuf .... bacon
hvau-vliêl .... sausage
iuv-gai .... cream
iuv-jluz .... butter
nriô-iuv .... cheese
due.uem .... soup
uem-due .... gravy
<u>uos</u> .... cake
nriô-uos .... biscuit
plif-uem .... candy
rie-jluz .... jam

tûu-aif-jluz .... chocolate
bluên-aif .... ice cream
ôip .... sauce
jom-ôip .... vinegar
zvôt-aif .... mustard
piev.ôi .... beverage
luû-vlaul .... aerated water
plif-due .... syrup
aot .... wine or any alcoholic beverage
rjok-aot .... beer
uûk .... medicine
uûk .... drug
bôi-uûk .... pill, tablet
shu-gai .... balm, ointment
rnû-due .... vaccine
phi-nos-uûk .... quinine
fluam .... poison
krois.muir.ôi .... insecticide
plauf .... tobacco
uam-plauf .... cigarette
fi.thuas .... narcotic
thuas .... opium
thuas-due .... laudanum
thuas-jluz .... morphine
ûp-thuas .... heroin
sdôus .... cloth
nriô-sdôus .... canvas
nê.sdôus .... ribbon
drô-sdôus .... bandage
nuap-sdôus .... rag
sruêm .... cotton
smuas .... linen

truar .... silk
sû-truar .... satin
sku.truar .... rayon
hiû-truar .... velvet
huûl-sdôus .... crêpe
sfuom-sdôus .... tapestry
sfuom-truar .... brocade
sdôus-sfuom .... embroidery
êz-hiû .... felt
dêl-dê-sdôus .... gauze
nio .... leather
krauf .... clothing
crêus-jlec .... sleeve
crêus-blop-zfê .... cuff, wristband
krauf-phêuz .... pocket
gsô-krauf .... button
rbo-krauf .... pyjamas
plia-krauf .... uniform
drof-roic .... shawl
val-crêus .... gown, robe
crêus .... coat or upper garment
brem-jaz .... collar
lûk-crêus .... overcoat
grêun-crêus .... raincoat
nu-crêus .... shirt
zrôp-krauf .... armour
stuôm .... trousers or lower garment
nôh-stuôm .... short pants
jza-stuôm .... skirt
sgon-stuôm .... sarong
svair .... hat or headgear
dluô-blê-svair .... cap

sku-svair	helmet
zoû-sdôus	veil
lkô-zoû	mask
brem-roic	necktie
stuôm-czuûb	belt
blop-roic	glove
riam-sdôus	handkerchief
sku-krauf	apron
snuim	shoe or outer foot covering
suz-snuim	slippers
jêh-snuim	boot
jrot-roic	sock, stocking
bluên-snuim	skate
vlaul-sdôus	towel
cgi-zoc	cushion
tluem	bedclothes
gûi-tluem	pillow
snêul-tluem	bedcover
hê-tluem	blanket
lô-tluem	mattress
chaim	cosmetic
pliz-chaim	lipstick
phuûf	perfume
lûr-brôn	incense
khôis	soap
êz-khôis	lather
roic-vlaul	sponge
côh-nui	curio
sfuom	ornament (ornamental article)
ef.sag.sfuom	trinket
jain-tbo-sfuom	pendant
crêus-sfuom	brooch

jlec-jaz ... bracelet

jaz-sfuom ... ring

truem ... comb (for hair)

hiû-kruod ... hairpin

glif-auf ... spectacles, eyeglasses

nrûs-phaiv ... razor

spôis ... mirror

svaup ... fan

tluat ... umbrella

chauk-phêuz ... purse

chauk ... money

buf-chauk ... cash

glup-chauk ... coin

lkô-chauk ... pension

prel-chauk ... capital

thô-sjie ... shares (of company)

rie-chauk ... interest

rôef ... price

rpû-chauk ... income

coet-chauk ... expenditure

plaz-maûs ... revenue

viûr-chauk ... alms

pruv-suêt ... postage

rdêup ... pen or any writing implement

rdêup-sgon ... penholder

rdêup-jluz ... nip

smuat ... ink

bih-brat-rdêup ... pencil

kraut ... book

kraut-jluz ... page

jiaz-kraut ... textbook

mro-kraut ... manuscript

hlan-sfo .... diary
cim-flêl-kraut .... encyclopaedia
cua-kraut .... dictionary
dak-kraut .... magazine, periodical
ftuêp .... newspaper
hlan-kraut .... calendar
sfo-nui .... file
seêm-blêh-kraut .... album
jzi-uam .... document
jzi-uam .... certificate
vrê-uam .... passport
sfu-uam .... permit
nu-vrê-uam .... ticket
pimrô .... affidavit
cuem-uam .... will, testament
clu-uam .... bill (account of money)
maûs-uam .... receipt
roiz-gsô-uam .... poster
sfo-uam .... label
jzu-nui .... stamp
suêt-uam .... cheque
pruv-nio .... envelope
aiz-thôuh-kraut .... atlas
aiz-thôuh .... map
vrôih-thôuh .... chart
flaic .... musical instrument
flaic.czuûb .... chord
troi-phuet .... trumpet
phuet .... pipe (musical instrument)
sû-phuet .... flute
chôik .... drum
ûp-spuin .... gong

rial-flaic .... cymbals
sguit .... violin
glik-sguit .... guitar
svaup-flaic .... accordion
truop .... piano
vlub.rze.aê .... gramophone
rial-blêh .... bat (used in sports)
saic-hlua .... dice
luû-vlêô .... balloon
êun-uam .... kite
stuûc-grêl .... firework
vlub-uam .... firecracker
ûp-stuûc .... bauble
stuûc .... a toy
hia-stuûc .... doll

II

Luif-English Alphabetical Dictionary

-a-

a.êun .... light wind: breeze
aif.............................. fine meal obtained from grinding any cereal: flour; mass of fine particles: powder
aif-nuap.................... crush to powder: grind
aif-nuap.czaf............. machine for grinding solid substances: mill
aif-jluz....................... baked flour of wheat: bread
aif-jluz.broit .... maker of bread: baker
aif-jluz.krat............... building where bread is made: bakery
aiz .... name of a planet: earth
aiz-laz........................ an end of earth's axis: pole
aiz-zru .... movement of earth's surface: earthquake
aiz-ba-jaz.................. imaginary line round middle of earth equidistant from poles: equator
aiz-thôuh.................. outline representation of earth's surface: map
aiz-thôuh-kraut .... book of maps: atlas
aot............................ alcoholic liquor: wine
aot-srêm .... building where alcoholic liquors are sold for consumption therein: bar
aot-jzû...................... have condition produced by drinking alcoholic liquor: drunk
aot.krat .... shop for selling alcoholic liquors: wine seller's shop
auf............................ transparent, brittle substance made by fusing certain oxides: glass
auf.kraug .... drinking vessel made of glass: glass
al .... position in front: in front of; following in time: after
al-êh .... alternately move backwards and forwards: to and fro
al-mli .... taking place after a person's death: posthumous
al nôu.ba .... after midday: *post meridiem,* p.m.

al.vrê .... go before in place: precede
al.jlô .... come after in time: follow
ar.............................. what thing: which; a thing of whatever kind: anything
a.mai .... district locality with a small population: village
a.meuh.aê................. small pincers: tweezers
an.lil.......................... shedding a little light only: dim
an.sor .... neither much nor little: moderate
a.fkal .... fictitious narrative of short length: short story
a.vlair .... small hill: mound
a.slar.......................... small ship: boat
a.srêm........................ small house: hut
azoh ....the necessary changes having been made: *mutatis mutandis*
az.hne........................ look momentarily: glance
az.vêu .... point of time: instant
az.vuêl .... shine momentarily: flash
az.vuô........................ particular place: locality
az.vlêr........................ particle of dust: mote
az.thin .... thin piece of wood split off: splinter
a.czuûb...................... spun filament of cotton or other textile: thread
a.pue .... narow road: lane
a.phaiv .... small knife with blades folded into handle: penknife
a.kruin .... small timepiece worn on the person: watch
a.grêun .... light rain in drops: drizzle
a.grôiv .... small pool: puddle

-e-

eiz .... one working for and carrying out the orders of another person: servant
eiz.lu .... work for a person under his directions: serve
eiz-cua...................... in Luif a word of the same part of speech as another but of lesser importance: subordinate word
eul............................ unit of protoplasm: cell
eul-fiûl .... morbid growth of cells: tumour
euf............................ lengthened posterior part of animal: tail
euf-êol...................... heavenly body with train of light: comet
euk........................... one of species of big birds of prey: eagle
eûd........................... one who receives: receiver
eûd-cua .... noun signifying that which receives the action of a verb: object
eûk........................... animal resembling human (excluding anthropoid apes): monkey
em.nôh.pue.............. way shorter than normal route: shortcut
em.nôf.û................... older person: elder
em.nru .... make faster: accelerate
em.dêl.lu .... make liquid thinner by adding water or other liquid: dilute
en............................. the cause being: because
ef.ril......................... a few: several
ef.sag.sfuom............. small ornament of little value: trinket
ef.dak .... now and then: sometimes
es............................. relating to: concerning
es-fri........................ remark on: mention
es-zle .... applicable to a particular matter: relevant
es-ztê....................... get involved in an affair: interfere
es-jzu....................... have recourse to: refer

-ê-

êol .... heavenly body appearing at night as a point of light: star

êol.ia .... assemblage of stars: constellation

êol-crul .... divination by reference to the stars: astrology

êol-jrual .... cloudy patch in sky consisting of stars or gaseous matter: nebula

êol-brail .... cloudy band of stars across the sky: Milky Way

êun .... moving air: wind; common report spreading by hearsay: rumour (v. êun-roiz)

êun-uam .... contrivance of wood and paper for flying on string: kite

êun-roiz .... common report spreading by hearsay: rumour

êun.fcô.aê .... pointer indicating direction of wind: vane

êus .... piece of furniture for storing food and crockery: cupboard

êh .... at back of: behind; preceding in time: before

ê.hlût .... female sexual organ: vulva

êh-hne .... see beforehand: foresee

êh nôu.ba .... before midday: *ante meridiem*, a.m.

êh-flua .... previous instance serving as example: precedent

êh-fri .... tell beforehand: predict

êh-vêu .... occur before normal time: premature

êh.vrê .... move behind: follow

êh.vrê.io .... one who moves behind another: follower

êh.jlô .... go before in time: precede

êh.jlô.io .... one who has done some particular thing before another: predecessor

êh-piôs .... realize in advance: anticipate

êh-trê .... speak badly of behind one's back: backbite

êh-dlû .... hold opinion before having sufficient knowledge: prejudice
ên.lil .... intensely bright: vivid
ên.hiôp .... passionate anger: fury
ên.rza .... sell goods in great quantities to retailers: wholesale
ên.rbo .... sound sleep
ên.hne .... look fixedly: gaze
ên.fiôp .... pierce strongly: stab
ên.vuêl .... shine brilliantly: glare
ên.vce-jlô .... tremendous disaster: calamity
ên.sla .... work hard: toil
ên.zis .... intensely delightful: charming
ên.zto .... hate intensely: loathe
ên.zgu .... extremely forceful: violent
ên.jza .... spread to fullest extent: outspread
ên.jci .... love intensely: adore
ên.prû .... mistake grossly: blunder
ên.bre .... intense emotion: passion
ên.krô .... beg earnestly: implore
êfpec .... inclined beam of room: rafter
êz .... signifying starting point: from; to position apart: away
êz-ian-czuûb .... blood vessel transporting blood from heart: artery
êz-ud .... position of point relative to another: direction
êz-hiû .... type of fabric made from wool: felt
êz-hrô .... take origin from: derive
êz.hea .... move away: remove
êz-nad .... inclined from direct line: oblique
êz-fzi .... deviating from the horizontal: sloping
êz.seêm .... keep away: avoid
êz.pauk .... obtain use of on loan: borrow

êz-toif........................ get rid of by rubbing: wipe
êz-khôis..................... froth produced by rubbing wet soap: lather

-i-

iar.............................. any animate being excluding human: creature
iar.seêm.uô................. place where animals are kept for exhibition: zoo
iar-sdut...................... open-work prison for birds or other creatures: cage
ian............................. liquid circulating in animal bodies: blood
ian-rseut.................... blood-sucking fly: gnat
ian-smiûp.................. blood-sucking worm: leech
ian-stû....................... shed blood: bleed
ian-czuûb .... tube in body transporting blood: blood vessel
ian-bliaz .... intestinal disease characterized by passage of blood in faeces: dysentery
ian-krois.................... blood-sucking, wingless insect: flea
iep............................. heavy, shaggy, carnivorous quadruped: bear; gruff and unfriendly: surly
iêt.............................. any feathered creature: bird
iêt-reu .... extinct flying reptile: pterodactyl
iêt-hê......................... comb on head of bird: crest
iêt-hrôz...................... mythical bird of wondrous character: phoenix
iêt-jeûp...................... human figure made of straw and cloth set up in field to scare birds away: scarecrow
iôm .... flying organ of bird: wing; swimming organ of fish: fin
iôm-hsa..................... move the wings: flap
iolia.......................... all together: en masse
iov............................ one who has control: master

iov-cua .... in Luif, a word of the same part of speech as another but of greater importance: principal word
iob.............................. one who performs an action: doer
iob-cua .... noun signifying that which performs an action: subject
iot .... ungulate, ruminant animal with antlers: deer
iuv...............................liquid food secreted by mammary glands: milk
iuv-zrar....................... amorphous hydrated silica marked by changing hues: opal
iuv-jluz....................... solidified fat obtained by churning cream: butter
iuv-phûl-tzif.............. leafy vegetable often eaten as a salad: lettuce
iuv-gai.........................fatty substance gathering at top of milk: cream
ius .... shelled body generated by fowl or other creatures: egg; shaped like a hen's egg: oval
ius-rie......................... oval, bitter fruit which yields oil: olive
ius-rze .... bring forth young from egg: hatch
ius-hiz .... yellow core of egg: yolk
ius-voi .... organ producing ova: ovary
ius-zel......................... white contents of egg: albumen
iûr .... four-footed mammal: animal; fiercely cruel: brutal
iûr-uô......................... hollow shelter of wild beast: den
iûr.muir.uô .... place where domesticated animals are killed for food: abattoir
iûr.muir.vriam .... one who kills animals for the market: butcher
iûh .... respectble man, used as a term of address: Mister
iûn .... one who inhabits a territory: inhabitant; one belonging to a group or society: member

iûn-ril........................ number of persons inhabiting a territory: population
iûn-plaz...................... state where the people elect the government: democracy
ih .... denoting the idea following: that; in the form or character of: as
im .... in a manner corresponding to: according to
im lêr .... as the ultimate outcome: in the long run
im sa hrô .... as stated hereunder: as follows
ifu .... in a few words: in a word
isô .... in most cases: in general
izuz .... looking at each other: face-to-face
ijoh .... the other way round: vice versa
ib............................... for the purpose of: in order to; object aimed at: purpose
itcioc .... word for word: verbatim

-Ô-

ô.es........................... subject engaging attention: matter
ô.êz........................... beginning from a source: origin
ôêp........................... piece of furniture with level top on supports and used for diverse purposes: table
ôêp-sdôus .... piece of cloth for laying over table: tablecloth
ôêp-jroz..................... one sitting at the same table
ôin .... heavenly body revolving round the earth: moon
ôip............................ liquid stuff used to give relish to food: sauce
ôuv............................ violent wind accompanied by heavy fall of rain, hail, or snow: storm
ôuv-muir................... indiscriminate killing of human beings: massacre
ôuv-sjie..................... sunder with force: tear

ôuv-klû..................... highly dangerous disease marked by frequent purging: cholera

ôuv-khe..................... wanton act of injury: outrage

ôut........................... seat of any kind for a single person: chair

ô.ud.......................... place constituting the object of a journey: destination

ôr.hlût....................... male sexual organ: penis

ôr.mêus.io................ married man

ô.nlo......................... a particular sensation perceived by the olfactory sense: smell

ô.frê......................... a meeting arranged for talking over things together: conference

ôv............................. on farther side: beyond

ôv.lu......................... represent beyond what is true: exaggerate

ôv-hmav.................... light present in sky before sunrise and after sunset: twilight

ôv-hsa....................... intrude into land of others: encroach

ôv-fiûl....................... project beyond a surface: jut

ôv-fiûl-nêz................ elevated strip of land: ridge

ôv-fiûl-blêh............... what juts out beyond a surface: hump

ôv.sne....................... live longer than: survive

ôv-sko...................... beyond what is needed: redundant

ôv-cab...................... exceeding the usual limits: extravagant

ôv.pan...................... beyond usual operations of nature: supernatural

ôs............................ pertaining to what person or thing: whose

ô.czu........................ cultivation of land: agriculture

ô.jlô.......................... anything that happens: event

ô.dlû......................... that which is conceived by the mind: idea

ô.guin....................... binding written agreeement: bond

-O-

oi.lziap .... military officer: officer
oi.lziap-a .... chief commander of an army: general
oi.rmuêz.................. big vessel for boiling liquids: cauldron
oih............................ person above ordinary grade
oih.i .... persons above ordinary grade collectively: elite
oih-plaz .... state governed by a small class of allegedly superior persons: aristocracy
oim .... hard excrescence on head of some animals like oxen: horn
oi.mai....................... town of a great size: city
oin .... respectable woman, used as a term of address: Madam
oi.flêc .... large enclosed structure for subjecting diverse materials to heat: furnace
oi.fruc .... institution of higher learning: university
oi.vlioc-a .... chief commander of a fleet of ships: admiral
oi.vrôih .... main division of expanse of water on earth's surface: ocean
oi.srêm .... big house: mansion
oi.sfas .... principal room in a house: hall
oic............................ large, striped carnivore of cat family: tiger; violent in behaviour: fierce
oic-eûk..................... huge and ferocious Afrian ape: gorilla
oic-flier..................... voracious wild animal of same genus as dog: wolf
oic-flier-htug .... human being assuming form of wolf: werewolf
oi-czuûb .... strong twist of fibre of some thickness: rope
oi-jui .... large block of stone: rock
oi.jluêm.................... principal division of land surface of the earth: continent

oi.jlûv .... community of families of common descent: clan
oi.phôs .... big mounted gun: cannon
oi.khuêj .... large vessel for holding fluids: tank
oi.gzauf .... extensive territories under one sovereign power: empire
ouz............................... fibre transmitting impulses between a centre like the brain and some other part of body: nerve
ol................................. up to such time: until
of .... come to be: become
of-rseut....................... larva of fly: maggot
of-fries........................ larva of frog: tadpole
of-brian .... tough, white, elastic tissue commonly developing into bone: cartilage
of-kleuc .... larva of butterfly: caterpillar
o.vûil.......................... found only in the imagination: imaginary
o.sjie.pom.................. that side of vulgar fraction indicating number of parts taken: numerator
ocêgi........................... if other things remain the same: *ceteris paribus*
o.jci .... much loved: dear
o.kri.vce .... deserving of sorrow: deplorable
o.kri.ceûl .... capable of exciting amusement: funny
o.kri.biôm .... capable of exciting admiration: admirable
og............................... on condition that: if

-u-

ual.............................. gaseous mixture surrounding earth: air; surrounding conditions: environment
ual-luû....................... gaseous element constituting nearly four-fifths of atmosphere: nitrogen
ual-htê....................... provide for passage of air: ventilate

ual-mul .... local atmospheric conditions at a particular time: weather
ual-mrail .... instrument that measures atmospheric pressure: barometer
ual-vlaul .... gathering of bubbles on liquid: foam
ual-csû...................... mechanically make air attain required temperature: air-conditioning
ual-jza .... expand with air or gas: inflate
uam.......................... thin, easily torn material fabricated from pulp: paper
uam-plauf ....tobacco encased in small paper cylinder: cigarette
uac .... sliding receptacle in an article of furniture: drawer
ueh........................... heavenly body round which earth revolves: sun
ueh-rial..................... physical affliction caused by exposure to intense heat of sun: sunstroke
uem.......................... what is eaten for sustenance: food
uem.eu .... article of food: viand
uem-hse.................... great dearth of food in an area: famine
uem-fleu-puô .... list of articles of food available: menu
uem-sviu .... a pair of rods for picking up food: chopsticks
uem.zri..................... desire to eat: appetite
uem-jro .... unduly fond of eating: greedy
uem-due....................sauce and juice in which food is cooked: gravy
uêr............................ material for colouring a surface: paint
uêr-vuêl................... resinous solution imparting glossy appearance: varnish
uêj .... vapour generated from water: steam
uêj.rôûn .... cook with the aid of steam: steam
uêj.slar...................... ship using steam as motive power: steamship
uêj-phêuz .... vessel in which steam is generated from boiling water: boiler

uos .... sweet delicacy made of flour, sugar and other ingredients: cake
uûd .... surface of earth viewed as a place of human habitation: world
uûk.......................... substance used internally or externally in treatment of disease: medicine; substance taken internally as a remedy, tonic, or for some physical effect: drug
uûk-csû .... deal medically with: treat
u.lkû......................... uncomfortable in presence of others: shy
u.rza .... sell goods in small quantities to consumers: retail
u.rbo .... sleep lightly for a short period: doze
u.hêun...................... flow lightly: trickle
u.hiôp .... slightly angry: annoyed
u.huûl .... light wave: ripple
u.hne......................... see cursorily: glimpse
um .... what person: who
un .... on this side: hither
u.not .... moderately warm: lukewarm
u.fiôv........................ jump lightly: skip
u.vuêl .... shine faintly: glimmer
u.sag......................... of little importance: trifling
u.siut .... make a slight cut: notch
u.sla.......................... light work
u.snôi .... slightly wet: damp
u.spiû .... weak point in character: foible
u.zsû......................... having mild enjoyment: comfortable
u.jci .... find pleasing: like
u.poc......................... small hollow in yieldable surface: dimple
uput .... to each distributively: respectively
ud .... in the direction of: to

ud-ian-czuûb .... blood vessel tranporting blood back to heart: vein
ud.nu .... to inside of: into
ud-vrôih-cêi............. structure projecting into sea for use as landing stage etc.: pier
ud.pauk.................... grant use of temporarily: lend
ud-piev..................... drink to: toast
ud-krôf..................... structure forming approach to doorway of building: porch
u.grê......................... stop irresolutely: hesitate

-û-

ûil .... one characterized by a certain quality
ûif .... huge, thick-skinned quadruped with tusks and trunk: elephant
ûif-iêt .... biggest of birds, very swift of foot and given to swallowing hard articles: ostrich
ûif-reu .... extinct type of elephant: mammoth
ûif.vhoil.................... long, protruding tooth of elephant: tusk
ûif-poi .... large citrus fruit with thick, green rind: pomelo
ûif-priog.................. large, aquatic animal with huge tusks inhabiting arctic regions: walrus
ûuc........................... shelter built by birds: nest; place to which one retreats for safety: refuge
ûuc-fzi...................... lie comfortably against: nestle
ûuc-srêm .... house for lodging travellers: lodging house
ûz............................. as a result: thus
ûp .... similar to: like
ûp-euf .... train of attendants: retinue
ûp-euk...................... bird of prey similar to but smaller than eagle: hawk

ûp-eûk........................ big animal resembling monkey but without a tail: ape
ûpoci........................ for a particular purpose: ad hoc
ûp.lu .... make alike: assimilate
ûp-rcûf........................ edible seed of a certain leguminous plant: pea
ûp-rtam........................ portable contrivance with steps for climbing purposes: ladder
ûp-hsa .... remove from one place or person to another: transfer
ûp-hpi .... relieve from distress with mild words: soothe
ûp-mro........................ produce literature or music: compose
ûp-fiem .... explanation that highlights the similarities between two things: analogy
ûp-flêc........................ closed box for producing heat for cooking or warning purposes: stove
ûp-flier........................ small, gregarious quadruped similar to a dog: jackal
ûp-fluaz........................ utensil with perforations for sifting: sieve
ûp-fries........................ tailless, frog-like creature: toad
ûp-fnoôl........................ crow-like chattering bird with black-and-white feathers: magpie
ûp-fjûb........................ marsh plant resembling grass with pithy stalk: rush
ûp-ftuav .... piece of metal or wood with sloping sides that form a thin edge, used for diverse purposes requiring force: wedge
ûp-vsud........................ incorporeal part of a person deemed capable of independent existence: soul
ûp-saic........................ risk money on something turning up as expected: bet
ûp-siû........................ fleshy, tapered fruit allied to apple: pear
ûp-slôn........................ set of regulations on any subject: code

ûp-srû .... speak aloud what is memorized: recite
ûp-smior .... marine creature allied to tortoise: turtle
ûp-spuin.................. metal disk emitting ringing sound when struck: gong
ûp-stuûc.................. showy article of little value: bauble
ûp-sdôus.................. coarse fabric for covering floor, etc.: mat
ûp-zle .... beat lightly with fingers: pat
ûp-crum .... overhanging cover: hood
ûp-cheud................. smooth and iridescent part of certain shells: mother-of-pearl
ûp-chûn .... black residue of charred wood: charcoal
ûp-cri .... examine critically: test
ûp-criôm .... timid woolly quadruped of goat family: sheep
ûp-criôm.hiû .... hair of sheep: wool
ûp-crif .... edible tuber of tropical plant resembling potato: yam
up-cvo .... make sounds resulting from laryngeal spasms: hiccup
ûp-czûus.................. small quadruped with long ears of same genus as the horse: donkey; stupid person: fool
ûp-cgi....................... sit with haunches near heels and knees bent: squat
ûp-jzêk .... white, hard, malleable metal: nickel
ûp-pleuf .... one of species of small rodent: mouse
ûp-plo .... afflicted with a usually temporary mental disorder manifesting itself in wild excitement and incoherent talk: delirious
ûp-pre .... established practice of a community: custom
ûp-ba....................... point of convergence: focus
ûp-bef-nio .... coarse type of cinnamon: cassia
ûp-blêh.................... insubtantial likeness as in a mirror or in the mind: image

ûp-tliô .... attach as addition: append
ûp-tres...................... pungent bulb of a liliaceous plant: garlic
ûp-truôz .... vessel of some size, not too shallow and usually not circular, for holding food at table: dish
ûp-thien .... large bird of duck family with beautiful plumage and long, flexible neck: swan
ûp-tho .... infectious disease accompanied by fever, headache, feeling of exhaustion, etc.: influenza
ûp-thuas .... drug derived from morphine: heroin
ûp-kêu...................... short descriptive appellation: title
up-kraun .... broad scooping instrument: shovel
ûp-kruod................. small, commonly cylindrical and pointed or tapered piece of wood, for various purposes: peg
ûp-khe...................... cause hurt other than of a physical nature: injure
ûp-khov.................... black substance deposited by burning fuel: soot
ûp-khuêj.................. open wooden vessel for holding liquid, etc.: tub
ûp-kzoêp .... insect of order hymenoptera with slender waist and poisonous sting: wasp
ûp-gêd...................... parallelogram with oblique, equal sides: rhombus
ûp-giûk .... feel chagrin at the advantages of others: envy
ûp-grê...................... rule that prohibits inhabitants of a locality from going out of doors at certain hours: curfew

-l-

lai..............................substance that cannot break down chemically into other substances: element; one of the parts of a thing: component; branch of an administration or other organization: department
la.lva....................... no longer alive: deceased

laz .... dot or very small spot: point
laz-oic........................ carnivorous feline quadruped with dark spots: leopard
laz.lu .... scatter in drops: spatter
laz-rpû........................ extract in drops: distil
laz.fleu....................... minute bit of matter: particle
laz-chuf .... long, sharp, pointed weapon for throwing: spear
laz-dba .... collect at one point: concentrate
lac .... at that time: then
leliv .... identification of the Supreme Being with the universe: pantheism
lemtêh .... belief in existence of only one god: monotheism
lesotêh .... belief in existence of plural gods: polytheism
leg .... colour like that of blood or ruby: red; intense emotion: passion (v. ên.bre)
leg-laz........................ infectious fever marked by red spots on skin: measles
leg-luû....................... inert gas found in atmosphere used in electric discharge lamps: neon
leg-vric .... big wading bird with red legs: stork
leg-zrar .... transparent red jewel: ruby
leg-cli .... hard, red, painful swelling on surface of body: boil
leg-chiûv .... big gallinaceous bird of pheasant family: turkey
leg-poi-bik................. of reddish brown colour: auburn
leg-phi....................... acute disease marked by intestinal ulceration, fever, and rose-coloured spots: typhoid
leg-due .... element of red liquid with suffocating odour: bromine
leg-dûn...................... bluish purple in colour: violet
leg-dûn-lai................. crystalline element producing corrosive, violet vapour: iodine

leg-dûn-zrar .... bluish violet gemstone, a kind of quartz: amethyst
lêr.............................. long in duration: long; long in use: old (v. hrô.lêr)
lêr.jû......................... long afterwards
lêr-tbo .... keep back progress: delay
lêr.do .... for as long a time as: as long as
lêr.gzô....................... stay for an undue length of time: linger
lên .... measuring a good distance from side to side: broad; comprising much: comprehensive
lên-aiz-nêz................ distance recorded in degrees north or south of equator: latitude
lên.o.jci .... liked by many people: popular
lên-roiz...................... announce publicly: proclaim
lên-ruûs..................... choose by vote: elect
lên-rnû .... any disease spreading widely among a community at any one time: epidemic
lên-ceûl .... smile with lips stretched wide: grin
lên-bûuj .... draw attention of the public: advertise
lên.dê .... from one side to the other: across
lên.guz....................... obtuse angle
li................................ and not
lie .... entire physical organism of living thing: body
lie.môip.io .... one who steals what is carried on the person: pickpocket
lien .... retain in memory: remember
lien.ôi .... object serving as a reminder: souvenir
lien-puô..................... brief record to help one to remember: memorandum
lie-vêg........................ incline body forward and downward: stoop
lie-vlaul .... liquid exuded from skin: sweat
lie-sla......................... physical work: labour
lie-czû .... enclose with arms: embrace
lie-jluê .... assume a certain posture of the body: attitude

lie.jziû .... worn out by work: tired
lie-ba .... contracted section of body between hips and ribs: waist
lie.kiûr .... clean body with water: bathe
lie.kiûr.sfas .... room where one can bathe: bathroom
liôl .... make scheme beforehand: plan; course of action to be followed: policy
liôl-uam .... series of events proposed: programme
liôl-rnê .... conceive and draw plan for execution: design
liôl-zku .... conceive and make: devise
liu .... female child: girl
liûz .... have no knowledge of: don't know
liûz.e .... person whom one does not know: stranger
liûz-drû .... pay no due attention: careless
liûgued .... solid figure with equal, parallel polygons as bases and parallelograms as sides: prism
lil .... shedding much light: bright; plainly visible clear (v. hne-lil); evident to understanding; obvious; mentally bright: intelligent
lil-czu .... cultivate intellectual accomplishments: culture
lil-cto .... lose a quality gradually: fade
lil-buv-jui .... transparent mineral with symmetrical form of plane faces: crystal
lif .... having taste like that of sugar: sweet; softly captivating
lifûe .... substance consisting of a collection of similar cells: tissue
lif.nos .... fortune and misfortune
lô .... in a lower position: under; lesser in value: minor
lô.êz .... in a position lower than but not contiguous to: below

lô.û........................... one below another in respect of rank or other quality: inferior
lô-laz-rnû .... mild disease mainly affecting children and characterized by a rash: chicken pox
lô.lu........................... yield and accept control: submit
lô.rêe .... small division of a country for administrative purposes: district
lô-rza......................... sell cheaper than others: undersell
lô-rtam...................... to or on floor below stairs: downstairs
lô.mi .... beneath and touching: under
lô-vlaul-slar .... ship sailing under the sea: submarine
lô-vluar-pue............. passage excavated below surface of land: tunnel
lô-vrê......................... move downwards by force of gravity: fall
lô-vric........................ that part of leg below knee: leg
lô-vric-al................... forepart of leg below knee: shin
lô-vrôih-chuf............ missile launched under the sea that explodes upon hitting an object: torpedo
lô-stô .... serve in a minor capacity to promote: subserve
lô-zcos .... area at base of trunk formed by hip bones: pelvis
lô-cua-sjie................. minor vocabulary division (Luif)
lô.pom.vlul............... fixed time interval, division of a minute: second
lô.tûu .... smaller type of flora: plant
lô-tluem .... fabric case filled with padding on which one sleeps: mattress
lô-tbo .... bring under control: subdue
lua............................. original entity from which all others proceed: First Cause
luam.......................... fix defects: repair
luav .... turn into liquid from application of heat: melt
luav-spuc.................. building where things are made by melting and moulding: foundry

luav-jui .... molten matter ejected from volcano: lava
luav-glup .... piece of metal in electric circuit that melts at danger point: fuse
luisehi .... member of a race that chiefly inhabits East Asia: Mongolian
luû .... substance normally in an aeriform state: gas
luû-vlaul .... aerated drink: aerated water
luû-vlêô .... inflated ball capable of rising upwards: balloon
lub .... cubical quantity: volume; solid figure: solid
lub-hsa .... movement of people and vehicles on a road: traffic
lub-feur .... reduce in volume by drawing together: shrink
lub.fleu .... three-dimensional piece of anything: block
lub-vlic .... person with hump on back: hunchback
lub-zca .... grow in size: swell
lub.plia .... assemblage of things lying closely together: heap
lub.thin .... piece of wood with the three dimensions not too different: block
lûur .... mild in behaviour: gentle
lûr .... sweet in smell: fragrant; conductive to advantage: favourable; well disposed towards others: benevolent
lûr-lrim .... aromatic labiate plant: mint
lûr-foi .... aromatic kernel of evergreen tropical tree used as spice: nutmeg
lûr-brôn .... substance emitting fragrant smell on burning: incense
lûr-thin .... fragrant wood of various trees: sandalwood
lûporazû .... ammonium chloride: sal ammoniac
lûk .... low in temperature: cold
lûkora .... compound of nitrogen and hydrogen, a pungent, colourless gas: ammonia
lûk-crêus .... long outermost coat worn for warmth: overcoat

lûk-phi .... disease with recurrent fever caused by parasite and conveyed by a mosquito: malaria
lrai............................ once more: again
lrai.lu........................ say or do once more: repeat
lrai.rpû .... regain prossession: recover
lrai-vlub.................... sound repeated by reflection: echo
lrai.vrê...................... go back
lrai.suêt .... give similar treatment in return: requite
lrai.sne...................... restore to consciousness: revive
lrai.zlog .... son of spouse by previous marriage: stepson
lrai.zma .... begin again: resume
lrai.cuem .... give back
lrai.czo...................... take back: retract
lrai.pci .... gain back what is lost: regain
lrai.tbo .... put back: restore
lrai.drô .... turn back to former position: return
lreon......................... internal, muscular, pear-shaped bag for digesting food: stomach
lreon-luav................. dissolve in stomach for assimilation: digest
lrim .... either of fleshy flaps closing the mouth: lip
lrim-piev .... drink with lips a little at a time: sip
lro .... signifying possibility: may
lro.vlô....................... it may happen: maybe
lrob .... one descended from an ancestor: descendant
lruic.......................... land where trees or plants are grown for their commercial produce: plantation
lruic-gzauf................ a country occupied by a foreign power: colony
lhôm .... disintegrated matter in surface layer of land: earth
lhôm-uem .... any matter added to soil to make it fertile: manure or fertilizer
lhôm-smiûp............. the common worm inhibiting the ground: earthworm

lhôm-plat.................. channel dug in the ground to convey water: ditch
lnu .... appear to be: seem
lnu.fa........................ appearing to be so: ostensible
lnu-znû.û .... one who seems wise but is not so: wiseacre
lnu-kuv .... resembling but not really so: quasi
lfe............................ exercise choice of action: will; fix the features of a thing: determine (v. nriô-lfe)
lfe-zri........................ voluntaily ready to do: willing
lfe.pa .... without any choice: *nolens volens*
lva .... have being: exist
lva-rêh...................... prevailing usage or custom: fashion
lva.fa .... expressing presence of a quality: positive
lva-sko...................... necessary for some particular purpose: essential
lziap .... one employed to fight a war: soldier
lziap.ia..................... group of soldiers: troop
lziap.ia-mo .... main division of the military forces of a country: army
lpa........................... hold in equilibrium: balance; agreement of parts with one another: harmony (v. gûin-lpa)
lpa.aê....................... apparatus for weighing: balance, scale
lpa-suêt .... make an equivalent return: compensate
lpa-plêm.................. motor-driven, two-wheeled vehicle: motorcycle
lpa.plia .... group of things that go together making one whole: set
lbe........................... of feeble intelligence: foolish
lbe.jci .... love to a foolish degree: dote
lbion .... organ for breathing air: lung
lbu .... bring about a result: effect; perform and complete a task: fulfill
lbu-ian-voi............... located behind a stomach, a soft organ capable of inducing modifications in the blood: spleen
lbu-lgi .... have firm belief: convince

lbu-zgu .... the act or power to effect: influence
lbu-cua .... type of compound word in Luif whose meaning differs little from the combined meanings of its component words: resultant word
lbu-pom .... part that follows later: sequel
lbu.blê .... without intended result: futile
lbu-blêh .... that by which something is effected: means
lto .... feel inconvenience or confusion: trouble
lto-nuap .... complete disorder: chaos
lto-siab .... mutter in dissatisfaction: grumble
lto-suêf .... applied to a crowd, break out in disorder: riot
lto-jluê .... a trying situation: predicament
lto-beûl .... have trouble and worry: bother
ldêi .... direction of setting sun: west
lkô .... eliminate an opening: close; place something over: cover
lkô.ôi .... thing made of any substance for plugging a hole: stopper; anything that serves as a cover: lid
lkô-mau .... alphabetical letter contradistinguished from vowel: consonant
lkô-mau-plia .... in Luif, a group of consonants classified for purposes of vocabulary formation: consonant group
lkô-nuê .... open area enclosed by walls: court
lkô-zoû .... covering worn over face for concealment: mask
lkô-zgu .... press together: squeeze
lkô-chauk .... periodical payment for past services: pension
lkô-blop .... hand closed tightly: fist
lkô-truôz .... device for fastening door, etc., usually operated by key: lock
lkô-daul .... cook by boiling slowly with some liquid: stew

lkû............................ uncomfortable feeling of humiliation induced by something discreditable: shame
lkû-jlô .... say or do something that shocks people generally: scandal
lgi............................ consider it true: believe; rely on other person's integrity: trust (v. fe-lgi)
lgi-raz .... certain of fulfilment of expectations: confident
lgi-roiz...................... trustfully impart secret to: confide
lgi-mli .... one who encounters death or intense suffering for his beliefs: martyr
lgi-jza .... disseminate ideas with a view to influencing people: propagandize
lgi-kuv...................... constant in adherence to: loyal

-r-

ralûkoje.................... strong, corrosive, nitrogenous acid: nitric acid
raz .... feeling no doubt: certain
razû .... acid compounded of hydrogen and chlorine: hydrochloric acid
raciz .... mineral oil consisting of natural mixture of hydrocarbons: petroleum
raciz-jluz................... oil obtained chiefly from distillation of crude petroleum and used for lighting, etc.: kerosene
racip .... organic compound of only hydrogen and carbon: hydrocarbon
reu............................ whatever has become extinct: extinct thing
reu.fa .... no longer existing: extinct
rev .... one of two equal parts: half
rev-rev .... settle by mutual concession: compromise
rev.zten..................... brother by only one parent: half brother

rev-bauz .... almost fall down while walking: stumble
rev-bôi...................... anything of a semi-solid nature like jelly: gel
rev.drô .... turn so as to face the opposite direction: turn about, turn around
rez .... integral number just above eight: nine
rec .... to that extent: so; of that kind: such
rec-fleu .... such person or thing: so-and-so
rêe .... division of a country: province, district, state
rêe.kûz..................... one who has charge of a province or district: governor
rêh............................ way in which a thing is done: manner
rêh.lu........................ conduct oneself: behave
rêh-chêb .... stereotyped rule of polite behaviour: etiquette
rial............................ deal repeated blows: beat; make forcible contact: knock
rial-liôl .... plan for overcoming opponent: stratagem
rial-rza...................... public sale in which items are sold to the highest bidder: auction
rial-hsa .... move or remove with brushing strokes: sweep
rial-flaic.................... musical instrument consisting of a pair of clashing brass plates: cymbals
rial-siut..................... cut out with blows of axe, etc.: hew
rial-zru .... beat forcibly like the heart: throb
rial-czuûb .... flexible instrument for beating: whip
rial-pfe...................... contend physically: fight
rial-blêh.................... sports implement for hitting ball: bat
rial-tiûn.................... eat by striking with beak: peck
rial-khe..................... hurt by means of a blow that does not break the skin: bruise
riam .... convey on person or by vehicle: carry
riam.ôi .... thing carried: load
riam-hmav................ light carried in the hand: torch

riam-sdôus................ cloth carried on person for wiping purposes: handkerchief
riam-bloek................ labourer engaged to carry things: porter
riam-truôz................ shallow vessel for carrying articles: tray
rie............................ edible product of plant associated with seed: fruit
rie.lruic..................... plantation of fruit trees: orchard
rie.nio....................... skin of fruit: peel
rie.vê .... fruit season
rie-zoc .... soft part of fruit: pulp
rie-chauk.................. payment made for use of money: interest
rie-jluz...................... conserve made by boiling fruit with sugar: jam
rie-pom .... segment of fruit like orange
ril .... amount counted in units: number
ril-rûus .... signify choice in a formal way: vote
ril.fleu .... discrete unit
rilvafvi...................... disease caused by germs found in soil and characterized by painful spasm of muscles: tetanus
ril-kuv .... numerical facts gathered and tabulated: statistics
rin .... sound like a bell: ring
ri.nôf.û..................... younger person: junior
ris............................. smaller in quantity: less
ris-ril .... the part smaller in number: minority
rô .... what place: where
rôef........................... give one thing in return for another: exchange; sum of money paid for purchase of a thing: price
rôef.rial-pfê.............. fight one another
rôef-jêh..................... high in price: dear
rôef-gûin .... with parts agreeing with one another: consistent
rôu .... numerical symbol: figure
rôûn .... prepare for the table using heat: cook; prepare from various ingredients: concoct

rôûn.rkec .... cooked rice
rôûn.sfas .... room for cooking food: kitchen
rôûn-pluiz .... big, long-handled spoon used in cooking: ladle
rôhipoje .... ferrous sulphate: copperas
rôs .... belonging to you: your
ro .... comprehending as part: including
roih .... shed tears: weep, cry
roih.siab .... give vent to loud sounds as in distress: cry out
roiz .... give utterance to works: talk
roiz-liôl .... confer in order to arrive at some arrangement: negotiate
roiz-htê .... honest and forthright in speech: frank
roiz-vlô .... make known: declare
roiz-sgam .... electrical apparatus for conveying speech by wire over a distance: telephone
roiz-crul .... eloquent public speech: oratory
roiz-jroi .... inconsiderate in behaviour or speech: rude
roiz-jziû .... weary by talking tediously: bore
roiz-pêa .... punctuation mark indicating directly reported dialogue: speech or quotation mark
roiz-blêh .... subject dealt with: theme
roiz-gsô-uam .... printed paper posted for public information: poster
roiz-gbo .... deliberately utter falsehood: lie
roic .... have on a person: wear
roic-vlaul .... elastic skeleton of an aquatic animal, used by people for absorbing liquids: sponge
roic-vce .... grieve over loss: mourn
roic-tau .... distinguishing mark worn on person: badge
ro-ril .... total prior to making deductions: gross
rua .... medium of communication of thought consisting of words: language

rua-rêh .... manner of use of words in expressing oneself: diction
rua-hpu .... render from one language to another: translate
ruam .... vie with others for something: compete
ruam.io .... one competing with another: rival
ruam.ôi .... reward won in competition: prize
ruam-soun................ compete by running: race
rua-sjie .... variety of language spoken by particular community: dialect
ruap .... treat hospitably: entertain; engage the attention pleasurably: amuse (v. zu.gle); behave towards: treat
ruap.e .... one who is entertained: guest
ruap.io...................... one who entertains: host
rui .... place off coast intended for reception of ships: harbour
rui.mai .... town having a harbour: port
rum .... belonging to him, her, or it: his, hers, or its
rud .... of poor quality: bad
rud.rêh.czûus........... vicious horse
rud-hsa..................... handle awkwardly: fumble
rud.mul.czûus .... horse in miserably bad condition: jade, nag
rud-za-fien................ noxious exhalation: miasma
rud-ciam .... use in a bad way: abuse
rud-jzu .... mar with something wrong: blemish; undesirable mark: stigma
rud.gun .... small and contemptible: petty
rûif........................... take as one's own: adopt
rûif.zlog.................... adopted son
rûo .... large nut with white flesh and tasty liquid: coconut
rûus.......................... pick out the most desirable: choose
rûus-vliêc.................. elected ruler of a country: president

rûus-zku .... choose for an office: appoint
rûm .... greatest in quantity or degree: most; to a very great extent: extremely
rûm-laz .... highest possible: maximum
rûg .... ten thousand; very numerous: multitudinous
rlu .... impart knowledge: teach
rlu.eu .... information taught at one sitting: lesson
rlu-roiz .... deliver instructional discourse to an audience: lecture
rlu-tuê .... rule of conduct purporting to be a truth gathered from experience: maxim
rhez .... large white flower of genus *Lilium*: lily
rmed .... small green plant, widely distributed, and with closely arranged leaves: moss
rmuêz .... vessel for boiling water, normally with lid, handle, and spout: kettle
rnê .... use any instrument or material to represent in the form of a picture, coloured or not: draw
rnê-fri .... explain or ornament with pictures: illustrate
rnû .... disorder affecting body: disease
rnû-cuem .... of disease communicable by contact or in some other way: contagious, infectious
rna-jzu .... sign characteristic of a disease: symptom
rnû-due .... preparation containing germs administered by inoculation or injection to make one immune to a disease: vaccine
rfom .... common culinary vegetable with round head or heart: cabbage
rvoh .... needle-like growth of plant: thorn
rvoh-srûuf .... small, spiny insectivore: hedgehog
rvoh-thin-tûu .... wild prickly shrub of various kinds: bramble

rseut .... any dipterous insect: fly; whatever is obtrusively annoying: nuisance

rseut-lto .... be active and particular over: fuss

rseut-fnoôl .... small bird similar to crow: jackdaw

rseut-sgon .... slender axis of plant: stalk

rseut-czil .... small branch: twig

rseut-czûus .... small horse: pony

rseut-kêg .... on a small scale: miniature

rsûh .... green, bladed, food-manufacturing organ of plant: leaf

rsûh-ius .... beaten egg fried without stirring and folded over: omelette

rsûh-hiû .... growth on bird's skin consisting of shaft and barbs: feather

rsûh-zrar .... green precious stone, a variety of beryl: emerald

rza .... exchange goods for money: sell

rza-viô .... woman who trades her body indiscriminately for money: prostitute

rza-seêm .... store goods for sale: stock

rze .... bring into existence: bear

rze.ôi .... thing produced: product

rze-leg .... climbing plant from which a red dye is obtained: madder

rze-fûl .... render ineffective: frustrate

rze.vam.phiom .... kitten

rze-voi .... organ in which embryo develops: womb

rze.vliêc .... hereditary ruler of a country: monarch

rze-vliêc-plaz .... state ruled by a monarch: monarchy

rze-srah .... social science dealing with production, distribution and consumption of wealth: economics

rze-sma .... assistance in delivering a child: midwifery

roûf .... kidney-shaped seed of leguminous plant: bean

rjok .... grain of a particular hardy grass: barley
rjok-aot .... alcoholic drink made from malted barley: beer
rpê.......................... profess falsely: pretend
rpê.biôm .... praise unduly for one's own purposes: flatter
rpû .... obtain or acquire: get; gain money by work: earn (v. chauk.pci)
rpû-suêt.................... total amount expended on making or acquiring an article: cost
rpû-chauk................. earnings from business, etc.: income
rpû-czû..................... take and hold: occupy
rpû-piûj.................... find answer, explanation of way out: solve
rpû-pom................... apportioned share: quota
rpû-gzô..................... obtain by transmission: inherit
rbo .... rest by becoming unaware of things: sleep
rbo-mul.................... be in temporary state of inactivity: abeyance
rbo-siab .... make hoarse breathing sounds in sleep: snore
rbo.sfas..................... room used for sleeping: bedroom
rbo-piûj.................... artificially induced state of profound sleep: hypnosis
rbo-krauf................. clothing worn for sleeping: pyjamas
rtam .... series of steps for getting from one floor to another: stairs; system of graduations: scale
rtam.eu..................... a tread in a flight of stairs: step
rti.............................ascertain extent: measure; ascertain weight: weigh
rdêup....................... any implement for writing: pen
rdêup-sgon .... the rod of a pen: penholder
rdêup-jluz................ pointed writing part of pen: nib
rkec .... white grain of plant widely cultivated in warm climes: rice
rkec.druap .... land where rice is grown: rice field
rgêp......................... building where the staff of a government department work: office

-h-

hau............................ assumed world
haracikoje................. sodium bicarbonate
has............................ in the early part of life: young
hajera .... sodium hydroxide
heu........................... male child: boy
heun......................... consider probable: guess
heu.vê....................... period when one is a boy: boyhood
hem.......................... offensive in smell: foul; exciting aversion: repellent; harbouring ill-will: malicious
hem-vliêl .... big bird of prey given to eating carrion: vulture
hev .... appearance caused by reflection of rays of light: colour
hev.ia....................... range of colours obtained by diffraction: spectrum
hev-hpu.................... spoil with spots of different colour: stain
hev-jzab.................... dissolved substance used for colouring cloth, etc.: dye
hec .... disagreable to senses: unpleasant
hê............................ in contact with upper surface of at a higher point: on, above; greater in value, etc.: major
hê.êz......................... at a higher point: above
hêun......................... move along (applied to wind): blow; move along (applied to water): flow
hêun.aê.................... contrivance for making air, used to fan a fire: bellows
hêun-êol .... small body journeying through space made luminous when in contact with earth's atmosphere: meteor
hêun-lbu .... influence mind in lofty way: inspire

hêun-roiz.................. speak readily and flowingly: fluent: talk much and idly: chatter

hêun-hsa .... incite to action by infusing with spirit: encourage

hêun-vrê.................... sail here and there: cruise

hêun-jzêk .... white liquid element: mercury

hêun-kiûr .... apparatus for purifying liquid by passing it through sand or other medium: filter

hê.û.......................... one above others in rank or in some other way: superior

hê-laz-rnû................. severe contagious disease marked by eruption of pustules: smallpox

hê-lô.......................... with the upper part below: upside down

hê.rêe .... major division of a country: province

hê-rtam .... to or on the floor or storey above stairs: upstairs

hê.mi......................... in contact with a surface: on

hê-vrê .... move upwards: rise

hê-vric....................... leg from hip to knee: thigh

hê-cua-sjie .... in Luif a principal division of the vocabulary: major vocabulary division

hê.pom.vlul .... fixed time interval, division of an hour: minute

hê.tûu........................ large perennial plant with a single, woody trunk: tree

hê-tluem.................... large sheet of cloth for covering the body while in bed: blanket

hia............................ human being

hia-eûk .... large arboreal anthropoid ape native to Sumatra and Borneo: orangutang

hia.i.......................... all human beings considered collectively: humankind

hia.ia .... a number of people closely united for some common purpose: party

hia-muir .... killing of a human being: homicide
hia-stuûc .... toy representing human being: doll
hia.zku.brail .... waterway dug for navigation: canal
hia.tiûn.io .... person who feeds on human flesh: cannibal
hia-thôuh .... picture representing real person: portrait
hiêm......................... in accordance with what is rightfully due: just
hiôp .... inflamed with displeasure: angry
hiôp-lto .... hurt the feelings of: offend
hiôp-miôz................ deep rumbling sound of angry dog: growl
hiû .... filament growing from skin: hair; growth on bird's skin consisting of shaft and barbs: feather (v. rsûh-hiû)
hiû-rie .... oval fruit with hairy rind: rambutan
hiû.siut.vriam .... one whose occupation is to crop hair: barber
hiû.zel .... with hair of head largely turned grey: grey-haired
hiû.blê...................... bare of hair on head: bald
hiû-truar.................. silk fabric with fine pile on one side: velvet
hiû-krois.................. parasitic wingless insect infesting hair: louse
hiû-kruod................ metal device for fastening the hair: hairpin
hiz .... of colour resembling that of gold: yellow; of great value: precious
hiz-lai .... yellow non-metallic element, insoluble in water and burning with strong smell: sulphur
hiz-rnû .... disease due to presence of bile in blood causing eyes and skin to turn yellow: jaundice
hiz-hmav .... metallic element of alkali group burning with yellow light: sodium
hiz-phûl-jluz............ translucent yellow fossil resin capable of taking high polish: amber
hôi........................... anything of a material nature: concrete object
hôi.fa....................... of a material nature: concrete

hôi-pauk.................. give as security for money borrowed: pawn
hôj.......................... superficial extent: area; outer part of a thing: surface; plane figure; extent of activity: scope
hôj.fleu.................... flat piece
hôj.czal.................... science dealing with surface of earth and its phenomena: geography
hôj.plia.................... group spread over a surface
hôj.thin.................... thin, flat piece of timber, usually much greater in length than in width: board
hôj-dluô.................. flat side
hozôo....................... indispensable condition: *sine qua non*
hue.......................... substance that occupies space: matter
hue-laz.................... smallest possible unit of a substance capable of retaining its chemical identity: molecule
hue-nuap................. emitting invisible rays from nuclear disintegration: radioactive
hues......................... grow better: improve; help advance: promote (v. stô-al)
hue.sô...................... theory that the universe contains only matter: materialism
hue.suô.................... faculty for exciting sensation: sense
hue.be..................... one who believes that only matter exists: materialist
hui.......................... produce shrill sound with breath through lips: whistle
huûl........................ movement of water in a ridge-and-trough form: wave
huûl-hsa.................. vary from one position to the other alternately: fluctuate
huûl-hpu................. twist out of regular shape: distort
huûl-sdôus.............. thin fabric with wrinkly surface: crêpe

huûl-zgu.................. energy moving in electromagnetic waves: radiation
huûl-jui.................. suspended weight swinging freely: pendulum
huûl-tûu.................. plant with slender, flexible branches: willow
hum.................. without delay: immediately
hum-vam.................. not long after: soon
hum.su.................. as soon as
hum.jû.................. and immediately
huv.................. of little width: narrow; of restricted extent: confined
huv-guz.................. acute angle
hû.................. notwithstanding the fact that: though
hlan.................. time taken by earth to complete one rotation round its axis: day; particular time specified in terms of day, month, and year: date
hlan-a.................. Monday
hlan-sfo.................. daily record of events: diary
hlan-kraut.................. tabulated register of months and days of the year: calendar
hli.................. perceive with the ear: hear
hlier.................. one devoted to philosophy: philosopher
hli.io.ia.................. gathering of listeners: audience
hli-cua.................. what is told by others: hearsay
hlu.................. isn't
hlua.................. figure composed of six equal square faces: cube
hlût.................. sexual organ of generation of either sex: sexual organ
hriûp.................. one engaged in a manual art: craftsman
hriûp.sla.................. work of a craftsman: craftsmanship
hriûp-crul.................. skilled trade involving making of artistic objects: arts
hrô.................. move in one's direction: come; get to a place: arrive

hrô.lêr .... long in use or existance: old
hrô.vam.................... just or recently come into use or existance: new
hrôz.......................... assumed thing
hrô-zvê .... come into view: appear
hron .... relative apart by one more generation
hron.nrûn................. parent's father: grandfather
hmaf......................... fine-grained metamorphic rock that easily splits into flat plates: slate
hmav .... radiant energy that makes things visible: light
hmav-cto .... temporary concealment of light of a heavenly object by another: eclipse
hmav-phêuz .... case enclosing light shining through it: lantern
hmav-krois .... insect capable of glowing at night: firefly
hne........................... apprehend with the eye: see
hne.ih....................... seeing that: considering
hne.ôi .... something seen: sight
hne-lil....................... plainly visible: clear; make intelligible: explain
hne-lil-blêh-suô .... in Luif a noun set before a name to explain to what the name relates: explanatory noun
hne-sgam................. electrical apparatus to enable distant things to be viewed on a screen: television
hne-bûuj .... see or have direct knowledge: witness
hne-dluô .... look obliquely from the eyes: squint
hnuv......................... one of four natural divisions of year: season
hnuv-a...................... first season of the year when vegetation begins: spring
hnuv-e...................... second season of the year when the heat is greatest: summer
hnuv-ê...................... third season of the year when the heat retreats: autumn
hnuv-i .... final season of the year when the temperature is lowest: winter

hfios .... one who creates drawings or paints pictures: painter
hfo .... cannot but: must
hfo-zla .... that cannot be dispensed with: indispensable
hfo.jlô .... cannot be avoided: inevitable
hvau .... solid figure resembling a roller: cylinder
hvau.ôi .... any cylindrical object: cylinder
hvau.lkô.fleu............. sheet rolled up to assume cylindrical form: scroll
hvau-vliêl.................. minced, seasoned meat stuffed into cylindrical casings: sausage
hvau-sor-vric .... cylindrical, vegeratian myriapod with numerous legs: millipede
hvau-sgiel .... cylindrical, slippery fish: eel
hvau-khuêj .... cylindrical vessel with wide mouth: jar
hvo .... perceive with tongue: taste
hvo-nriô .... be particular in taste: fastidious
hvo.zis .... pleasant in flavour: tasty
hvo.blê .... wanting in flavour: tasteless
hsa............................ change place: move
hsa-êol...................... heavenly body revolving about sun: planet
hsa-liôl .... plan of journey: itinerary
hsa-lô .... towards or in a lower position: down
hsa-rpû..................... come up with: overtake
hsa-hê....................... towards or in a higher position: up
hsa-hvau................... cylindrical piece sliding in tube of engine, etc.: piston
hsa-vlêr..................... cloth or brush for clearing dust from furniture: duster
hsa-vza .... devoid of power of motion or action: inert
hsa-slar .... pole with blade for rowing boat: oar

hsa-sdôus.................. piece of canvas, etc., for catching wind and thus moving ship: sail
hsa-sku...................... go round on protective duties: patrol
hsa-sgon.................. stem of slender palm like rattan or giant grass like bamboo: cane
hsa-zfê...................... insert to produce organic unon: graft
hsa-zca...................... remove plant and grow it elsewhere: transplant
hsa-czaf..................... machine imparting motion: motor
hsa-paz...................... put in proper order or position: adjust
hsa-gai...................... refined petroleum that powers vehicles: petrol, gasoline
hsa-glu...................... that which incites to action: incentive
hse............................ desire to have or do: want; be without what is required: lack
hse-ril....................... minimum number of members required to be present for transaction of business: quorum
hzi............................ innate impulse that inspires action: instinct
hzi-lgi....................... belief without rational foundation: faith
hzô............................ produce effect: cause
hzô-lgi...................... talk and induce belief or action: persuade
hzô-jeûp................... produce a sense of danger: alarm
hjuez........................ water that issues from the ground: spring; place from which river starts: source; of novel character: original; have whatever excites to action: motive (v. nzo-hsa)
hjuez-iûn.................. original inhabitants of a place: aborigines
hpi........................... tranquil in mind: calm; free from disturbance: quiet
hpim........................ one of the two protuberances on chest: nipple
hpi-zlu...................... calmly endure delay, misery, etc.: patient
hpu.......................... pass from one state to another: change

hpu-auf .... transparent glass, etc., made so as to refract light: lens
hpu-ûp .... drawing or other representation rendered grotesque through distortion: caricature
hpu-hev..................... small lizard given to changing colour: chameleon
hpu-mro .... write in characters of another language: transliterate
hpu-fôb .... of an institution, etc., change for the better: reform
hpu-fcô .... change appearance to conceal identity: disguise
hpu-suô .... in Luif, part of speech a word assumes different from what is specific to it: transformed part of speech
hpu-piem .... change residence: move house
hpu-dlû .... arbitrary change of mind or behaviour: caprice
hpu-drô .... speak evasively, shifting from side to side: prevaricate
hbel .... person related by blood: relative
hbel.jzon .... person related either by blood or marriage: relative
htê .... make aperture so as to expose to view or permit passage: open
htê-roiz .... speak and make known: reveal
htê-mau .... letter representing open sound: vowel
htê-mau-plia .... in Luif, a group of vowels classified for purposes of vocabulary formation: vowel group
htê-hôj .... area in town not covered by buildings: open space
htê-fcô .... take away cover: expose
htê-skêf .... raised level placc open to skies: terrace
htê-zca .... advance to higher state: develop
htê-prus .... horizontal timber, etc., over opening in wall: lintel

htê-kruod................ that which opens a lock: key; answer to a problem: solution

htug......................... man or manlike being assumed to exist: assumed man

hkaip........................ place excavated for minerals: mine; source of supply

-m-

mai........................... area developed with streets and houses and containing a considerable population: town

mai-jroz.................... fellow citizen

mai.dluô.................... outskits of town: suburbs

mai.kûz..................... ruler of a town: mayor

mau.......................... symbol denoting an elementary sound of a language: letter; first principles: rudiments

mau.i........................ system of letter pertaining to a language: alphabet

mau-srû.................... recite in order the letters that make up a word: spell

mau-khôn................ branch of mathematics using symbols in calculations: algebra

maûs........................ take what is given: receive

maûs-uam................ written paper ackowledging that something has been received: receipt

maûs-czo.................. agree to receive: accept

man.......................... halfway between two sides or opposites: intermediate

mac.......................... not bound by something or subject to another person: free

mac-hlan.................. day of leisure or recreation: holiday mac-vrê .... move from place to place with no fixed route: wander

mac-jza..................... spread in disorder, as hair or clothing: dishevel

meuh........................ use force to draw in one's direction: pull; pull off or gather bit by bit: pick

meuh.aê .... gripping tool consisting of two pivoted limbs: pincers

meuh-stû................. remove covering: strip

meuh-drô-truôz........ wheel for raising weights, etc.: pulley

mêus .... take in marriage: marry

mêus.noê................. man at or about time of his marriage: bridegroom

mêus.viô.................. woman at or about time of her marriage: bride

mêus-gûin .... bind oneself to mary: engage

mêj .... resplendently impressive: glorious; lofty and stately: majestic

mi .... in possession of: with; in company: together; presence in association: company; by means of: using

miôz......................... sound made by living thing other than human

mi.û .... one who keeps company with another: companion

mi-liôl .... plot together: conspire

mi-rial .... strike two things together, as hands, to produce sound: clap

mi-rze....................... each of two children born together: twin

mi-rkec..................... food eaten with rice

mi-hsa-êol .... heavenly body revolving around a planet: satellite

mi-vrê .... go together: accompany

mi.ztê .... mix together: intermingle

mi.cgi .... sit together

mij .... number equal to ten times ten: one hundred; many sorts of

mi-jlô .... surroundings of an action or a person: circumstances

mij.ghal.ia .... period of a hundred years: century

mij.ghal.û.................. one aged a hundred years: centenarian

mip .... denoting person or thing close at hand: this; second-mentioned of two: latter

mi-paf .... with child: pregnant

mi-bre .... feeling for others: sympathy

mi-thô .... business establishment with more than one owner: company

môip .... take secretly without permission: steal; move quietly

môip.ôi .... stolen goods

moês.......................... look for: seek; inquire into: investigate; pursue wild animals: hunt; discover by search: find (v. moês.rpû)

moês.rpû .... discover by search: find

moês.sûig .... make request for job, etc.: apply

moês-jci.................... endeavour to win love: woo

moês-buûj .... seek to discover by travel: explore

moês-trê .... find fault

moil .... strike with foot: kick

mov........................... of unit number: one; entire amount: whole (v. cim.mov)

mov.lu .... cause to become one: unify

mov-vliêc-plaz .... state with absolute ruler: autocracy

mov-zrôp-nio .... shell having only one valve: univalve

mov-cûg.................... giving and receiving: mutual

mov-drin-zriv .... practive of being married to only one wife or husband at a time: monogamy

mov-kol.................... indivisible by two integrally: odd
muir......................... put to death: kill
muir-luû.................. gas intended to injure or kill: poison gas
mul .... state in which a thing is: condition
mul-seêm .... keep in a particular condition: maintain
mûn .... being one part out of a hundred: hundredth
mlê........................... disinclined to work: lazy
mlê-coôl.................. walk leisurely here and there: stroll
mli .... cease to be alive: die
mli.lie....................... dead body: corpse
mli.hia...................... dead person
mli-htug.................. spirit conceived of as existing after a person's death: ghost
mloû .... obtain product of two numbers: multiply; frequently repeated
mloû.lu .... combine resources: pool
mloû.lto .... feel persistently troubled: harass
mloû-hev................. of various colours: motley
mloû.vêg .... curving in wave-like form: undulating; showing abrupt turns to right and left alternately: zigzag
mloû.vuêl................ shine by a succession of rapid flashes: twinkle; close and open eyes rapidly: wink
mloû.jaz-hsa............ revolve round and round
mloû-tbo................. impress by frequent repetitions: inculcate
mloû.grê.................. stops and starts now and then: intermittent
mlûhum.................... always reverts quickly to original condition: elastic
mlûhum-glup........... elastic contrivance of coiled metal: spring
mrail .... recording meter
mrak......................... building where the sick are treated: hospital
mrean....................... brilliant-hued bird able to repeat human speech: parrot

mrêl......................... science that investigates phenomena of organic mind: psychology
mro......................... mark paper, etc., with words: write
mro.io...................... one who writes: writer
mro-êôp.................... table for writing: desk
mro-rêh.................... way in which a person expresses himself in words: style
mro-roiz................... speak for another person to write down: dictate
mro-fleu................... written task for pupils to do: exercise
mro-czaf................... machine used for printing letters, etc.: typewriter
mro-piôs................... prepare writings of others for publication: edit
mro-piôs.io.............. one who edits books or directs the content and style of a magazine or newspaper: editor
mro-pra.................... make formal written application to an authority: petition
mro.blê..................... having no writing or other marking: blank
mro-droim .... one who composes music: composer
mro-kraut................. book in handwritten or typed, not printed, form: manuscript
mru......................... draw towards oneself: attract; induce to action by exciting desire: tempt; dispose to do: incline
mru.rbo.................... inclined to sleep: drowsy
mru-hsa.................... tend towards by force of gravitation: gravitate; one-sided inclination: bias
mru-fcô.................... brilliant show: pageant
mru-vlêr.................. domestic appliance for removing dust, etc., by suction: vacuum cleaner
mru-seêm................. disinclined to change: conservative
mru-sgiel................. food used to entice fish: bait
mru-cua................... an expression intended to catch the fancy of the public by constant repetition: slogan
mru-pra.................... persuade by blandishment: cajole

msê.......................... appoint one to act for another: deputize; stand for something: represent; put in place of another person or thing: substitute

msê.io...................... one transacting business on behalf of another: agent

msê.rûus-vliêc........... deputy of president of a country: vice president

mcu......................... strive to resemble: imitate

mcu-flua.................. person or thing intended to be imitated: model

mcu-mro.................. reproduce writing or picture: copy

mjê.......................... originate material contrivance: invent; produce a literary work or other work of art: create

mjê-znû.................... natural power of origination in intellectual and artistic pursuits: genius

-n-

nad.......................... in a line extending evenly without any curve: straight; without deviating from the shortest course: direct (v. dê-nad)

nad.lu...................... set right: redress

nad-roiz-puô .... words of speech reported as spoken: quotation

nad-nriô.................. lacking in flexibility: stiff

nad-vlair.................. steep, high rock: cliff

nad-jêh.................... rising almost perpendicularly: steep

ne........................... connecting words, etc., and signifying addition: and

neufla...................... doubt about truth of existing religions or any other idea: scepticism

ne cûg .... and the rest: *et cetera*

nê.laz....................... series of points

nê.roiz .... continuous spoken address delivered to an audience: speech
hê.hmav .... shaft of light: ray
nê.nui .... long, slender piece of wood or other firm material: bar
nêftêh .... belief that personal god or gods do not exist: atheism
nê.sdôus .... narrow strip of silk or other fine material: ribbon
nêz .... what is traced by a continuously moving point: line
nêz.fleu .... long piece: length
nêz-fcô .... diagram showing variation of quantity: graph
nêz-siut .... cut marks into a hard surface: engrave
nêz.zku.aê .... straight piece of wood or other hard material for drawing lines: ruler
nêz-czûus .... striped quadruped related to horses: zebra
nêz-plia .... line of persons or things: row
nêz-dluô .... sharp or narrow side of anything: edge
nê.cze-fiôp .... continuous discharge of firearms: fusillade
nê.plêm .... row of railway carriages connected and running together: train
nê.thin .... long, slender, round piece of wood: stick
nê.glup .... flexible, thread-like piece of metal: wire
ni .... sound made by mosquito: hum
niav .... feel uncertain: doubt; incline to believe: suspect
niav-drû .... be on one's guard: beware
nio .... external flexible covering of body: skin; skin of animal tanned or otherwise treated: leather; whatever is spread over for protection of concealment: covering

nio-laz .... tumour on skin, commonly dark coloured: mole
nio-laz-plia .... eruption on skin in spots: rash
nio-leg...................... grow red in face with shame, etc.: blush
nio.rkec .... rice in the husk: paddy
nio-hev-laz .... brownish spot on skin: freckle
nion .... identify as known before: recognise
nio.blê.rkec.............. hulled rice: rice
nius .... emotion produced by what is unexpected: surprise; bewildered surprise caused by what is strange: wonder (v. nius-dlû)
nius.cêôm................ surprise attack
nius-dlû................... bewildered surprise caused by what is stange: wonder
niûh .... see things during sleep: dream
nôu .... time while sun is shining: daytime
nôu.ba...................... time at the middle of the period of daytime: noon
nôh .... little in length: short; insufficient in quantity, etc.: deficient
nôh.lu .... make short: shorten; reduce length of writing by omitting details: summarize
nôh-hsa .... make a short, abrupt movement: jerk
nôh-stuôm .... short trousers: shorts
nôh-pêa................... punctuation mark indicating a short pause: comma
nôf .... having existed a long time: old
nôf.has .... length of time lived or in existence: age
nôf-blêh-thêh .... science that interprets ancient artefacts: archaeology
noê........................... male adult human being: man
noê.mul.................... state of being a man: manhood

nos .... tasting like quinine: bitter; bitter in feeling: acrimonius; partially dark: gloomy

nos-tûu..................... bitter, perennial herb: wormwood

not .... high in temperature: hot; violent in feeling: vehement

not.lûk .... degree of hotness: temperature; that which produces sensation of warmth: heat

not-mrail.................. device for measuring temperature: thermometer

not-jaz...................... region of earth between Tropic of Cancer and Tropic of Capricorn: tropics

nu .... indicating position within boundaries of: in

nuah......................... consume with fire: burn

nuah.rôûn .... cook by exposure to fire: roast

nuah-hue................. material for burning: fuel

nuah-zru.................. burn unsteadily: flicker

nuah-khuêj.............. vessel for holding burning charcoal: brazier

nuap......................... divide partly or wholly by use of force: break; break continuity of speech, etc.: interrupt

nuap.htê................... break open forcibly: burst; to burst with a loud report: explode

nuap-nuê.................. intervening space: interval

nuap-vêu .... intervening time: interval

nuap-vle .... make unconscious: stun

nuap-vrê................... spread in various directions: disperse

nuap-siab.................. speak haltingly, tending to repeat spasmodically the same sounds: stammer

nuap-sdôus.............. torn scrap of cloth: rag

nuap-chiûs .... large snake that forcibly crushes its prey: python

nuap-jroi .... broken and rough of surface: ragged

nuap-pêa .... punctuation mark denoting a break in the sense: dash

nuap-khe................. wrench joint and injure ligaments: sprain nuap-gaif.................. reduce to broken-down state: ruin; damage and disable, of ship: wreck

nuê........................... continuous entity in which matter has extension: space

nuê-sgam ....apparatus for receiving sound without conducting wires: radio

nuê-czuûb .... piece of string, etc., folded upon itself so as to leave an open space: loop

nui .... lifeless thing

nu-lifûe .... soft tissue inside stems of plants or in bones of animals: pith, marrow

nu.lkô....................... shut inside something: enclose

nu-fal .... intrinsic, distinctive nature: essence

nu-vêg...................... with surface curved inwards: concave

nu-vluar .... interior section of country: inland

nu.vrê....................... go inside: enter (v. vrê nu)

nu-vrê-uam .... printed slip of paper giving right of admission to a place: ticket

nu.vrê.uô.................. place by which one enters: entrance

nu-za........................ inside out

nu-za-vlaul .... periodical ebb and flow of sea: tide

nu-zgu...................... force in, of liquid: inject

nu-zgu.aê................. tube with piston for injecting liquid: syringe

nu-crêus .... man's loose-sleeved garment worn under coat: shirt

nu-gzauf.................. pertaining to a country itself: intestine (internal affairs relating to state or country)

ni-gzauf puêr .... civil war

nûu .... used by speaker when referring to himself: I

nûh .... with little or no light: dark; full of secret or incomprehensible things: mysterious

nûh-lgi .... irrational belief engendered by fear of the unknown: superstition
nûh-hmav .... nonmetallic element capable of appearing luminous in the dark: phosphorus
nûh-fri...................... refer indirectly: allude
nûh-vuêl................... emit light in the dark like phosphorus: phosphoresce
nûh-zve .... watch or investigate secretly: spy
nûmhi .... rubber treated with sulphur: vulcanite
nlai.......................... pertaining to that side west of a person facing north: left
nlep.......................... rear lower part of body: buttock
nlep-poc................... opening of alimentary canal at buttocks: anus
nlê............................ not in a state of being: do not exist
nlê.fa .... expressing absence of a quilty: negative
nliôr .... one who originates or establishes: founder
nlôl........................... day following today: tomorrow
nlôl.guê .... night of tomorrow: next night
nlo............................ perceive by nasal sense: smell
nrel........................... entire body of people of same period: generation
nriô .... unyielding to touch: hard; difficult (v. pa.suz); severe in behaviour: stern; lacking kind feelings: unfeeling
nriô-iôm................... insect with hard wing cases: beetle
nriô-iuv .... curd coagulated and pressed solid: cheese
nriô-uam .... thick, stiff paper: cardboard
nriô-uos.................... dry, crisp cake made of unleavened dough: biscuit
nriô-lûk.................... repellently harsh: severe
nriô-lfe .... fix the features of a thing: determine; unyielding in opinion: obstinate
nriô-hêun .... stongly resistant to flow: viscous

nriô-nru .... rough and abrupt in manner: brusque
nriô-fri .... maintain emphatically: insist
nriô-suêf.................... rise up against: revolt
nriô-suz-nuap .... hard, brittle metallic element: manganese
nriô-sdôus .... strong coarse cloth of hemp, cotton, etc., used for tents, etc.: canvas
nriô-sdôus-srêm........ temporary shelter constucted usually of canvas stretched over poles: tent
nriô-zrop .... iron with high carbon content, melted and shaped in mould: cast iron
nriô-zpe..................... hardened and unfeeling: callous
nriô-pra..................... ask for as of right or peremptorily: demand
nriô-phûl.................. coagulated juice of some tropical plants: rubber
nriô-thaid.................. network of cross laths: trellis
nriô-dlû..................... consider seriously and deeply: contemplate
nrôus .... mass of land surrounded by water: island
nrôus.ia .... group of islands: archipelago
nrôus-priog .... large marine mammal of fish-like form: whale
nru .... with high speed: quick
nru-hsa...................... move with urgent speed: make haste
nru-mro .... speedy kind of writing for recording speech: shorthand
nru-siut .... cut with quick blow: chop
nru-creu .... able to move swiftly and lightly: nimble
nru.jra .... rate of motion: speed
nrû .... do as bidden: obey
nrûn .... male parent: father
nrûn.mul................... state of being a father: fatherhood
nrûn.srel.jci .... love from parents: parental love
nrûs........................... hair growing on face: beard
nrûs-phaiv .... bladed implement for removing hair: razor

nziop .... one versed in the design or construction of public works, machinery, etc.: engineer

nzo .... deduce conclusions in a systematic way: reason

nzo.ûz........................ resulting from that reason: therefore

nzo-rpû .... derive conclusion from what precedes in a rational way: deduce

nzo-hsa...................... have whatever excites to action: motive

nzo-flêl .... branch of knowledge dealing with correct rules of reasoning: logic

nzo-dlû...................... consider carefully and rationally: deliberate

-f-

faê .... body of rules governing a language: grammar; set of rules; manner of organization: structure

faur .... keep from happening: prevent

fal............................. distinctive character: quality

fal-suô .... in Luif, a word that signifies a quality and modifies the meaning of another word: qualifier

fal.plia .... step in quality or standing: rank, grade

fe.............................. belonging to: of

feur .... bring together: gather; collect into a heap or mass: heap

feur-mro.................... collect material or information from various sources: compile

feur-sfo..................... list of subjects: index

feur-cim .... entire amount: total

fe.lu.......................... be the possession of: belong

fe-lgi......................... rely on another person's integrity: trust

fe-ruap .... pleasant diversion after toil, etc.: recreation

fe-rûus...................... like one rather than others: prefer

fe-rbo .... lying motionless and inactive: torpid
fem............................ greater in quantity or degree: more
fe-mi .... connected with: related
fem-lfe....................... more willingly: rather
fem-rec .... to a degree exceeding that required: too
fem-ril .... greater part: majority
fem-ris....................... more or less: about
fem-vlô .... to be more than: exceed (v. vlô fem gi)
fe-nuah...................... burn without flame, but usually with smoke: smoulder
fef............................. small in quantity or size: little
fe-faur .... stop progress: impede
fe-faur.ôi.................... anything standing in way of advance: obstacle
fe.foz .... one of ten equal parts: tenth
fe-frê-cuem............... provide with all requirements: equip
fe-fcô .... give an idea of: indicate
fe-vêg .... winding while advancing like thread of screw: spiral
fe-sag........................ excellence worthy of praise: merit
fe-siut........................ cut short: crop
fe-suêf .... prevent advance: resist
fe-sla......................... employment for pay: job
fe-sto .... belonging specially: peculiar
fe-stû .... hand over: deliver
fe-sgô .... belonging to the practical arts based on science: technical
fe-zru........................ make slight tremulous movements: shiver; move unsteadily: stagger
fe-zmo .... meet requirements: satisfy
fe-zkû .... kind thought and beneficial action: charity
fe-zgu .... acquired power to carry through any action: authority

fe-cab .... according to established doctrines: orthodox
fe-ceûl .... quality associated with mirth: humour
fe-cêôm .... enter with hostile intent: invade
fe-ciam .... activity proper to a person or thing: function
fe-cri.......................... contend against difficulties: strive
fe-chauk .... money affairs: finance
fe-cfe .... possessed of special skill: expert
fe-jain-tbo .... incline downwards: droop
fe.poh........................ one of four equal parts: quarter
fe-pûuk .... make one pass of needle in sewing; stitch
fe-biôm .... hold in esteem: honour
fe-buf .... of present or recent time: modern
fe-bke .... disregard intentionally: ignore
fe-tras .... piece of wood or other material at foot of window: sill
fe-trê .... judge as guilty or bad: condemn
fe-tbo .... ascribe as pertaining to: attribute
fe-dhô .... happening irregularly without design: casual
fe-kiuf .... deteriorate in quality: decay
fe.kol .... one of three equal parts: third
fe-krôf .... piece of wood or stone at bottom of doorway: threshold
fe-gûin....................... agree or correspond exactly or nearly so: tally
fe-gsô .... stick easily to: sticky
fê.............................. what reply: whether
fêr .... belonging to me: my
fêz .... consisting of one element or not complex: simple; unmixed with extraneous stuff: pure
fêz-tuê .... sentence without subordinate clauses: simple sentence
fiem.......................... estimate similarity or relative value: compare
fiem-csû .... control by making comparison: check

fiem-kaê .... figure of speech whereby an object is given a property only on the basis of resemblance: metaphor

fien........................... take into and expel air from lungs: breathe

fien-ual..................... air breathed in and out: breath

fien-rnû.................... chronic respiratory disease marked by breathlessness, cough, and tightness in chest: asthma

fien-faur .... stop breathing by squeezing throat: choke

fien-voi..................... respiratory organ of fish: gill

fien-siab .... speak under the breath: whisper

fien-zru .... gasp for breath: pant

fien-dhûiv .... main air passage between mouth and lungs: windpipe

fien-gaif.................... kill by squeezing throat: strangle

fi.êol......................... heavenly body

fi.ôêp......................... movable equipment of house: furniture

fiôf .... keep out of sight: hide; conceal from knowledge of other people: secret (v. fiôf-nûh)

fiôf-hne .... look from concealment or through narrow opening: peep

fiôf-moês.................. game played by children: hide-and-seek

fiôf-nuap-chuf.......... hidden charge of explosives: mine

fiôf-nûh.................... conceal from knowledge of other people: secret

fiôf-vrê .... disappear secretly: abscond

fiôf-sdôus .... hanging screen of cloth: curtain

fiôf-tuês-iar............... small, furtive quadruped that preys on mice, etc.: weasel

fiôv-nru.................... spring suddenly: bounce

fiôv-soun .... run like horse with all feet off ground at each stride: gallop

fiôv-bûuj.................... clearly understand all of a sudden: suddenly realize fiôv-brail .... stream of water descending presicipitously: waterfall

fiôv-glu...................... act without due caution: rash

fiôp .... make tiny hole: prick; let fly as bullet with intent to injure: shoot (v. cze-fiôp)

fiôp.aê .... instrument for pricking small holes: awl

fiôp-chuf.................. short, pointed weapon for stabbing: dagger

fiôp-tûu..................... plant characterized by stinging hairs: nettle

fiôp-troih.................. arachnid with claws like lobster's and sting in tail: scorpion

fiûl .... take upright position on one's feet: stand; perpendicular to the ground: vertical

fiûl.prus..................... vertical piece of timber, etc., for supporting load in building: post

fiûl-guz...................... right angle

fiûl-guz-nêz .... at right angles to given line: perpendicular

fi.rcûf .... edible seed of any leguminous plant: pulse

fi.flec .... any pungent vegetable substance giving flavour to food: spice

fi.frûin....................... any of a large class of hard-shelled, mostly aquatic animals: crustacean

fi.fjûb .... any plant without woody stem: herb

fi.slôp .... any long, cylindrical, hollow body: tube

fi.smôn...................... narrative of incidents of any kind, true or fictitious: story

fi.smôn.eu .... section of a story forming a detachable unit: episode

fi.spom...................... plant without chlorophyll, like mushroom, toadstool, and mould: fungus

fi.chiûs .... any crawling vertebrate like snake, crocodile, and turtle: reptile fi.plêm...................... a conveyance of any kind including motorcar, ship, and airplane: vehicle

fi.phêuz..................... anything hollow and capable of holding other things like bag, sheath, or vessel: receptacle

fi.thôd...................... quantity serving as a standard for measuring others: unit

fi.thuas..................... anything that induces drowsiness, torpor, insensibility, etc.: narcotic

fôb.......................... possessed of the right qualities: good

fôb-mul...................... in good condition physically and in other respects: well; live in good condition; a word used as a parting wish: farewell

fôb.fal.czûus............ horse of a superior quality: steed

fôb-sag..................... high in quality: fine

fôb-zku..................... make the best of

fôb-dlû...................... possessed of good sense: sensible

foi........................... fruit consisting of kernel in hard shell: nut

foi-vliêl..................... edible part within shell of nut: kernel

fois.......................... set burning: light; urge to action: incite; influence mind in a lofty way: inspire (v. heûn-lbu)

foz........................... integral number just above nine: ten

foz-sen..................... decimal fraction

foz-sen-tau.............. mark denoting decimal fraction: decimal mark

foz-phuê................... decimal system

focitera..................... white hydrocarbon solid derived from coal-tar: naphtalene

fot........................... denoting person or thing the more distant: that; first mentioned of two: former

fuû.......................... land where flowers are cultivated: garden

fus........................... belonging to them: their

fûl........................... no number: zero

fûl.lu........................ declare nonexistent or not true: deny

fûl.hia....................... no person: nobody
fûl-hue-nuê .... space completely without matter: vacuum
fûl.flêl.û.................... person without knowledge: ignoramus
fûl.sme .... meaningless or foolish language: nonsense
fûl.blêh..................... no thing: nothing
fûl-tpê .... condition in which no government operates: anarchy
fûfel.......................... no knowledge of First Cause: agnosticism
flaic .... musical instrument
flaic.czuûb .... string of musical instrument: chord
fleu........................... denoting single, separate thing or person: unit; particular but unspecified: some
fleu.rev.bôi .... small mass of semi-solid matter: clot
fleu-hsa..................... advance step by step: gradual
fleu-puô .... catalogue of articles, etc.: list
fleu.blêh .... some undefined thing: something
flec .... pungent condiment obtained from some plants: pepper
flêl............................ that which is known: knowledge
flêl-niav.................... inclined to doubt truth of what is proffered as such: sceptical
flêl-fri .... set expression of some principle, rule, etc.: formula
flêl-cri....................... systematically search for facts to advance scientific knowledge: research
flêl-czil .... branch of knowledge: subject
flêl-blêh.................... theme or topic: subject matter
flêl-tuê..................... short saying containing some observation regarding human behaviour: proverb
flêz .... whatever is to be sung: song
flêz-iêt .... bird of a kind noted for singing: thrush
flêz-stôh .... short poem of emotional character: lyric

flêc .... receptacle or chamber for baking, drying, etc.: oven
flier .... wild or domesticated animal of same genus as wolf: dog
flô .... play music
flo .... in good health: healthy
flo-hsa .... exert body for health purposes: exercise
flo-jzab .... one of a number of accessory food factors essential for health: vitamin
flua............................ thing serving to illustrate a class or rule: example
flua.ro .... for example
fluam.......................... any substance capable of injuring health or destroying life: poison
fluam-lai...................... semimetallic element, most of whose compounds are poisonous: arsenic
fluam-chiûs .... venomous snake of various kinds: viper
fluaz .... plaited receptacle of cane, etc.: basket
flua-jlô .... one of a number of occurrences of related character: case
frê.............................. come face to face: meet
frê-sûig....................... meet formally for getting information: interview
frê-ceud...................... accost with words or some gesture: greet
frê-cuem..................... give requirements: supply
frê-bûuj .... have direct knowledge of: experience
fri .... put into word: express
fria .... of great weight: heavy
fria-lai .... heavy, ductile, radioactive metallic element: uranium
fria.rnû....................... serious disease
fria.creu...................... amount a thing weighs: weight
fries .... tailless amphibian of genus *Rana*: frog

friêm .... large, cloven-footed ruminant beast of pasture: ox
friêm-rseut................ blood-sucking fly given to biting cattle: gadfly
friêm.vliêl .... meat of ox: beef
friêm.seêm.io........... one who tends cattle: cowherd
fri-rud .... treat with contempt: insult
fri-vza....................... command not to do: forbid
fri-vce........................express grief: lament; express grievance: complain
fri-suêf...................... express opposition: protest
fri-sto .... demand as a due: claim
fri-zla........................ admit possession or receipt of: acknowledge
fri-zsû .... express sympathetic joy: congratulate
fri-biôm.................... express respect or praise: compliment
fri-tuê .... in Luif a sentence simply conveying an idea: statement sentence
fri-kôz .... express regret for offence: apologize
fri-khe .... announce intention to injure: threaten
fri-gsô....................... assure as correct: confirm
frôj .... unit of weight
fruc .... institution for education: school
fruc.vê........................period when one was a pupil at school: school time
fruc-jroz .... one at same school at same time: schoolfellow
frûin......................... crustacean with ten feet and given to travelling sideways: crab
frûin-vliêl .... malignant tumour that damages adjacent tissue: cancer
frûin-troih............... large marine crustacean with long tail and strong claws: lobster
fnoôl .... large bird with black plumage: crow
fsep ....grain of hardy grass cultivated in cool climes: oats
fzi............................ make body assume horizontal posture on some surface: lie; parallel to horizon: horizontal; set in specified place: situate

fzi.prus .... horizontal or inclined piece of timber, etc., for transmitting load in building: beam

fcô .... present to view: show; take away cover: expose (v. htê-fcô); bear a certain appearance: look

fcô-êus .... case for diplaying articles of value: cabinet

fcô-ûp-kuv .... delineate objects in such a way as to convey the same impression as the objects themselves: perspective

fcô-rua .... grandiose language: bombast

fcô-hôi-srêm .... building exhibiting objects of interest historically, scientifically, etc.: museum

fcô-flua .... little something to show qualities of group: sample

fcô-vuêl .... given to pretentious display: ostentatious

fcô-jlô .... sign of future occurrence: omen

fcô-jzi .... exhibit and explain: demonstrate

fcô-biôm .... express approbation loudly as by clapping hands: applaud

fcô-glu .... unusual, showy feat: stunt

fjûb .... common herbaceous vegetation covering ground: grass

fjûb-siut .... cut down with scythe or machine: mow

fjûb-siut.aê .... manual mowing implement with long, curved blade: scythe

fjûb-chiûs .... secret danger

fpies .... jumping, chirping insect that lurks among blades of grass: grasshopper

fbun .... science of the structure and properties of substances and their transformations: chemistry

fbun-thôuh .... picture produced by action of light on chemically prepared surface: photograph

fbun-thôuh-phêuz .... apparatus for taking photographs: camera

ftiûn .... mollusc capable of ejecting inky liquid: cuttlefish
ftuav .... heavy chopping tool consisting of a wedge-shaped piece of iron and a wooden handle: axe
ftuêp .... publication issued regularly, usually daily, giving news, etc.: newspaper
ftûuv .... small, plain, brown bird: sparrow
fdem........................... beverage prepared from roasted and ground seeds of the coffee plant: coffee
fdem-srêm .... place for selling coffee and other refreshments: café
fdem.poc.ôi .... pot for preparing and serving coffee: coffeepot
fkal .... imagined story: fiction
fkal.driôs .... one who writes works of fiction: novelist
fkal-kêu .... fictitious name: pseudonym

-V-

va .... signifying position in space, etc.: at
vaekô .... as much as possible
vaekô nru .... as fast as possible
vaekô vam .... as soon as possible
vaê .... totality of existing things: universe
vaê-snuv .... philosophy of the fundamental nature of being and thought: metaphysics
vaê.jluz .... what really exists prior to modifications made by the mind: noumenon
val .... measuring much between the extremities in space: long; in high degree: intense
val-aiz-nêz .... angular distance between meridian of a place and a standard meridian: longitude

val-euf-krois .... neuropterous insect with slender body and long tail: dragonfly
val-ôut...................... long, upholstered seat with back: sofa
val-lên-zal................. extent in terms of length, breadth, or thickness: dimension
val.lu .... increase in length: lengthen
val-vric .... wading bird with long legs, neck, and bill: crane
val-sgon-tûu .... tropical climbing palm with long, thin, flexible stem: rattan
val-crêus .... long, loose outer garment: gown
val-jaz....................... regular, closed curve, longer than broad: ellipse
val-jaz-foi .... fruit of tree allied to peach, the dry kernel being shaped like ellipse with one pointed end: almond
val-pêa...................... punctuation mark that is placed at the end of a sentence: full stop or period
val-poc .... long, narrow hollow on any surface: groove
val-brem.................... ruminant characterized by extremely long neck: giraffe
val.dê........................ through length of: along
val-gêd...................... plane four-sided figure with adjacent sides unequal and all angles right angles: rectangle
vam .... of short duration: short; just or recently come into use: new (v. hrô.vam)
vam.lziap.................. newly enlisted soldier: recruit
vam-ris .... a little while ago: just
vam-fem.................... a little while more: about to
vam-zca .... rudimentary flower, etc.: bud
vam.jôm.................... not long past: recent
vam-jlô..................... report of fresh event: news
vam.piem .... stay temporalily: sojourn
vam-bauz.................. get under water for a short time: dip

vam-thêt................... residence for students or some particular group of people: hostel

vêi .... smallest possible particle of an element still retaining its properties: atom; extremely small: minute

vêi-poc .... minute opening in skin for passage of sweat: pore

vêu .... that which continues and in which things change: time; uninterrupted in connection or sequence: continuous

vêu.êz .... from that time on: since

vêu.sê.dba................. existing without beginning or end: eternal

vêu-slôn.................... recurrent period of time with its phenomena: cycle

vêu.cav .... keeping appointed time: punctual

vêu-ciam................... pass or spend the time

vêu.tis....................... happening at the same time: simultaneous

vêu-kôz..................... anything lagging behind the times: anachronism

vêg .... with such form that no part is straight: curved

vêg.ôi .... bent piece of metal, etc., for holding things: hook

vêg.ôin .... moon curved as in its first and last quarters: crescent

vêg.lu .... make into curved form: bend; incline neck or body in salutation, etc.: bow

vêg-roiz-puô .... words of speech reported with some change: indirect speech

vêg-hsa .... twist body with regular short movements: wriggle

vêg-fri....................... mode of expression deviating from the normal for special effects: figure of speech

vêg-vrê...................... make a circuitous way: detour

vêg-sme .... indicate indirectly: imply
vêg-sdu..................... a curved structure supporting a load: arch
vêg-znû..................... clever by way of using strategems: cunning
vêg-crum .... arched roof: vault
vêg-chuf .... contrivance for shooting arrows: bow
vêg-cfe...................... execute something in cunning fashion: trick
vêg-drô .... move tortuously: twist
viaf........................... think highly of oneself: conceited
viaf-rêh.................... exhibit great self-esteem in one's manner: proud
viaf.roiz .... extol oneself: boast
viô............................ female adult human being: woman
viûr .... feel sorrow for the sufferings of others: pity
viûr-chauk............... money given to the poor out of pity: alms
vôp........................... by that time: already
vo............................. introducing an alternative: or; one of two possibilities: alternative
voi............................ a part of the body adapted for a particular vital function: organ
voi-nio...................... filmy structure covering bodily organ, etc.: membrane
von.......................... partially dark from interception of light: shady
vo-nriô .... position where either alternative course is evil: dilemma
vuêl .... emit light: shine
vuêl-crêus................. glassy hard coating given to metal surface: enamel
vuêl-jzu .... mark with festivities, etc.: celebrate
vuêl-beûl .... confuse with strong light: dazzle
vuô.......................... position in space or a surface of earth: place
vuô.ud .... in position facing each other: opposite
vuô-rze..................... born in the place: native
vuô-hpu .... move from one place to another
vuô-vrê.................... go to a distance place: travel

vuô.tû........................ in place of: instead
vuô-tbo .... give directions about location: address
vuô-gsô...................... fixed to one place
vûil............................. form mental image: imagine; found only in the imagination: imaginary (v. o.vûil); full of imagination: imaginative (v. vûil.zla)
vûil-mêj..................... given to what is captivating and remote from experience: romantic
vûil-zla .... full of imagination: imaginative
vûil-plo....................... fantastic and ludicrous: grotesque
vlair........................... high mass of land: hill
vlair-laz .... pointed top of mountain: peak
vlair-mul .... elevation of condition, character, mien, etc.: dignity
vlair-pue.................... narrow passage over mountains: pass
vlaul .... natural liquid colourless and transparent when pure: water
vlaul.uô .... large basin for storing public water supply: reservoir
vlaul-lô .... plunge under water: dive
vlaul-riam.................. transport by boat or barge over strait or river: ferry
vlaul-hue .... matter settling at bottom of liquid: sediment
vlaul-hsa.................... travel over water under power of wind: sail
vlaul-hse.................... prolonged lack of rain: drought
vlaul-fiôv .... rush into water: plunge
vlaul-fjûb................... tall, straight, stiff grass growing in water: reed
vlaul-seêm .... steep in water: soak
vlaul-smer.................. large fruit with smooth skin and very juicy pulp: watermelon
vlaul-sdôus .... cloth for drying body: towel

vlaul-sgon................. plant with thick fleshy stem storing water and performing work of leaves: cactus
vlaul-zfê.................... combine chemically with water: hydrate
vlaul-coôl .... walk through water: wade
vlaul-cto .... make dry and hot: parch; fade from want of water: wither
vlaul-jlo .... feel vehement desire for drink: thirst
vlaul-pue .... passage for water: channel
vlaul-pca.................... supply water to crops by means of channels: irrigate
vlaul-bliaz................. frequent looseness of bowels: diarrhoea
vlaul-troi .... impervious to water: waterproof
vlaul.khau................. undesirably filled or saturated with water: waterlogged
vle .... what is perceived through any of the senses: sensation; aware of things: conscious (v. sdû-bûuj)
vle-nzo .... reasoning from the particular to the general: induction
vlez............................ female relative born of same parents: sister
vle.blêh...................... thing as it appears to the senses: phenomenon
vlêô .... solid, three-dimensional figure with all points on surface equidistant from centre: sphere
vlêô.ôi .... any spherical concrete thing: ball
vlêô-mêj-spol............ magnificent, large, globular flower: peony
vlêô-chôud .... deep, rounded cooking vessel: pot
vlêô-chuf.................. hollow spherical case packed with explosive: bomb
vlêr .... powdery earth or other matter: dust
vlêr-rmed.................. woolly growth of small fungi: mould
vliê .... sounding strongly: loud; prominently noticeable: conspicuous; unduly thrusting oneself forward: obtrusive

vliêl .... soft substance like muscular tissue between skin and bones: flesh
vliê.lu.aê .... instrument for intensifying sound: microphone
vliê-lto .... loud, confused noise: clamour
vliêl.gloit .... one who sells meat: meat seller
vliê-zsû .... noisily joyous: merry
vliêc.......................... one who rules a country: ruler
vliêc-nêz .... line of monarches of same family: dynasty
vliêc.vê .... period of rule of monarch: reign
vliêc.srêm .... residence of a monarch: palace
vliê-krois .... homopterous, shrilly chirping insect: cicada
vlioc .... one who works on board a ship: sailor
vlil .... person conceived of as a distinctive unit: self; relating to the individual: personal; having no connection with the public: private
vlil.lfe .... of one's own volition: voluntary
vlil.roiz .... speech made to oneself: soliloquy
vlil-hsa .... moving or acting without external force: automatic
vlil-hsa-czaf .... self-moving machine: automaton
vlil.muir .... self-inflicted death: suicide
vlil-nuap-lai .... radioactive element, a white metal: radium
vlil-fal .... mental trait peculiar to a person: idiosyncrasy
vlil-blêh-suô .... in Luif, a noun indicating person: self-noun
vlic .... rear part of human torso: back
vlic-hne .... a look back: retrospect
vlic-hsa .... start back: recoil
vlic-vuêl .... throw back light: reflect
vlic-vluar .... scenery serving as setting: background
vlic.vrê .... draw back from untenable position: retreat
vlic.zgu .... drive back by force: repulse
vlic-blê-ôut .... seat that has no back: stool

vlic.brian .... firm supporting column of bone extending from base of head to base of back: spine
vlô .... have description mentioned: is
vlôi .... direction to right of person facing setting sun: north
vlôi-mrail .... instrument for showing direction: compass
vlôi-zrôp .... piece of iron capable of attracting other iron: magnet
vlô fem gi .... is more than: exceed (v. fem-vlô)
vluar .... solid part of surface of the earth: land
vluar-laz .... point of land jutting out into sea: cape
vluar.lu .... come onto land from air or water travel: land
vluar-rti .... make measurements of land for making plan or map: survey; examine carefully in detail
vluar-foi .... pod growing under ground and containing edible seeds: ground nut
vluar-ftuav .... tool for breaking ground, with head having point at one end and chisel edge at the other: pickaxe
vluar-vrer .... hollow place under hill: cave
vluar-siut .... long, narrow, deep excavation: trench
vluar-sfas .... room under the ground: cellar
vluar-sjie .... distribute land, as a policy: agrarian
vluar.sto.io .... one who owns land: landowner
vluar-jrual .... cloud near the ground: mist
vluar-pêa .... features of an expanse of land: topography
vluar-poc .... hole in ground, natural or artificial: pit
vluar-glu-skêf .... platform along shore for ships to load and unload: wharf
vlul .... division of a day: hour
vlub .... phenomenon that is perceived by the ear: sound

vlub-uam.................. contrivance for exploding with loud noise, for entertainment and without intent of harm: firecracker

vlub.rze.aê .... instrument that automatically reproduces sound: record player

vlub-fal...................... character of sound: tone

vlub-fien.................... draw long, deep, audible breath: sigh

vlub.sor .... full of loud sound: noisy

vlub-cua .... word formed in imitation of sound associated with some particular thing: onomatopoeia

vlub-thaid................. regulated poetic rhythm: metre

vlû............................. experience physical sensation as by touch: feel; permeate with water, dye, etc.: imbue

vlûr .... part of face above eyebrows: forehead

vlû-fiôp .... prickling sensation: tingle

vlû.klû....................... inclination to vomit: nausea

vraid.......................... pit constructed for obtaining supply of subterranean water: well

vreuc .... one employed to keep records and do work involving some writing: clerk

vrer .... orifice in head for eating and speaking: mouth; place by which one enters: entrance (v. nu.vrê.uô)

vrer-htê .... open mouth wide and take deep breath: yawn

vrer-meuh .... draw in with mouth: suck

vrer-val...................... push lips outwards: pout

vrer-vrôih .... large inlet of sea with wide mouth: bay

vrer-crum .... roof of mouth: palate

vrer-czû .... hold in mouth

vrer-brian .... bony structure of mouth: jaw

vrê............................. move in direction away from one: go; start from a place: depart

vrê-ôv .... be better than others: surpass

vrêu .... every time: always; existing indefinitely: permanent (v. zlu.lêr)
vrê-uam .... document authorizing one to travel to other countries: passport
vrê-rpû .... go and get: bring
vrê-hrô .... have passage to and fro: communicate
vrê-hne .... go to see: visit
vrê-nêz .... line of persons walking along for some specific purpose: procession
vrê nu .... go inside: enter (v. nu.vrê)
vrê-nu-slar .... go on board ship: embark
vrê za .... go outside: emerge (v. za.vrê)
vrê-plia .... company of people journeying together: caravan
vrê-phêuz .... bags, etc., of a traveller: luggage
vri .... don't want
vriam .... one who works: worker
vriam.ia .... body of persons working in an organization: staff
vriôb .... glandular organ for secreting urine: kidney
vrih .... person of a long past generation from whom one is descended: ancestor
vrih-lgi .... belief handed down through successive generations: tradition
vri-stû .... let go of a possession or claim: renounce
vriz .... daughter of brother or sister: niece
vric .... limb used for walking: leg
vric-zal .... thick back part of leg below knee: calf
vric-zma .... region where leg joins trunk of body: hip
vric-zfê .... place where thigh and lower leg join: knee
vric-zfê.lu .... fall and rest on knees: kneel
vric-chiûs .... large amphibious reptile with horny scales: crocodile

vric-plêm.................. two-wheeled vehicle propelled by legs: bicycle
vrôih .... any great expanse of salt water: sea; continuous expanse
vrôih-hmav............... building with beacon light to guide or warn ships at sea: lighthouse
vrôih-môip............... rob at sea by capture of ships: pirate
vrôih-flier................. furred and paddle-footed marine mammal that preys on fish: seal
vrôih-slû.................... feel sick owing to motion of ship: seasick
vrôih-stô................... thing that keeps person afloat at sea until rescued: lifebuoy
vrôih-jzêm................ calcareous substance of various colours deposited at bottom of sea by kinds of marine polyps: coral
vrôih-phiom............. furred aquatic mammal of weasel family feeding on fish: otter
vrôih-bôz.................. mean level of surface of sea: sea level
vrôih-thôuh.............. map of sea showing coasts, currents, etc.: chart
vrôih.dluô.vluar........ land at edge of sea: shore
vrouh .... fibrous tissue controlling bodily movement: muscle
vrouh-lreon .... muscular second stomach of bird: gizzard
vrouh-hsa .... violent involuntary contraction of muscles of body: spasm
vrouh-bli .... disease characterized by pain in the joints and muscles: rheumatism
vhoil......................... one of hard structures in mouth for masticating purposes: tooth
vhoil.lu.aê .... instrument with toothed bar for drawing together, smoothing, as fallen leaves or earth, etc.: rake
vhoil-vliêl .... firm flesh surrounding bases of teeth: gum
vhoil-siut.................. cut with teeth: bite

vhoil-toif .... grind with teeth: chew
vmac .... reddish metallic element which is ductile and malleable: copper
vmac-vtuk .... alloy of copper and zinc: brass
vmac-drês .... alloy of copper and tin: bronze
vnên .... division of year based on length of time taken by moon to make one revolution round earth: month
vnên-rze .... child born recently: baby
vnên-jluz .... conventional period of time of seven days: week
vsud .... that which has consciousness and thinks: mind
vsud-raz .... firm in pursuit of purpose: resolute
vsud.rnû.flêl .... science of diseases of the mind: psychiatry
vsud-hsa .... sudden inclination to act: impulse
vsud-htug .... being consisting only of mind: spirit
vsud-maûs .... quick to receive ideas: receptive
vsud-mul .... frame of mind: temper
vsud-fal .... individual nature or sum of qualities: character
vsud.suô .... mental faculty
vsud-srô .... give heed: attention
vsud-stû .... heedless of untoward consequences: reckless
vsud-zvê .... presence of mind
vza .... don't do
vza-krois .... insect in torpid stage of development: pupa
vzôn .... phenomenon of energy produced by electrons in motion: electricity
vzôn-auf .... electric bulb
vzôn-nziop .... electrical engineer
vzôn.svuan .... any device giving light produced by electricity: electric light
vzû .... perceive meaning of: understand; correspond secretly: fit

vzû-csû........................ adroit in handling people under the circumstances: tact
vzû-jci .... understand and like qualities of: appreciate
vce............................. feeling sorrow: sad
vce-jlô .... sad event: tragedy
vce-kôz........................ feel sorrow for the wrong that one has done: repent
vtuk........................... bluish-white metallic element used to protect other metals against corrosion: zinc
vgep .... horny growth at tip of finger or toe: nail
vgep-toif..................... draw fingernails over: scratch

-S-

sa.............................. used in a question regarding identity or specification: what; one unspecified: any
saic .... play games of chance: gamble
saic-hlua..................... small cubes used in gambling: dice
saic.srêm..................... house used for public gambling: casino
sa.lbu.......................... what result
sa.ril .... how many
sa.hzô .... what cause
sam .... belonging to you: yours
sa.mul .... what condition or state
sa.fleu......................... which one
sa.sor .... how much
sa.kêg .... what type
sag............................. of great value: valuable; of great moment: important (v. sag-zên)
sag.ôi .... any valuable thing: treasure
sag-ris .... diminish in worth: depreciate

sag-fria .... valuable white metallic element, hard, heavy, ductile and malleable: platinum
sag-zên .... of great meaning: important
sag-jbe...................... judge value of: estimate
sag.pa .... that quality which makes a thing estimable or desirable: value
sag-pci...................... increase in value: enchance
sag-tû .... equal in value to: worth
seêm......................... retain in possession: keep; preserve from spending, loss or danger: save (v. tbo-seêm); go on in time: continue
seêm-flo.................... practice of principles of health: hygiene
seêm-viô.................... woman who lives with a man without being married: mistress
seêm-vuô................... place where plant, vehicles, or stores are kept: depot
seêm-srêm .... building for storing goods: storehouse
seêm-srêm.vriam ...... one in charge of stores: storekeeper
seêm-sku .... keep under observation to prevent damage, loss, etc.: watch
seêm.cuem.ôi........... thing kept in memory of the giver or as a reminder of a person or experience: keepsake
seêm-czû .... hold back for later use: reserve
seêm-blêh-kraut........ blank book for keeping photographs, stamps, etc.: album
seêm.grêun.lu........... continue raining
sehi.......................... division of humankind deemed of common stock: race
sen........................... number less than one: fraction; part separated from a unit or not forming a whole: fragment
sen.nuap.................. break in pieces
sen.cze-stû .... disperse here and there: scatter

ses .... sound of splashing water
sêûm .... deposit below ground as corpse: bury; put out a sight
sêûm-poc.................. place where corpse is buried: grave
sêûm-poc.uô............ piece of ground for burying the dead: cemetery
sêûm-thin................ wooden case to contain dead body: coffin
sê.ris .... considering this, not to say a lesser thing: even
sê.ris.tû..................... not the less for: nevertheless
sê.mêus.io................ unmarried person: bachelor
sê.mi .... not having: without
sêf .... belonging to us: our
sêv .... expressing absence of quality, etc., signified: not
sêv-rôûn-tzif............ vegetable eaten uncooked: salad
sêv-vriam................. person not engaged in a given occupation: layman
sê.sla......................... not engaged in work: idle
sê.sfuom .... without anything added by way of elaboration or ornamentation: plain
sê.tis .... not the same: different
sê.grê .... going on without end: continual
sia............................. any living thing, including vegetable, animal, and human
sia.ia.......................... group of living things with common characteristics: species
sia.fiôp .... prick with poison-injecting weapon of living thing: sting
sia-czuûb.................. thread-like thing in vegetable or animal structure: fibre
siab........................... sound uttered by human beings: voice
siab-biôm .... speak highly of: praise
siab-biômb.sag.......... worthy of praise: praiseworthy
siab-trê .... give utterance to words of rebuke: scold

siêpi........................... on the spur of the moment: extempore
siut........................... divide with sharpe edge: cut; shape by cutting: carve (v. siut.zku)
siut-lub..................... block of wood on which things are chopped: chopping block
siut.hôj.fleu.............. thin, broad piece cut out: slice
siut-hpu.io .... one who deserts a party or an ideology: renegade
siut-mêus.viô............ woman whose husband has died: widow
siut-nui .... tool with one end a cutting edge for shaping: chisel
siut-fjûb .... grass cut and dried: hay
siut-stû........................ withdraw from employment, public life, etc.: retire
siut.zku .... shape by cutting: carve
siut-czo...................... cut and gather: reap
siut-jav .... trim by lopping off superfluous branches, etc.: prune
siû .... round fruit with firm pulp and red skin: apple
siû-prel...................... round, fleshy, edible root: turnip
sik .... without cavities: solid; possessed of the character assigned: genuine
sik-jaz........................ flat, circular, solid object: disk
sôp .... secure from danger: safe
sôp.lu .... deliver from danger: rescue
sôp.seêm................... keep in safety: preserve
sôp-tluat..................... umbrella-like device that slows the descent of those who jump from airborn aircraft: parachute
sôp-gûin................... vouch for: guarantee
soun .... move speedily: run
son-vlaul.................... body of water flowing in a certain direction: current
soun-cze .... flee from danger, etc.: fugitive
soun-czo.................... follow to overtake from some purpose: chase

sor .... in great quantity: much; high degree: very
sor.fef .... measurable amount: quantity
sor-vric-iar .... flattened, carnivorous myriapod: centipede
sor-snil .... red fruit with thick, tough rind enclosing numerous seeds surrounded by white pulp: pomegranate
so.vrê .... visit often: frequent
so.sla .... much occupied: busy
sod .... ten hundred: thousand
so.dak .... many times: often
so.glu .... given to action: active
su .... what time: when; any time: ever
suêf .... set oneself against: oppose
suêf.ud .... in opposition to: against
suêf-fri .... assert contrary of: contradict
suêt .... give money due in exchange for goods received, etc.: pay; periodical payment to employee: salary (v. sla-suêt)
suêt.e .... one to whom money is paid: payee
suêt-uam .... written order on bank to make payment: cheque
suêt-ciam .... pay for use of something: hire
suêt-plêm .... motorcar plying for hire: taxi
suô .... part of speech; any power inherent in the body or mind: faculty
suô.lien .... faculty of remembering: memory
suô.nlo .... sense for preceiving odours: smell
suô.vûil .... faculty for conceiving mental images: imagination
suô-cua-sjie .... in Luif, a division of the vocabulary containing words all of the same part of speech: part-of-speech division
suô.kut .... moral senses resident in a person's mind directing him or her about right and wrong: conscience

suo .... area of land owned by one entity for cultivating crops: farm

suz............................ involving hardly any labour and trouble to do: easy

suz-ûuc..................... bird with distinctive note and given to laying eggs in nests of small birds: cuckoo

suz.lgi....................... inclined to believe without careful consideration: credulous

suz.hpu..................... likely to change easily: fickle

suz.nuap................... likely to break easily: brittle

suz-nuap-lai............. brittle, bluish-white metallic element: antimony

suz-vêg .... able to bend easily: pliant

suz-snuim................. soft, loose shoes for indoor wear: slippers

sujôj .... compound which in aqueous solution readily neutralizes acids: alkali

sû .... in the number of: among

sûig .... put an inquiry: ask

sûig-cua.................... in Luif, a word used in the framing of questions: interrogatory term

sûig-jbe..................... question and test: examine

sûig-pêa.................... punctuation mark placed at the end of a question: question mark

sûig-blêh .... matter requiring a solution: problem

sûig-tuê .... sentence in which a question is expressed: interrogative sentence

sû-ôut........................ long seat, usually unpadded and without a back: bench

sû-lhôm.................... soil composed of clay and sand with vegetable matter: loam

sû-roiz .... talk with one another: converse

sû-rfom .... kind of cabbage with large flower head which is eaten: cauliflower

sû-mrean .... large crested parrot: cockatoo
sû-suêt........................ make payment along with others for a common purpose: subscribe
sû-smer....................... green, juicy, oblong fruit of creeping plant: cucumber
sû-cuem...................... do along with others to bring about: contribute
sû-jae.......................... allotrope of oxygen found in atmosphere: ozone
sû-puô .... comment appended to text: note
sû-plia .... a different form of a thing: variant
sû-phuet .... musical pipe with finger holes along it and a hole for blowing through near one end: flute
sû-trêf........................ low wall alongside of bridge, etc.: parapet
sû-truar .... kind of silk with lustrous surface: satin
sû.tbo .... place in or among: insert
sû-grib .... one associated in work, etc., and on very familiar terms: comrade
sla.............................. expend energy to achieve something: work; work habitually undertaken for a living: occupation; bring about by work: operate (v. sla-lbu)
sla-liôl .... scheme to be undertaken: project
sla-lbu .... bring about by work: operate
slar .... any large vessel for travelling on water: ship
slar.ia......................... group of ships operating together: fleet; total collection of ships of war belonging to a country: navy
slar.uô........................ basin for keeping ships: dock
slar-sgon .... long pole for supporting sails of ship: mast
slar.kûz .... one who commands a ship: captain
sla-hsa .... operate a vehicle to make it move along: drive
sla-hsa.aê .... apparatus for steering any vessel or vehicle: helm

sla-hsa-nui .... shaft with blades for propelling ship or airplane: propeller
sla.mac .... free from work: leisure
sla-fal......................... quality fitting one for a post: qualification
sla-vrê........................ progress in some line of work: career
sla-suêt .... periodical payment to employee: salary
sla-stû........................ relinquish an employment: resign
sla-ciam .... use a person for regular work, paying him for it: employ
sla-jroz....................... person with whom one works: colleague
sla-jza .... agitate and swell by action of some agent like yeast: ferment
sla-piô .... viscous substance made up of minute fungi used in fermentation: yeast
sla-bhon .... association of workers to promote their common interest: trade union
slôn .... body of connected ideas: system
slôn-mau .... general basic idea: principle
slôp .... tube for conveying liquids: pipe
sluj .... series of sounds produced for aesthetic enjoyment: music
sluj-buv .... pleasing measured flow of sound: rhythm
slû .... physically not in sound condition: sick
slû-hev....................... be of bloodless, sickly complexion: wan
slû-nuah .... morbid condition with swelling, heat, redness and pain: inflammation
sraô .... morally bad: immoral
sraô.û .... wicked person: villain
sraô-htug................. evil incorporeal being: devil
sraô-muir.................. wrongfully kill a person: murder
sraô-drû.................... moral objection deterring action: scruple

srah .... any branch of knowledge dealing with some aspect of society: social science or philosophy
srêm .... building serving as abode or for other purposes: house
srêm.iûn .... one inhabiting a particular house: inmate
srêm.uô .... land on which a building stands: site
srêm-sko-gloit........... shopkeeper selling foodstuff and household supplies: grocer
srêm.ciam.io .... one who rents a house from its owner: tenant
srêm-crul .... art of building houses: architecture
srêm.jriêf .... one who designs and builds houses: architect
srêm-pue .... road lined with houses: street
srêm.gûi .... one who lets his house: landlord
sriol .... small, thin plate covering fish: scale
sriol-rie..................... large tropical fruit with scaly rind: pineapple
criol-rsûh.................. scaly plant with edible shoot: asparagus
sriol-nio.................... chronic wasting disease producing scales and deformities on skin: leprosy
srô .... get implicated: involve
srô-rial...................... strike together: collide
sruêl .... implement with bristles for cleaning, etc.: brush
sruêm .... soft, white, fibrous substance covering seeds of cotton plant: cotton
srû .... look at written words to gather their meaning: read
srûuf......................... omnivorous ungulate reared for its meat: pig
srûuf.uô.................... pen where pigs are kept: pigsty
srûuf.vliêl .... pig's flesh as food: pork
srûuf-priog .... marine mammal of dolphin family with short, blunt snout: porpoise
srûuf.dlos .... projecting nose of pig or other animal: snout
srû-bûuj .... able to read and write in some language: literate

shail........................ tool with solid head for driving nails, striking, etc.: hammer
shail-zrôp .... iron block on which metal is hammered into shape: anvil
shu .... restore to healthy condition: cure; restore to former condition: recover
shu-fri .... write directions for making up medicines: prescribe
shu-gai .... oily preparation for soothing pain or healing skin diseases: balm
sma .... stay for some expected event: wait
sma-nêz.................... line of persons awaiting their turn for something: queue
sma-vriam .... one who waits at table in a restaurant: waiter
sma-poc.................... lightly covered pit for trapping animals: pitfall
sme.......................... intend a certain sense: mean
sme.ih .... that is to say: that is, i.e.
smer .... large, fleshy fruit with hard rind: gourd
sme-hsa .... make movement with arm, etc., to signify something: gesture
sme-niav.................. be of uncertain meaning: ambiguous
sme-gsô .... settle exact meaning of: define
smior....................... land or freshwater chelonian: tortoise
smiûp...................... any creeping, small, elongate invertebrate: worm
smôn....................... methodical account of past events of a country: history
smôn-hrôz............... ancient traditional story popularly deemed true: legend
smuas...................... cloth made of flax: linen
smuas.tûu................ plant from whose fibres linen is woven: flax
smuat...................... liquid, black or of some other colour, used for writing: ink

smuat-uam .... paper for absorbing extra ink right after writing: blotting paper
sne .... experience life: live
sne.hia .... live person
snêul .... thing on which one sleeps: bed
snêul-bauz .... forced to stay in bed by infirmity: bedridden
snêul-tluem .... upper covering for bed: bedcover
snêul-krois .... flat, blood-sucking insect living in beds: bedbug
snil .... that which a flowering plant bears to reproduce itself: seed
snil-tbo .... scatter seed on the ground: sow
snôi .... soaked with water or other liquid: wet
snou .... more than one: plural
snou-drin-zriv .... practice of being married to more than one person at a time: polygamy
snuim .... any outer covering for foot: shoe
snuim.luam.io .... one who makes and mends shoes: cobbler
snuv .... knowledge dealing with ultimate reality or abstract phenomena: philosophy
sfas .... space in house enclosed by partitions: room
sfas-pue .... passageway in a house onto which several rooms open: corridor
sfo .... set down in writing for reference: record
sfo-uam .... a slip attached to article pointing out its nature, etc.: label
sfo-nui .... appliance for keeping documents: file
sfu .... permit or let: allow
sfuom .... thing that serves to adorn: ornament
sfuom-vlêô-spol .... showy flower growing in spherical clusters: hydrangea
sfuom-sdôus .... fabric with ornamental designs used for curtains, etc.: tapestry

sfuom-truar .... silk fabric woven with figures: brocade
sfu-uam .... document granting permission: permit
svair .... any covering for the head: hat
svaup .... contrivance for stirring air to cool face: fan
svaup-iêt.................... bird with gaudy plumage and tail that can spread out like fan: peacock
svaup-rsûh .... tree with unbranched stem and crown of pinnate or fan-shaped leaves: palm-tree
svaup-flaic .... musical instrument with folding bellows: accordion
sviu .... set of two similar or corresponding articles: pair
sviu-lkô-mau .... in Luif, two consonants pronounced together: double consonant
sviu-htê-mau .... two vowels pronounced as one sound: diphthong
sviu-blê..................... child whose parents are both dead: orphan
svuan......................... any contrivance for producing light: lamp
svuan-czuûb .... thread of spongy material that draws up oil and keeps lamp or candle burning: wick
sca .... communication sent by one person to another: message
sca-sgam .... electrical apparatus for transmitting messages: telegraph
sci.............................. ascertain number or quantity: count
sci.aê .... machine capable of making arithmetical calculations: calculator
sci-sfo .... record of money transactions: account
sci-thaid ....frame with beads for reckoning purposes: abacus
sci-khôn .... science of computation by figures: arithmetic
sje.............................. usually competitive game or pastime involving physical exertion: sport; exercise or feat involving physical strength or skill: athletics

sjie............................ ascertain how many times a number contains another: divide
sjie.lu......................... have a part of: share
sjie-lrim-iûr.............. rodent that can run very swiftly and has a divided upper lip: hare
sjie-lbu .... result of dividing one number by another: quotient
sjie-nuap..................... break along a line: split
sjie-voi-nio .... dividing membrane: diaphragm
sjie-sen .... fraction with numerator and denominator expressed: vulgar fraction
sjie-sen-tau .... in Luif, marks used in conjunction with vulgar fractions: vulgar fraction mark
sjie-siut....................... cut lengthwise: slit; cut up in order to inspect: dissect
sjie-cuem.................... divide and give out: distribute
sjie.pom .... that side of vulgar fraction indicating total number of parts considered: denominator
spe.............................. do something for amusement: play
spe-kêu....................... name conferred playfully: nickname
spe-gle........................ pleasure derived from some form of activity: fun
spe-gbo....................... a deception for the sake of amusement: hoax
spiû .... lacking in strength: weak
spiû-ian .... physical condition in which blood lacks red cells or haemoglobin: anaemia
spôis........................... applicance with glass for reflecting image: mirror
spol .... part of plant containing reproductive organs: flower
spol.eu........................ division of corolla: petal
spol.ia......................... bunch of flowers: bouquet
spol-hiz .... dried yellow-orange stigmas of a species of crocus: saffron

spol.czû.ôi .... ornamental vessel for holding flowers: vase
spol-jaz .... wreath of flowers: garland
spol-pêm .... female organ of flower: pistil
spol-kôr .... male organ of flower: stamen
spol-kraug .... whorl of leaves making outer covering of flower: calyx
spol-kraug.eu .... division of calyx of flower: sepal
spom .... usually edible fungus: mushroom
spuin .... device of metal capable of emitting ringing sound: bell
spuc .... building where commodities are manufactured by machine: factory
sbaun .... part for holding a thing: handle
sbaun-khuêj .... deep vessel with handle to hold liquid: jug
sbaz .... unit of volume
sboif .... scaly, four-legged reptile: lizard
stêk .... building for dramatic performances: theatre
stô .... render assistance: help; sustain weight of: support (v. stô-czû)
stô-al .... help advance: promote
stô-roiz .... argue in support: plead
stôh .... composition in a form different from prose: poetry
stô-hue .... material for steadying ship: ballast
stô-nui .... that on which a thing like a building rests: foundation
stô.vriam .... one who assists another in work: assistant
stô-sko .... rest on another's efforts: rely
stô-zca .... advance the growth of: nourish
stô-cêi .... structure supporting a bridge: abutment
stô-crum .... framed structure supporting roof of building: truss

stô-czû........................ sustain weight of: support
stô.blê........................ lacking help: helpless
stô-tliô........................ contribute in a subordinate way: accessory
sto .... have as one's property: own; acknowledge as one's own: admit
sto.io .... one who owns: owner
sto.ôi .... what is owned: property
sto-blêh-suô.............. in Luif, a noun indicating possessor: possessive noun
stui .... having an abundance of possessions: rich; high in price: dear (v. rôef-jêh)
stui.ôi .... possessions in abundance: wealth
stui-uem.................... sumptuous meal: feast
stui-gle .... enjoyment of rich things: luxury
stuôm......................... garment for lower part of body having one segment for each leg: trousers
stuôm-czuûb .... band of any material encircling waist: belt
stuûc .... thing used in play: toy
stuûc-grêl .... device for engendering entertaining spectacle in fire: firework
stû .... release hold of: let go; cause to flow: pour; get free from confinement: escape; give free rein to one's desires: indulge
stû-roiz...................... reveal the truth about one's affairs: confess
stû-ruap..................... treat another person with extreme care and attention: pamper
stû-spe....................... given to lewd behaviour: wanton
stû-jain...................... cease to be firm: relax
stû-piev .... drink alcohol boisterously in company: carouse
stû-phôs .... device for firing gun by releasing catch: trigger
stû-blêa .... cone-shaped vessel for running liquid into small opening: funnel

sdôus .... woven material: cloth
sdôus-sfuom .... ornamental needlework on cloth: embroidery
sdôus-zku .... produce cloth from thread, etc.: weave
sdu .... construct, as house, etc.: build; form of parts
sdu.ôi .... thing constructed like bridge, tower, etc.: structure
sdu.nziop.................. one engaged in designing or constructing works of public utility like roads: civil engineer
sdu-ztê...................... building material formed of cement, sand, and stone: concrete
sdu-jhus .... building block of baked clay: brick
sdut .... building where persons are confined by government for violating the law: prison
sdut.û .... person confined in prison: prisoner
sdut.seêm.io .... one in charge of a jail: jailer
sdû .... cease sleeping: awake; stir to action: rouse
sdû-bûuj .... aware of things: conscious
skêf........................... lower surface of room: floor; one of horizontal divisions of building: storey
skêf-sruêl .... brush with long handle for sweeping floor: broom
skêf-sdôus................. fabric for covering floor: carpet
sko .... want what is essential for some purpose: need
sko-blê-zca .... abnormal outgrowth on living body: excrescence
sku .... keep safe: protect; maintain against attack: defend; keep under observation to prevent damage, loss, etc.: watch (v. seêm-sku); conceal from observation, etc.: screen
sku.uô .... place that provides protection against rain, danger, etc.: shelter; institution for care of afflicted persons, like the insane: asylum
sku-lziap .... soldier keeping guard: sentry
skun .... story for perfomance on the stage: drama

sku-sfas..................... covering over room below roof: ceiling
sku-svair.................... protective covering for head: helmet
sku-tbo...................... insert in something like a frame: set, frame
sku-krauf.................... covering to protect front part of clothing: apron
sku-glik..................... metal protective covering for finger used in sewing: thimble
agam......................... communicating instrument
sgêûn........................ cutting instrument consisting of a pair of pivoted blades: scissors
sgêûn-siut................... cut with scissors: clip
sgiel........................ cold-blooded aquatic vertebrate that breathes through gills: fish
sgiel-euk.................... large bird of prey living on fish: osprey
sgiel.uô..................... building where aquatic animals or plants are kept in tanks: aquarium
sgô.......................... work performed by engineers: engineering
sgon......................... main stem of tree: trunk; main part
sgon-vluar................... main part of a country in contradistinction from adjacent islands: mainland
sgon-srêm.................... lofty, narrow building: tower
sgon-stuôm................... garment for lower part of body hanging from waist loosely round both legs: sarong
sgon-gzô..................... remnant of tree trunk left in the ground: stump
sguit........................ four-stringed musical instrument played with bow: violin

-Z-

za........................... position external to: outside
za.ôi........................ soft material like paper enclosing something: wrapper

zal .... great in depth from surface to surface: thick; pressing closely together: dense; turning out well: flourishing; not acute in feeling: insensitive
zal-iûr-hiû .... thick, short, fine hair of some animals: fur
za.lu .... send away; dismiss
zal.lu .... become viscous: coagulate
za-rêh .... be detached in manner: aloof
zahipoje.................... magnesium sulphate
zam .... far on in a period of time: late
zam-uem .... late meal at night: supper
za-vêg .... with surface curved outwards: convex
za.vrê........................ go outside: emerge (v. vrê za)
za.vre.uô .... place by which one leaves: exit
za-slôp...................... outlet tube: nozzle
za-cab .... deviating from rule: anomalous
za-cuem.................... put forth: issue
zab .... plane figure with four sides: quadrilateral
za.kôof .... send out: emit
za-gzauf.................... pertaining to another country: foreign
ze .... on the other hand: but
zeu .... the persons addressed: you
zel .... of the colour of silver: white; without anything added by way of elaboration or ornamentation: plain (v. sê.sfuom)
zel.lu .... make white: bleach
zel-nuah .... light metallic element that burns with white light: magnesium
zel-dêl-glup .... brittle, thin, white metallic element: bismuth
zên .... large in size: big; of high degree: great
zên-hrôz .... any imaginary animal or thing of tremendous size: monster

zên.gun .... amount of space taken up by a thing: size
zêj .... of the shape of a plane figure bounded by three sides: triangular
zêj-khôn .... branch of mathematics dealing with relations between sides and angles of a triangle: trigonometry
zis.............................. agreeable to the senses; pleasant; of fine, soft quality: delicate
zis-côh .... pleasantly odd: quaint
zis-tuz......................... pleasing in respect of form or movement: elegant
zôa .... period of daytime between sunrise and noon: morning
zôa-uem .... first meal of the day: breakfast
zoû .... front part of head: face; appearance presented to view: aspect
zoû-hev .... colour and appearance of skin of face: complexion
zoû-hê .... lying with face upwards
zoû-hsa....................... make a wry face: grimace
zoû-nêz....................... furrow in skin of face: wrinkle
zoû-fri .... expression of face: countenance
zoû.vrê .... go forward: advance
zoû-sdôus .... cloth worn over face: veil
zov .... the colour of fresh foliage: green; in new, fine condition: fresh
zov-luû .... yellowish-green gaseous element with suffocating smell: chlorine
zov-sfuom-jui .... hard ornamental stone commonly green in colour: jade
zoc............................. readily yielding to pressure: soft
zoc-lie......................... soft-bodied marine animal: jellyfish
zoc.lu .... become less severe: relent

zoc-rial .... knock gently: tap
zoc-siû .... pulpy fruit of red or yellow colour in the potato family: tomato
zoc-zrôp .... malleable, fairly pure iron: wrought iron
zoc-zkû .... mild in treatment: lenient
zoc-glup .... soft, white, metallic element: potassium
zoc-griu .... soft gelatinous food: jelly
zulûkoje .... potassium nitrate: saltpetre
zu.mli .... causing death: fatal
zu.mlê .... make existence cease: extinguish
zusehi .... human being characteristics of dark skin, broad nose, etc.: Negroid
zucuhijef .... double sulphate of aluminium and potassium: alum
zu.jeûp .... cause a person to be frightened: scare
zu.bauz .... strike down, as a tree: fell
zu.gûin .... become friendly again after estrangement: reconcile
zu.gle .... engage the attention pleasurably: amuse
zûr .... with taste of salt: salty; useful and agreeable
zûr.zis.uem .... salty delicacy
zûfue .... compound of chlorine with some other element: chloride
zla .... hold in possession: have
zla-pom .... have a part in: partake
zle .... bring fingers or some other part of body into contact with: touch; be in contact with: abut
zle-lto .... touch lightly, producing a distubing sensation: tickle
zle-hsa .... feel about as in the dark: grope
zle.va .... in contact with: touching
zle-zru .... knock against and jar: jostle
zle-zfê .... make connection with: contact

zlêu .... in or to this place: here
zlêu-jzua-coôl .... walk at random: ramble
zlôn .... anything of an abstract nature: abstract object
zlôn.fa .... not of concrete form: abstract
zlog .... male offspring: son
zlog.jzez.jci .... love of children for parents: filial love
zlu .... remain the same: endure
zluû .... direction to left of person facing setting sun: south
zlu.lêr .... existing indefinitely: permanent
zlu-lva .... preserve from extinction: perpetrate
zlu.vam..................... lasting for a short time only: temporary
zrar .... precious stone: jewel
zrar-ôut .... monarch's chair of state: throne
zrel .... female parent: mother
zri.............................. have a desire: wish
zrir .... protruding bottom of face: chin
zri-rud .... wish evil upon: curse
zri-fôb .... wish good to befall on: bless
zriv .... woman to whom a person is married: wife
zri.vlô .... wish to be: would-be
zrôp.......................... ductile metal widely used for tools and other purposes: iron; unwavering in mind: firm
zrôp-nio .... hard outer case of eggs, etc.: shell
zrôp-vuô................... fortified place: fort
zrôp-zca.................... reddish-brown matter produced by oxidation of iron: rust
zrôp.zboec .... one who works iron with a hammer: blacksmith
zrôp-jui .... hard, granular, igneous rock: granite
zrôp-pue................... track of iron rails on which trains ride: railway
zrôp-tûu .... tree of beech family yielding hard timber: oak
zrôp-thaid................ frame of iron bars: grating

zrôp-krauf .... protective apparel for warfare: armour
zru .... make short, rapid movements: shake
zru-nui .... suspended seat that moves back and forth: swing
zru-ceud .... call by gesture: beckon
zhi .... experience quivering sensation: thrill
zhi-jlô .... hazardous enterprise: adventure
zma .... commence to do: start
zma-hia .... wild, primitive human: savage
zma.fe .... at the start of: beginning of
zma-sia .... animal in unborn state: embryo
zma-snêul .... rocking bed for infant: cradle
zma.zôa .... beginning of daylight: dawn
zma-zca .... begin to grow: sprout
zma-zku .... bring into existence: found
zma-cua .... preliminary statement at beginning of book: preface
zma-jroi .... of initial stage: elementary
zma-krois .... immature form of insect before metamophosing into adult form: larva
zma.ghal .... first few days of the year: New Year
zmeop .... one who cultivates land: farmer
zmo .... satisfied with amount possessed: contented
znaisib .... shelled aquatic invertebrate: shellfish
znû .... of good intellectual powers: wise
znû.û .... one of profound wisdom: sage
zfê .... come into close contact; join; seize by legal process: attach
zfê.uô .... place where two things join or meet: joint
zfê-hue .... substance with properties differing from those of the elements composing it: compound
zfê-nêz .... line of junction between two edges: seam

zfê-nuê .... extend from end to end: span
zfê-vrê .... go along with for protection or courtesy: escort
zfê-vrouh................. fibrous tissue joining muscle to bone or other structure: sinew
zfê-suô...................... in Luif, a word connecting other words and expressing a certain relationship between them: connective
zfê-stô....................... work jointly to achieve an objective: cooperate
zfê-cua...................... word composed of two or more words: compound word
zfê-pêa...................... punctuation mark used for joining component parts of compound word: hyphen
zfê.plia...................... number of things growing or fastened together: bunch
zfê-blêh .... associated thing
zfê-thô.io................. person running joint enterprise with others: partner
zfê-kaê...................... in Luif, a phrase made up of words of the same part of speech: aggregated phrase
zfê-krôf..................... movable device on which door turns: hinge
zfe-glu .... join some service or organization: enlist
zfê-gsô .... fasten together: bind
zfê-gsô.plia .... number of things loosely tied together or loosely wrapped up: bundle
zvê........................... be in specified place: present; come into view: appear (v. hrô-zvê); make known: introduce (v. czo-bûuj)
zvê.mi...................... in presence of
zvê-fôb .... introduce as suitable: recommend
zvê-cûg-vuô .... be present in another place: alibi
zvê-tbo .... guarantee prisoner's appearance in court: bail
zvôt........................... yellow precious metal of high specific gravity: gold

zvôt-aif .... ground seeds of various kinds of mustard plant made into a pungent condiment: mustard

zvôt-iêt .... golden bird with black wings: oriole

zvôt-rcûf .... a nutritious bean rich in protein and oil of an East Asian plant: soya bean

zvôt.hriûp .... one who works in gold: goldsmith

zvot-spol .... yellow flower of genus of composite plants: chrysanthemum

zvôt-sgiel .... small golden fresh-water fish allied to the carp: goldfish

zvôt-gsô .... cover with gold: gild

zsû .... emotion of gladness consequent on mental apprehension only: happy

zsû-maûs .... receive with gladness: welcome

zsû-skun .... drama calculated to excite laughter: comedy

zsû-hau .... blissful world where the good are supposed to dwell after death: heaven

zca .... advance in size by natural process: grow; advance to higher state: develop (v. htê-zca)

zca-lô .... small plants growing under trees of greater size: undergrowth

zca-stui .... bearing or growing profusely: fertile

zca-csû .... raise or bring up: rear

zca.pa .... wax and wane

zcos .... part of trunk of body below diaphragm: belly

zcos-laz ....small, wrinkled depression in middle of abdomen: navel

zcos-voi .... internal organs of body: viscera

zcos-vric-nêz .... furrowed part of body between abdomen and thigh: groin

zcos-zên-bli .... severe pain in abdomen due to spasmodic contractions: colic

zcos-bli .... pain in belly: stomach ache
zpe .... mainly or wholly concerned with one's own interests: selfish
zpiat .... one in charge of flying an aircraft: pilot
zboec .... skilled worker in engineering and allied trades: mechanic
zten .... male relative born of same parents: brother
zten.mul .... state of being a brother: brotherhood
ztê .... join together so that the components of one thing are diffused among those of another: mix; consisting of various kinds: miscellaneous (v. ztê.kêg)
ztê-iar .... animal of mixed breed: mongrel
ztê-rze....................... of mixed race: half-blooded
ztê-zfê....................... make into a confused mass: entangle
ztê-cua...................... in Luif, a word formed from other words: composite word
ztê-czûus .... animal born of ass and horse: mule
ztê-jzab..................... product of mixing: mixture
ztê-tuê .... sentence composed of clauses: complex sentence
ztê.kêg...................... consisting of various kinds: miscellaneous
ztê-glup .... mixture of metals: alloy
zto .... feel intense dislike: hate
zto-lto .... harass with intention to injure: persecute
zdoaf .... one receiving instruction in an institution of learning: student
zku .... fashion or bring about: make
zku.io .... one who makes: maker
zku-raz .... make agreement to secure payment in event of loss, etc.: insure
zku-hjuez................. structure with jet of water: fountain
zku-vzôn.................. machine for generating electricity: dynamo

zku.truar .... artificial silk: rayon
zku-kêg .... particular kind of goods: brand
zku-grêl .... small piece of wood tipped with inflammable material: match
zkû .... disposed to do good: kind
zgu .... strength or power: force
zgu-eiz .... one forced to serve another without pay: slave
zgu-hsa .... hasten forward precipitately: rush
zgu.môip.io .... one who wrongfully seizes property by force: robber
zgu-nêz .... crush into creased condition: crumple
zgu-nuap .... compress forcibly so as to damage or break: crush
zgu-fien .... strain for breath: gasp
zgu-frê .... violent collision: shock
zgu-vliêc .... absolute ruler of a country: dictator
zgu-vrê .... push violently: thrust
zgu-sla .... forced labour
zgu-sgon .... bar moving on fulcrum and designed to overcome resistance: lever
zgu-za .... cast out: eject
zgu-zfê .... join metal by means of heat or hammering or compressing: weld
zgu-csa .... exhort earnestly: urge
zgu-czo .... seize a person, usually for ransom: kidnap
zgu-czû .... grasp forcibly: seize; assume power unjustly and forcibly: usurp
zgu-pêa .... in Luif, a punctuation mark used to indicate emphasis: emphasis mark
zgu-pra .... order or bid: command
zgu-bauz .... treat unjustly and cruelly: oppress
zgu-bauz-vliêc .... oppressive ruler: tyrant

zgu-tbo.................... force into place: ram
zgu-kri...................... capacity for exerting force: power

-C-

ca .... what manner: how
car .... quality of being male or female: sex
car.lu .... sexual intercourse
car.lkû .... shame concerning sexual matters
car-rnû .... contagious veneral disease that begins as a sore: syphilis
car-môip.................. sexual intercourse between two persons of whom one at least is married to someone else: adultery
car-vza...................... innocent of sexual intercourse of an immoral nature: chaste
car-vza-liu................ person who has not experienced sexual intercourse: virgin
car-siut .... remove tesicles: castrate
car.srêm.................... house where prostitutes ply their trade: brothel
car.zri .... sexual desire: lust
car-zgu .... force sexual intercourse: rape
car.ceûl-spe.............. obscene jest
car-cûg .... one who is sexually attracted towards members of opposite sex: heterosexual
car-cto-noê.............. castrated man: eunuch
car.jci....................... sexual love
car-tis .... sexually attracted towards members of one's own sex: homosexual
cav........................... precise or accurate: exact; keeping appointed time: punctual (v. vêu.cav)

cab .... of what serves as a means of judging: standard; according to established doctrines: orthodox (v. fe-cab); guiding principle: rule
cab-fri.......................... form of expression peculiar to a language: idiom
cab-giêf .... outward formal observance: ceremony
ceud .... utter sounds or words expressing some emotion or in greeting, summoning, etc.: call
ceud-piôs.................... put armed forces in readiness for war: mobilize
ceud-piûj .... accountable for one's actions or control: responsible
ceud-puêr .... call to a contest: challenge
ceud-blêh-suô........... in Luif a noun employed as a term of address: vocative noun
ceud-glu .... call upon to appear or perform some action: summon
ceûl .... relax lips to express pleasure, etc.: smile
ceûl.siab .... emit sounds from mouth expressive of joy, etc.: laugh
ceûl-siab-flier ....carnivore allied to dog with a howl that resembles hysterical laughter: hyena
ceûl-suô...................... sense of humour
ceûl-spe .... say or do something to produce a laugh: joke; make fun of: mock
ceûl-znû .... power of producing pleasure by manipulating ideas of words: wit
ceûl-thôuh................. comic drawing: cartoon
cel .... one more than one: two
cel.fûl .... not either: neither
vel.vo........................... one or other of two: either
cel-sjie .... divide into two equal parts: bisect
cel-zrôp-nio .... mollusc with shell in two valves: bivalve
cel jû cel .... two by two

cel-poh .... divisible by two into integers: even
cel-pue-hêun .... ebb and flow
cel-drô .... double over upon itself: fold
cerahi .... sulphuretted hydrogen
cerahipoje.................. sulphuric acid
ceraceje...................... hydrogen peroxide
ceracikoje .... carbonic acid
cehacikoje.................. sodium carbonate
cez .... hundred million
cêi .... structure for carrying a road across river, etc.: bridge; means of solving a difficulty
cêôm .... fall upon forcibly: attack
cêôm-lkô .... surround place with armed forces to compel its surrender: siege
cêôm-sma.................. lie in wait to make surprise attack: ambush
ci .... not including: except; if not: unless
ciam .... apply to some purpose: use; do good to: benefit
ciam-sia..................... organism living on another: parasite
ciam-dak .... occasion capable of being utilized to advantage: opportunity
cietûem .... hold ceremony connected with disposal of the dead: funeral
cirakozû..................... volatile liquid capable of producing insensibility: chloroform
ci-ril .... free from any further deduction: net
cim............................ comprising everything there is: all
cim.mov .... entire amount: whole
cim-flêl-kraut .... book or set of books providing information on every department of knowledge: encyclopaedia
cim.cel....................... the two: both
cim.bûuj.................... have knowledge of all things: omniscient
cim-gûin.................... all of the same mind: unanimous

ciceje .... carbon dioxide
cipora .... colourless inflammable gas released by putrefying vegetation in marshes: methane
côh .... not commonly found: rare; occuring only now and then: seldom
côh-nui .... rare and curious thing: curio
coet .... pay out money: spend
coet-liôl .... estimate of income and expenditure: budget
coet-siut .... cut down expenses: retrench
coet-fcô .... grand display: pomp
coet-creu .... sparing in expenditure: economical
coet-chauk .... amount of money spent: expenditure
coet-bli .... meanly reluctant to spend: miserly
coôl .... move along unhurriedly by lifting each foot alternately: walk
coôl.eu .... one complete movement of the leg in walking: step
coôl-rêh .... manner of walking: gait
coôl-pue .... path for pedestrians: footpath
cofse .... cost of living
cua .... unit of language, spoken or written, embodying an idea: word
cua.i .... list of words with definitions: vocabulary
cua-lûur .... gentle in word and manner: polite
cua-hia .... direction of signification of a word indicating person speaking, spoken to or spoken of: person
cua-siab .... give the sound of a word: pronounce
cua-sjie .... in Luif, a systematic division of the vocabulary: vocabulary division
cua-pom .... part of a word pronounced as one sound: syllable
cua-kraut .... book giving the words of a language with their meanings: dictionary

cuem .... transfer to another: give
cuem.ôi .... thing given: gift
cuem-uam .... written document dictating disposition of one's property after death: will
cuem-ruap................ bestow in return for service or merit: reward
cuem-fôb................. possessed of good intentions: well meaning
cuem-zkû .... liberal in giving: generous
cuem-cto .... submit to demand: surrender
cuem-bûuj................ impart knowledge: inform
cuem-kuv .... things known or assumed: data
cuit .... impose contribution to state: tax
cun........................... without any defect: perfect
cun-cab .... highest conceivable: ideal
cun-cab.û .... one devoted to an ideal: idealist
cun-cab.jci................ devotion to what is ideal: idealism
cûn........................... integral number just abive six: seven
cûf............................ not more than: only
cûg........................... separate from the one in question: other; turn the other way about: reverse (v. cûg-drô)
cûg-fri .... give account of: report
cûg-fri.vriam .... one who makes reports for newspapers: reporter
cûg-jêh .... extending far down: deep
cûg-ban .... extending only a little way down: shallow
cûg-drô..................... turn the other way about: reverse
cûg-kêu .... another name: alias
cli............................. diseased spot on body: sore
cli-sriol .... crust resulting from sore: scab
cli-jluz .... thick fluid produced by suppuration: pus
cli-jluz-laz................ small spot on skin containing pus: pustule
clu............................ buying and selling of goods: trade
clu-ôêp .... table in shop where money and goods change hands: counter

clu.ôi .... things for sale: goods
clu-uam .... note giving particulars of payment required on a transaction: bill
clu-rze .... economic activity: industry
clu-cuit .... tax on goods: duty
clu-plêm .... motor vehicle for transporting goods: lorry, truck
clu-tau .... device marking out a firm's goods: trademark
creu .... of little weight: light
creu-uem .... drinks or light food: refreshments
creu-lai .... lightest of elements, a colourless, odourless, inflammable gas: hydrogen
creu-lu .... hold in slight regard
creu-luû .... light, inert, nonflammable gaseous element: helium
creu.rnû .... light illness: ailment
creu-srêm .... light building for amusement purposes: pavilion
creu.kiûr .... wash lightly: rinse
creu-glup .... white metallic element remarkable for lightness: aluminium
crêe .... not civilized: barbaric
crêus .... garment for upper part of body: coat
crêus-sfuom .... jewellery pinned to dress: brooch
crêus-jlec .... that portion of garment covering arm: sleeve
crêus-blop-zfê .... end of sleeve over or near wrist: cuff
cri .... attempt to do: try
criôm .... hardy ruminant allied to sheep: goat
crif .... farinaceous edible tuber of various plants: potato
cru .... express gratitude: thank
crul .... one of the fine arts: art
crul.eu .... a work of art
crul.flêl.û .... one well versed in the fine arts: connoisseur
crum .... topmost covering of house: roof

crum-fjûb................. covering for roof of straw, leaves, etc.: thatch
crum-chiûs............... venomous snake capable of dilating neck to look like hood: cobra
crum-jhus................. roofing slab of baked clay: tile
crum.dluô .... edge of roof jutting beyong wall: eave
chaêv......................... thing employed for doing some work: instrument
chaêv-bli................... inflict severe pain, usually by means of instruments: torture
chaim .... preparation for improving beauty of face, etc.: cosmetic
chauk.........................whatever is used as a medium of exhange: money
chauk-rgêp .... establishment for keeping, lending, and dealing with money generally: bank
chauk-nuap .... having sustained financial losses and become insolvent: bankrupt
chauk.seêm.uô.......... place where money and valuables are kept: treasury
chauk-sfo-vreuc........ one who works at keeping accounts: bookkeeper
chauk-csû................. illegally offer money to influence action: bribe
chauk-jro.................. inordinately desirous of wealth: avaricious
chauk-phêuz............. small pouch for carrying money: purse
chauk.pci.................. gain money by work: earn
chauk-bli .... impose a money penalty: fine
chav.......................... science dealing with the heavenly bodies: astronomy
cheud .... prized concretion formed by oyster: pearl
chê .... make rhythmical motions with legs or other parts of body: dance
chêô .... minute account: detail
chêô-fri..................... give account of: describe
chêô-fri-kêu............. descriptive title
chêô-sûig-jbe............ examine in detail: scrutinize

chêô-sla .... work out in detail: elaborate
chêô.plia.................. statement of details: schedule
chêb .... regulation made by a government: law
chêb-lruic................. assembly for making laws: legislative council
chêb-moês .... make claim in court: sue
chêb-siut .... deprive of legal protection: outlaw
chêb-czû.................. apprehend by legal authority: arrest
chiat......................... dark-brown, beetle-like, orthopterous insect: cockroach
chiul......................... nocturnal, mouse-like mammal with wings: bat
chiûv......................... common domestic bird of the poultry family: fowl
chiûs......................... long, scaly carnivorous reptile with forked tongue and no limbs: snake
chiûs-reu .... huge marine reptile, fossil of Mesozoic times: plesiosaur
chiûs-hrôz .... imaginary snake-like flying monster: dragon
chim......................... small round succulent fruit of whatever kind: berry
chôik........................ musical instrument consisting of parchment stretched on a frame and sounded by percussion: drum
chôud....................... any pot or container used in cooking: cooking vessel
chôk......................... any building devoted to worship: temple
chui.......................... soiled with foul matter: dirty
chui.ôi...................... filthy matter: dirt
chui-ban.................. of low, disgusting quality: sordid
chuit......................... tremulous sharp sound of birds: twitter
chuf.......................... any instrument of war
chuf.seêm.srêm......... public storehouse for weapons and ammunition: arsenal

chûn........................ firm, black, combustible, carbonized prehistoric vegetation: coal
chûn-iêt.................... black songbird: blackbird
chûn-lai.................... non-metallic element that is a constituent of all living matter: carbon
chûn-jluz.................. black, viscous liquid obtained from distillation of coal, etc.: tar
chûn-thin................. kind of wood that is black, heavy, and hard: ebony
chûp........................ any kind of edible grain: cereal
chûp-hue.................. food material, a carbohydrate forming the principal constituent of cereals: starch
chûp-nio .... husks of grain obtained by threshing: chaff
chûp-feur .... reap and gather in grain: harvest
chûp-vliêl................. meat cut small: mincemeat
chûp-siut.................. cut into small pieces: mince
chûp.srêm................. storehouse for grain: granary
chûp-sgon .... dried stalks of grain after threshing: straw
cfe .... ability in carrying out some action: skill
cfe.roiz .... able to speak fluently and persuasively: eloquent
cfe-nru .... dexterity in performing tricks: legerdemain
cvo .... expel air from chest and throat with explosive sound: cough; cast out: eject (v. zgu-za)
cvo-phûl................... viscid matter brought up by coughing: phlegm
csa .... give counsel: advise
csa-lruic.................... political assembly for giving advice: advisory council
csa-rlu .... expound to win over to some belief: preach
csa-sûig..................... seek advice of: consult
csa-pra...................... inform of danger in advance: warn
csû........................... conduct affairs: manage
csû.io........................ one who is in charge of a business, etc.: manager

csû-lruic .... body of persons appointed to perform some function: committee
csû-zfê .... arrange into a functional whole: organize
csû-cri .... conduct test to prove some theory: experiment
csû-kûz .... one who presides at an assembly: chairman
czal .... science of the earth: geology, geography
czaf .... contrivance for doing work: machine; device for converting one kind of energy to another: engine
czaf.nziop .... one who is versed in the design, construction, and operation of machinery: mechanical engineer
czaf-zku .... produce by machinery: manufacture
czaf-plêm .... vehicle driven by motor: motor vehicle
cze .... move through the atmosphere: fly; run for safety: flee
cze-hvau .... cylindrical contrivance projected through the air by force: rocket
cze-hjuez .... spring shooting up hot columns of water: geyser
cze-fiôp .... let fly as bullet or arrow with intent to injure: shoot
cze-stû .... fling through the air: throw
cze-chuf .... straight penetrating weapon released from bow: arrow
czil .... limb growing from tree: branch
czil-sjie .... divide into two branches: fork
czôn .... science dealing with plants and animals: biology
czo .... lay hold of: take
czo-roiz .... cite words of another person: quote
czo-nuê .... space occupied by a thing: space taken
czo-vêu .... time spent over something: time taken
czo-vrê .... take away
czo-saic .... scheme whereby one may win a prize by lot: lottery

czo-sto........................ take as one's own: appropriate
czo-sgiel..................... large voracious seabird: cormorant
czo-czû....................... lay hold of after pursuit: catch
czo-czû.aê................. contrivance for catching animals: trap
czo-czû.e .... person held as pledge: hostage
czo-buûj .... make known: introduce
czo-dlû .... assume as correct: suppose
czo-glu .... take upon oneself to do: undertake
czu .... prepare ground for growing crops: till
czu-aê........................ implement for cutting and turning up soil: plough
czuel.......................... any instrument for making measurements of whatever kind: measuring instrument
czuûb .... small cord for binding, etc.: string
czuûb-aif.................... paste made in long, slender strings: noodle
czuûb-rpû.................. catch fish with rod and line: angle
czuûb-hvau............... cylinder with helical thread round it: screw
czuûb-zfê.................. intertwining of parts of a cord or cords: knot
czuûb-zku................. draw out and twist into threads: spin
czuûb-cua................. in Luif, one of a class of words formed of a word and a letter or figure to distinguish between phenomena of similar nature: serial word
czuûb-tûu................. plant of mulberry family whose coarse cortical fibre is used for ropes, etc.: hemp
czuûb.gso .... bind with string or the like: tie
czû .... keep fast in the hand: hold; remain in contact by grasping: cling
czûa........................... deduct one quantity from another: subtract
czû.aê .... gripping instrument consisting of two limbs connected at one end: tongs
czûa.lu....................... become less: decrease
czûa-stô .... alleviate or eliminate distress, etc.: relieve

czûa-gzô .... remain over: surplus
czû.ôi .... thing held; what is contained in: contents
czûus .... swift-running mammal with solid hoofs: horse
czûus.srêm................ building for horses to dwell in: stable
czûus.cgi.ôi.............. seat placed on back of horse for rider: saddle
czû-ruam .... contend by grappling and throwing: wrestle
czû-fri....................... make an assertion in support: allege
czû.siut.aê................ pincers for holding small objects or bending wire, etc.: pliers
czû-sla .... occupy an office or post
czû-poc...................... hollow place for holding something: socket
czû-thin.................... staff carried in the hand by police officer, etc.: baton
czû-tbo .... place for safekeeping or as security: deposit
cto .... cease to have: lose
cto-roiz..................... without power of speech: dumb
cto-hli .... partially or wholly deprived of power of hearing: deaf
cto-hne..................... without power of sight: blind
cto-hne-rsûh............ clouding of lens of eye causing partial blindness: cataract
cto-vle .... lose power of sensation or motion in a part of the body: paralyse
cto-coôl .... deprived of power of walking normally: lame
cto-phûl-pler .... dried grape: raisin
ckô .... act against the law: crime
ckô-moês.................. detect crime
ckô-moês.io .... one engaged in secretly investigating cases of crime or unravelling cases of misbehaviour: detective
ckô-zrôp .... metal rings with chain for securing hands or feet: handcuffs, fetters
ckô-jzu .... having committed a crime: guilty

cgi .... rest on buttocks: sit; travel by sitting on horse or in vehicle: ride (v. cgi-vrê)
cgi.ôi .... thing for sitting on: seat
cgi-vrê .... travel by sitting on horse or in vehicle: ride
cgi-vric .... upper legs of person in sitting position: lap
cgi.sfas .... room where one may sit and converse or spend the time: parlour or living room
cgi-zoc .... pliable case stuffed with soft material for resting on: cushion

-j-

jae .... gaseous element found free in atmosphere and necessary to life: oxygen; necessary for some particular purpose: essential (v. lva-sko)
jain .... rest on liquid: float; remain aloft in the air: hover (v. jêh-jain)
jain-rhez .... plant with broad leaves and beautiful flowers floating on water: lotus
jain-hue .... matter rising to surface of liquid or floating thereon: scum
jain-jzu .... floating anchored object serving as guide or warning: buoy
jain-bôz .... flat structure of timber for use as transport on water: raft
jain-tbo .... sustain from falling down: hang
jain-tbo-sfuom .... ornament suspended from necklace: pendant
jav .... external form: shape
jav-rnê .... make a drawing showing only main lines: outline
jav-siut .... put into shape by clipping, etc.: trim

jav-czaf..................... machine for turning and shaping metal, wood, etc.: lathe

jav-khôn................... branch of mathematics dealing with lines, surfaces, etc.: geometry

jaz .... with regular curved outline like ring or globe: round; flat, circular, solid object: disk (v. sik-jaz); have unvarying course of action: routine

jaz-lên .... straight line through centre of circle or sphere with ends at widest part of circumference: diameter

jaz.lu .... extend all round: surround

jaz.rnê.aê .... instrument consisting of a pair of jointed limbs, used for drawing circles: compass

jaz-rnû....................... skin disease marked by circular patches: ringworm

jaz-hsa .... travel along circular course: revolve; move as though in a circle: circulate

jaz.fe.......................... on all sides of: around

jaz-fri......................... express an idea in a roundabout way: circumlocution

jaz-val....................... boundary line of circle or other figure: circumference

jaz-vlaul.................... circular current in sea, etc.: whirlpool

jaz-soun.................... circle a heavenly body: orbit

jaz-sfuom.................. ornamental circlet for finger: ring

jaz-jô .... round the outside of and near to: about

jaz-poc...................... nearly hemispherical vessel for holding food or drink: bowl

jaz-drô...................... twist into circular form: coil; turn round like wheel: rotate

jea .... the person addressed: thou

jeûp.......................... be afraid: fear

jeûp.ih .... for fear that: lest
jeûp.û .... one without courage: coward
jeûp.rze..................... deserved of fear: formidable
jeûp-htug .... imaginary man-eating giant: ogre
jeûp-nius .... struck with sudden fear: startled
jeup-niûh .... horrifying dream: nightmare
jeûp-soun .... sudden, fear-induced flight of a herd of animals: stampede
jeûp.blê .... without fear: brave
jeûp-drû .... careful for fear of consequences: cautious
jeûp-kiuv................. crawl in abject fear: grovel
jêu .... this present day: today
jêu.guê .... night of today: tonight
jêh .... of great extent upwards: height; great in bodily height: tall; extending far down: deep (v. cûg-jêh); of high rank or character: noble; aspiring for advancement: ambitious (v. pso-hse)
jêh-laz .... height above a base: altitude; reach highest point of a series of events, ideas, etc.: climax
jêh-luav-laz.............. heavy metallic element with high melting point: tungsten
jêh-htug .... fictitious person of great height: giant
jêh-mêj..................... of lofty, impressive character: sublime
jêh-snuim.................. outer covering for foot and lower part of leg: boot
jêh-skêf..................... raised floor: platform
jêh-zkû .... act patronizingly to inferiors: condescend
jêh-cze...................... rise to great height in the air: soar
jêh-jain..................... remain aloft in the air: hover
jêh-pci .... perform surpassingly well: excel
jêh-bluim .... flat, elevated land of great extent: plateau
jêh-kraut .... literary work of the highest quality: classic

jêh-khuêj .... deep, hand-held vessel with bail handle for holding water: bucket
jiaz .... gain knowledge by study: learn
jiaz.û .... person of extensive learning: scholar
jiaz-zên .... versed in scholarship: learned
jiaz.plia..................... group of students taught together: class
jiaz-kraut .... book for learning a subject: textbook
jivoi .... long-legged, screaming wading bird: heron
jô.............................. at short distance from: near
jô-lreon .... large gland behing stomach discharging digestive juice into small intestine: pancreas
jô.raz.......................... more likely to be the case than otherwise: probable
jô.rô .... about where: whereabouts
jô-hrô .... soon to happen: imminent
jôm .... gone by in time: past
jôm.rûus-vliêc .... former president of a country: ex-president
jô-nrôus.................... piece of land surrounded by water on nearly all sides: peninsula
jô.fa.......................... close in respect of position, etc.: nearly
jô.fiûl.io .... one who stands near and looks on: bystander
jô-vlêô .... nearly spherical figure: spheroid
jô-vlûr .... flat part of either side of head adjacent to foreheaad: temple
jô.sêv .... nearly not: scarcely
jôzue .... compound of basic and acid radicals: salt
jô.truûv .... optical instrument magnifying minute objects: microscope
jom .... acid in taste: sour; look sullen: scowl; fond of finding fault: captious
jom.ôi .... substance possessed of a sour taste: acid
jom-ôip...................... sour condiment produced from wine, etc.: vinegar
jom-jroi .... ungraceful in movement, etc.: awkward

jui .... small detached piece of rock: stone
jui.uô .... place where stone is extracted: quarry
jui-tûu......................... tropical tree with hard, durable timber: teak
jû .... after this; nearest in place, etc.: next
jûz .... without sound: silent
jleûp .... one who drives a vehicle: driver
jlec .... upper limb from shoulder to hand: arm
jlec.riam .... carry in arms
jlec-nuê .... part of body under shoulder: armpit
jlec-vrôih .... part of sea extending like an arm into recess in coast: gulf
jlec-zfê .... outer part of joint where arm bends: elbow
jlec-jaz .... ornament worn round wrist or arm: bracelet
jliun .... oily substance in adipose tissue: fat
jlô .... take place: happen; thing with which one is concerned: affair
jlô-nêz .... sequence of actions or operations: process
jlo .... feel uneasy sensation on account of need for food: hunger; feel intense desire: yearn
jloi .... piercing in sound: sharp; with keen edge: cutting; quick to understand; vigorously active: energetic
jloi.lu.aê .... instrument for making whistling sound: whistle
jloi.lu.jui .... stone prepared for sharpening tools: whetstone
jloi-jzu .... take notice: mark well, *nota bene*, N.B.
jloi-toif .... rub with sharp edge: scrape
jloi.kiaz .... utter a shrill cry: yell
jluê .... place occupied by a thing: position; assume a certain posture of the body: attitude (v. lie-jluê)
jluêm .... division of surface of earth: region
jluz .... anything which exists: real thing
jluz.fa .... actually existing or occurring: real

jlûv.......................... set of parents, children, and other relatives: family
jlûv.kêu .... name pertaining to a family: surname
jlûd .... daughter of one's uncle or aunt: cousin (female)
jra............................. deficient in speed: slow
jraim .... rural area: countryside
jraim.û .... one living in rural areas and engaged in pursuits connected with the land: peasant
jraim-ruap .... outing with repast, often to the countryside by a group of people: picnic
jriap.......................... medical practitioner: doctor
jriêf .... one practising an intellectual art
jriol .... large gland secreting bile: liver
jriol-due .... bitter fluid produced by liver: bile
jrôû .... at no time: never
jro .... filled with ardent desire: eager; intense interest: enthusiastic
jroi .... of uneven surface: rough; with coarse, abrupt projections and indentations: rugged; without skill: unskilled
jroi-srêm.................. rough building used for purposes other than for dwelling: shed
jroi-jloi..................... making sharp, harsh sound: creaking
jroi-piem .... temporary quarters of soldiers, travellers, etc.: camp
jroi-plêm .... rough, two-wheeled vehicle for transporting goods, etc.: cart
jroi-dluô.................. with sharp, notched edge: jagged
jroz........................... one who dwells near another: neighbour
jroz.uô...................... place lying near: neighbourhood
jroz-hia..................... one to be viewed sympathetically as member of same human race: fellow human

jroz-grib .... one associated with another: fellow
jrot .... extremity of leg: foot; lowest part of a thing: bottom
jrot-êh .... rear part of foot: heel
jrot-lô .... lower surface of foot: sole
jrot-roic .... close covering of cloth for foot and leg: sock
jrot-vlêô .... game in which large inflated ball is kicked about: football
jrot-zfê .... joint between foot and leg: ankle
jrot-jzu .... impression made by foot: footprint
jrual .... visible mass of water vapour floating high in atmosphere: cloud; lacking in clarity: vague
jrual-iêt .... small bird that sings as it flies high upwards: skylark
jruûn .... large mass of body surrounded by land: lake
jhus .... tenacious, impervious earth: clay; stick stiffly: tenacious; capable of being moulded: plastic
jhus-zrôp .... earth composed of clay and iron oxide: ochre
jhus-jzab .... mouldable synthetic substance: plastic
jhus.poc.ôi .... vessels of baked clay: crockery
jhus-phûl .... viscid substance exuding from some plants that hardens in air but dissolves in water: gum
jfi .... expect fulfilment of what is desired: hope
jfi-hrô .... inclined to take sanguine view: optimistic
jfi-sma .... look forward to happening: expect
jfi-cri .... allure by exciting hope: entice
jsôm .... brilliant, hard precious stone: diamond
jza .... extend more widely: spread
jza-rza .... make copies of book and offer for sale: publish
jza-rza-paz .... have exclusive right to reproduce book, etc., for sale: copyright

jza-stuôm .... garment or part of garment hanging from waist: skirt
jza-stû....................... throw liquid about: splash
jza-znû .... able to deal with many subjects: versatile
jzab .... essential part of an entity: substance
jzab.czal.................... science that treats of earth's crust: geology
jza-kaê...................... in Luif, phrase consisting of qualifier preceding noun, verb, or connective: expanded phrase
jzef .... fleshy side of face below eye: cheek
jzez .... female offspring: daughter
jzêu .... pertaining to that side east of a person facing north: right
jzêl .... sound or flash arising from electric discharge through air: thunder or lightning
jzêl-hêun .... flow out suddenly in a jet: spurt
jzêl-nru..................... swiftly and unexpectedly: sudden
jzêl-cêôm................. make sudden attack: raid
jzêm .... oxide or hydroxide of calcium: lime; stick easily to: sticky (v. fe-gsô)
jzêm-lai .... ductile metallic element found in lime, etc.: calcium
jzêm.jui .... sedimentary rock with calcium carbonate as the principal constituent: limestone
jzêm-buû................. plastic mixture of lime and sand for coating walls, etc.: plaster
jzêm-buû.lu.aê.......... short-handled, flat-bladed tool for laying plaster: trowel
jzêk........................... white, malleable, ductile, precious metallic element: silver
jzêk-sgiel.................. kinds of white fish: silverfish
jzêk-krois................. silvery insect found in books, etc.: silverfish

jzi............................ demonstrate truth by argument, etc.: prove; examine critically: test (v. ûp-cri)
jziem .... one who writes poetry: poet
jzi-uam..................... written paper giving information or evidence: document; formal written declaration attesting some fact about a person: certificate
jziû............................ muffled in sound: dull, with an obtuse edge: blunt; needing rest, especially sleep: tired (v. lie.jziû)
jziû-spiû .... lose strength and spirit: languish
jziû.tis .... dull and without variety: monotonous
jzi-ruam.................... contend by reason: argue
jzi-flêl....................... provable proposition: theorem
jzon .... person related by marriage: relative
jzon.zten................... brother of husband or wife or husband of sister: brother-in-law
jzod .... son of brother or sister; nephew
jzu............................ make distinctive modification to one spot on a surface: mark
jzua .... in or to that place: there
jzuis.......................... piece of land with phenomena as presented to the view: landscape; entire range of things seen by a spectator: scene
jzu.ôi .... device for stamping an impression: seal
jzu-roiz..................... remark critically or explanatorily: comment
jzu-rpû .... point at a target: aim
jzu-hlan.....................day devoted to celebration of something: festival
jzu-hmav .... light set up for guidance: beacon
jzu-hne..................... look into: inspect
jzu-mro .... impress on paper, etc., by applying inked types, etc.: print
jzu-mro-ril............... total number of copies of book printed at one time: edition

jzu-mro-czaf............ machine for printing books, etc.: printing press
jzu-nion.................... mark off by characteristic qualities: distinguish
jzu-nui....................... piece of printed paper for sticking to letter, etc.: stamp
jzu-siab .... stress some particular words in speaking: emphasize
jzu-sla........................ daring or unusual undertaking: enterprise
jzu-côh .... of a particular kind: special
jzu-côh-pci .... special advantage: privilege
jzu.plia .... designation of things differentiated from others: class
jzu.plia.lu .... arrange in classes: classify
jzu-blêh .... object that one aims at in shooting: target
jzu-glup..................... small piece of metal with inscription or device to commemorate event, etc.: medal
jzu-gsô...................... mark by pressure: impress
jzû .... unsound in mind: mad; in confusion: disordered
jzûut......................... one whose work is teaching: teacher
jci .... feel exceedingly well disposed towards: love
jci-roiz...................... talk a great deal: talkative
jci-vuô .... place popular for some particular recreational reason: resort
jci.stô .... inclined to assist: helpful
jci-sku .... to feel great affection: cherish
jbe .... ponder pros and cons and decide: judge; hold examination in court of law to find out the truth: trial
jbe-lgi .... hold view without certain proof: opinion
jbe.rgêp .... place where judicial trials are held: court
jbe-hpu..................... look over and correct: revise
jbe-muir .... put to death by process of law: execute
jbe-fri .... comment and pass judgement: criticize
jbe-siut .... examine and suppress: censor

jbe-sfu .... pronounce as accepted: approve
jbe-gsô..................... come to a resolution: decide
jbe-gsô-laz .... point where a decision is needed: crisis

-p-

pauh........................ turn up ground: dig
pauh.aê.................... instrument for loosening earth: hoe
pauh-iar.................... small burrowing rodent: rabbit
pauh-guê-iûr .... burrowing nocturnal plantigrade: badger
pauk........................ lend or borrow: loan
pal........................... of contrary kind: opposite
pa.lien .... fail to call back to mind: forget
pa.liôl...................... by chance: haphazard
pa.lva....................... put an end to: abolish
pa-biôm-prôh.......... literary composition holding up something to ridicule: satire
pa.rôûn .... in uncooked state: raw
pa.ro........................ without taking into account: excluding
pa.ro.lu .... do not take into account: exclude; leave out: omit
pa.rpû .... fail to get: miss
pa.hues.................... become worse: worsen; reduce to a lower rank: demote
pa.hsa...................... be stationary: motionless
pa.hse...................... decline to take: refuse
pa.hpi...................... aroused emotionally: excited
pa.hpu..................... not subject to change: constant
pa.meuh.................. move away by pressure: push
pa.mêus................... dissolve marriage: divorce
pa.mlê..................... given to working hard: diligent
pan.......................... pertaining to nature: natural
pan.raz .... by natural consequence: of course

pan.rze .... produced naturally in a place: indigenous
pan-nu .... belonging naturally: intrinsic
pa.nzo .... not in accordance with reason: absurd
pan.blêh .... world of things excluding human works: nature
pan.thêt.................... natural abode of animal or plant: habitat
pan-kri .... natural special aptitude: talent
pan-gaif.................... tremendous disaster produced by nature: natural calamity
paf........................... not complete in natural development of body and mind: immature
pa.fêz.lu.................... make intricate: complicate
paf-jroi .... in an unfinished state: crude
pa.viaf .... not proud or arrogant: humble
pa.vlair .... long hollow area between hills: valley
pa.vle........................ become unconscious: swoon
pa.sôp....................... full of peril: dangerous
pa.suêt...................... be in debt: owe
pa.suêt.ôi.................. what one owes to another: debt
pa.suz .... hard to do: difficult
pa.sla .... cease from work: rest
pa.snôi...................... free from moisture: dry
pa.spe .... not given to trifling: serious
pa.stui .... without adequate means to maintain a comfortable life: poor; low in price: cheap
paz .... according to what should be: right
pa.zla........................ remove from possession: deprive
paz.lu .... set right: rectify
paz.hfo .... must as a matter of right: ought
pa.zfê........................ become disunited: separate
paz-fôb...................... honest and correct in dealings with others: upright
paz-buv .... right and in accordance with what is ordinarily deemed correct: propriety

pa.cab........................ different from accepted standards: eccentric
pa.chui .... free from dirt: clean
pa.jeûp .... courage to do: dare
pa.jeûp.û .... one distinguished for acts of bravery: hero
pa.jro........................ unwilling to do: reluctant; lose heart: dispirit
pa.jza........................ put closely together: pack
pa.peôn .... climb down: descend
pa.pûuk...................... free from entanglement: unravel
pa.pso........................ miss achievement: fail
pa.bauz...................... move upwards: rise (v. hê-vrê)
pa.bûuj-sor .... having no previous knowledge of: strange
pa.tiûn .... go hungry: fast
pa.thuû...................... not domesticated: wild
pa.thuû.iûr .... wild animal
pa.dba .... having no limits: infinite
pa.dba.gun .... infinitely small: infinitesimal
pa.kul .... not commonly occuring: unusual
pa.kuv .... contrary to truth: false
pa.khau .... containing nothing: empty
pa.gsô .... make loose: unfix
pa.gbo .... free from deceit: honest
pe............................. in addition to: besides
peôn .... mount with help of limbs: climb
peôn-voi .... slender climbing organ of plant: tendril
peôn-jzu .... one of a series of steps on a scale: degree
peôn-thaid.................. temporary erection of poles and planks for workers employed on a building: scaffolding
per............................. little beyond all others: least
per-laz .... least amount: minimum
pet............................. sound made by footsteps
peb .... being at the end: last

pêa .... mark used in writing for dividing sentences, etc.: punctuation mark, subsidiary device; distinctive quality or trait: feature
pêm .... of the sex that bears offspring: female
piem .... has one's abode in: dwell; stay for an undue length of time: linger (v. lêr.gzô); rest on another's effors: rely (v. stô-sko)
piev .... swallow liquid: drink; suck in: absorb
piev.ôi .... any liquid for drinking: beverage
piô .... organism of that division other than the animal: vegetable
piôs .... make ready: prepare
piôs-iûn .... person appointed by a society to transact its business: secretary
piôs-hues .... free from impurities, crudities, or defects: refine
piôs-nru .... done at once: prompt
piôs-cuem .... present for acceptance or rejection: offer
piôs-blê .... performed without preparation: impromptu
piôs-bzê .... all prepared: ready
piûj .... say in answer: reply
piûj-glu .... act in return: react
pimrô .... written declaration made under oath: affidavit
pin .... integral number just above five: six
picikerajera .... toxic acid used as germicide: carbolic acid
poi .... round fruit of several related kins consisting of a tough rind enclosing juicy segments: orange; colour between red and yellow: orange
poi-bih .... of colour obtained by mixing orange and black: brown
poi-bih-foi .... edible nut with husk of deep reddish-brown colour: chestnut
pom .... less than the whole: part

pom-fiem .... with comparative relation in magnitude: proportion
pom.fleu.................. detached portion of a thing: piece
pom.plia.................. smaller group divided from bigger group: subdivision
pom-chêô .... relating to a distinct part or unit: particular
poh.......................... integral number just above three: four
poh.mloû .... four times as much: fourfold
poz.......................... before all others: first; in the chief place: primarily
poz-mau.................. first letter of a word, especially a name: initial
poz-suô .... in Luif, part of speech to which a word primarily belongs: original part of speech
poz-sme.................. in Luif, original meaning of a word: primary meaning
poz.brik.................. largest toe of foot: big toe
poz.glik .... short, thick finger of two phalanges: thumb
poc.......................... having empty space inside: hollow; hollow place: hole (v. poc.uô); without intended result: futile (v. lbu.blê)
poc.ôi .... hollow receptacle for liquids: vessel
poc.uô .... hollow place: hole
poc-luav-jui............. light, spongy lava: pumice
poc-roiz.................. talk idly: gossip
poc-hêun................. flow through crack, etc., in vessel: leak
poc-suêf.................. object captiously: cavil
poc-zku .... force hole through: pierce
poc-zku.aê............... instrument for boring holes: drill
poc.czû.ôi................ tubular, close-fitting covering: sheath
poc-jaz.................... anything in shape of hollow circle: ring
poc-due................... round film of liquid enclosing air or other gas: bubble

puaf.......................... overcome by force: conquer; extend widely: pervade
puaf.io...................... one who has beaten all competitors: champion
pue........................... artificial track on land on which people travel from place to place: road
pue-pca .... direct the way: guide
pue-cto..................... wander from the right way: stray
pue.dê .... by way of: via
pue-kôz .... away from the right course of action: astray
pue-guz .... place where roads intersect: crossroad
puêr.......................... engage in armed conflict as between states: war
puêr.eu .... combat between armies on a specific terrain and of limited continuous duration: battle
puêr-hue................... all material used for warfare: ammunition
puêr.slar.................... armed ship for warfare: warship
puêr-csû .... art of conducting military campaign: strategy
puêr-tuês .... things captured in war: booty
puô........................... short piece of written material: written passage
puô-og...................... condition in document: proviso
pûen......................... touch with lips as sign of affection, etc.: kiss
pûuk .... fasten by means of thread and needle: sew
pûuk.aê .... slender, pointed tool for sewing: needle
plaul......................... representation in stone, etc., of human or other figure: statue; person in fiction or history: character
plaul-zku .... carve or make statues: sculpture
plaul.jriêf................. one who carves or makes statues: sculptor
plauf......................... leaves prepared for smoking from plant of American origin: tobacco
plal........................... system of belief and conduct: religion
plal-roiz.................... instructive lecture on religious matters: sermon
plal-fri .... assert on oath: swear

plal-sraô .... transgression of a dictate of religion: sin
plal-bhon................... religious organization
plal-kut .... good from a religious point of view: holy
plaz .... political community with government: state
plaz.û .... member of a state: citizen
plaz-lai .... one of main departments of government: ministry
plaz.lu .... take over as property of the state: nationalize
plaz-rêh .... system of principles governing a state: constitution
plaz-maûs .... income of a state: revenue
plaz-msê-dliôt........... representative of a government in a foreign country: ambassador
plaz-chaêv................. civil service
plaz-czo .... seize property for the state by way of penalty: confiscate
plaz-blêh .... political affairs: politics
plaz-bhon .... body of persons organized for political purposes: party
plat............................ channel for refuse water: drain
pleuf.......................... rodent related to mouse but of larger size: rat; low in behaviour: mean (v. ban)
pleuf-rnû .... deadly infectious disease in which the germs are conveyed from rats to humans by fleas: plague
pleuf-fjûb .... any useless or unwanted herb: weed
pleuf-vêg .... crouch servilely: cringe
pler............................ small fruit that grows in clusters on vine: grape
pler.tûu..................... climbing woody plant producing grapes: vine
plê .... utter words in musical sucession: sing
plê.ia .... company of singers singing simultaneously: chorus
plê.io .... one who sings: singer
plêm .... conveyance for use on land: vehicle

plêm.uô .... building for keeping motor vehicles: garage
plêm.riam.................. carry by vehicle
plêm.cgi.io .... one who is conveyed in a vehicle: passenger
plia .... a number of persons or things together: group
plia.hia .... people in considerable number gathered close together: crowd
plia.hôj.fleu .... one of several strata of a thing: layer
plia-mru .... given to living in groups: gregarious
plia.fleu .... unit in an enumeration: item
plia-jlec .... person holding a post in a private organization: official
plia-krauf................... same garb worn by members of a body: uniform
plia-grê .... collectively cease work: strike
plif .... sweet substance from diverse plants used in food and drink: sugar
plif-uem .... shaped morsel of boiled, crystallized sugar: candy
plif-prel .... succulent root of a plant yielding sugar: beetroot
plif-due .... saturated solution of boiled sugar: syrup
plif-krev...................... tall, woody grass yielding sugar: sugarcane
pliz .... fragrant, beautiful flower of genus *Rosa*: rose; having pink colour of rose: rosy; extremely delightful: enchanting
pliz-rie........................ sweet, juicy stone fruit with downy yellowish skin tinged with red: peach
pliz-chaim .... cosmetic for reddening lips: lipstick
plo.............................. sensation of unsteadiness: giddy
ploil............................ web-footed bird between duck and swan in size: goose
plo-ztê .... throw into disorder: confuse
plo-coôl...................... walk to and fro irresolutely

pluiz........................ eating implement consisting of bowl and handle: spoon
pra............................ ask for something: request
pra-hse..................... ask as a need: require
pra-pêa..................... in Luif, punctuation mark to indicate address, request or command: request mark
pra-tuê..................... in Luif, sentence containing request or command: request sentence
pre............................ get into settled practice of: habituate
prel........................... lowest part of plant attaching it to earth: root; that on which a thing like a building rests: foundation (v. stô-nui)
prel-hpu.................. make fundamental change in state organization: revolutionize
prel-nuap................. break into component parts: analyse
prel-siut.................... destroy down to the roots: eradicate
prel-cua.................... in Luif, monosyllabic word that goes to form foundation of vocabulary: basic word
prel-chauk................ money utilized to make earnings: capital
prel-czil.................... Indian tree with big branches rooting widely: banyan
pre-seêm.................. habitual practice
prêc......................... building in which people are placd regularly for specific purpose: station
priêk......................... small, long-legged insect whose female sucks blood: mosquito; any irritating thing
priêk-thaid.............. net to keep off mosquitoes: mosquito net
priôh........................ long-winged, swift-flying, migratory bird feeding on insects: swallow
priog........................ any mammal living in the sea: sea animal
priog-reu.................. gigantic extinct marine reptile: ichtyosaur
priûm....................... shiny, creeping, air-breathing gasteropod: snail

prôu .... developed in culture: civilized
prôh .... written composition of cultural value: literature
prôh.jaz .... literary circle
proic.......................... microscopic living thing: germ
pruv .... written communication dispatched to a person: letter
pruv.lu....................... communicate by letter: correspond
pruv.rgêp .... office for transmitting letters, etc.: post office
pruv-nio .... cover in which letter is dispatched: envelope
pruv-suêt................... sum paid for conveyance of letter: postage
prus........................... long, straight piece of timber placed horizontally or vertically as a support of a building: beam or post
prû .... a misunderstanding in thought or action: mistake
prû-kôz .... faulty in some respect: defective
phaiv .... cutting tool consisting of sharpened blade with handle: knife
phaiv-chuf................ offensive weapon with long, sharp blade for cutting or thrusting: sword
pahiv-jluz .... cutting part of knife, etc.: blade
phêuz .... receptacle capable of being closed, of leather, wood, etc., for solid objects: bag or box
phêuz-vrer .... waterfowl with large, pouched bill: pelican
phêuz-plêm .... conveyance with one wheel and two shafts for one person to push along: wheelbarrow
phi .... morbid condition marked by raised body temperature: fever
phiôk......................... shrill-sounding, saltatory insect: cricket
phiom .... small carnivorous mammal, especially domesticated: cat
phi-nos-uûk .... bitter alkaloid from cinchona bark: quinine

phit .... yellow American cereal: maize
phôs .... metal-tubed weapon for explosively releasing projectiles: gun
phôs-vlêô................. projectile of lead, etc., used in guns: bullet
phôs-vlêr .... explosive mixture of potassium nitrate, sulphur, and charcoal used in guns, etc.: gunpowder
phôs-phaiv .... stabbing steel weapon fixed to muzzle of gun: bayonet
phoôz .... bivalve mollusc, a kind of which bears pearls: oyster
phoôz.uô .... place where oysters breed: oyster bed
phuet........................ musical wind instrument in form of tube: pipe
phuê......................... orderly arrangement: method; sequence of actions or operations: process (v. jlô-nêz)
phuê-fôb .... in good order: neat
phuê-cab .... regular and conventional: formal
phuê.plia .... group of people or things arranged in a systematic manner: array
phuê-tpê.................. control to enforce obedience to rules: discipline
phuê-tbo .... set in order: arrange
phuê-drô .... exercise in military evolutions: drill
phuûf .... liquid made fragrant for use as scent: perfume
phun .... science of physical properties like force, light, etc.: physics
phûun .... nocturnal bird of prey with large head and eyes, short hooked beak, and hooting cry: owl; marked by grave dignity: solemn
phûl .... liquid produced by plants: juice; any liquid produced and separated by action of living matter: secretion
phûl-smer................. any of several kinds of juicy gourd: melon
phûl-jaz.................... rubber band encircling rim of wheel: tyre (or tire)

phûl-jluz.................... adhesive substance obtained from plants that is insoluble in water: resin

pfê............................ contend angrily: quarrel

pfê-miôz.................... make surly, quarrelsome noise like a dog: snarl

pso .... accomplish what one attempts: succeed

pso-hse .... aspiring for advancement: ambitious

pso-zsû .... exult over victory: triumph

pso.pa........................ success and failure

pca .... direct actions of: lead

pca-laz....................... anything suggesting the solution of problem: clue

pca-nêz...................... line about which a body rotates: axis

pca-zma..................... take early part in enterprise, exploration, etc.: pioneer

pca-csû .... guide ship entering or leaving harbour: pilot

pca-czuûb.................. long strap used to guide horse: rein

pci............................. obtain some benefit: gain; interest of: sake

pci-mru .... have attention engaged: interest

pci-zdoaf .... person who has won academic degree: graduate

pci-cuem .... give benefit: avail

pci-khu...................... negotiate to obtain a lower purchase price: bargain

pdi .... move along in water bodily: swim

-b-

ba.............................. equally distant from ends: middle; in intervening space or time: between

ba-uem...................... meal about midday: lunch

bauz .... move downwards in liquid: sink; move downwards by force of gravity: fall (v. lô-vrê);

sink in worth: decline; apply oneself habitually to: addict

ba.û .... one occupying middle position: middleman

ban .... not extending far up: low; small in stature: short; extending far up: low; small in stature: short; extending only a little way down: shallow (v. cûg-ban); low in behaviour: mean (v. pleuf)

ba-nad .... straight line from centre of circle or sphere to circumference: radius; bar radiating from hub to rim of wheel: spoke

ban.û .... person much below ordinary stature: dwarf

ban-rud .... of low, despicable worth: base

ba-vêu .... intervening time: interim

ba-vêg .... bulge downwards in middle: sag

ba-sag .... medial value: average

ba-jzab .... central portion of mass: nucleus

ba-plia-hia .... person of the middle class of society: bourgeois

ba.tbo .... place between: interpose

ba-gloit .... person engaged in buying and selling for others: broker

beo .... organ of hearing: ear

beo-rze .... waxy secretion in ear: earwax

beo-troi .... perveiving sound through the ear: hearing

beûl .... puzzle with intricacies: perplex; throw into disorder: confuse (v. plo-ztê)

beûl-lto .... agitate the mind: disturb

beûl-sûig .... enigmatic problem: riddle

bef .... acrid in taste: pungent; make wounding remark: sarcastic; smile derisively: sneer; tensely active

bef-lûr .... pungent, aromatic kind of mint: peppermint

bef-hiz .... food cooked with turmeric, chillis, etc.: curry

bef-nio .... aromatic bark of tropical tree: cinnamon

bef-prel..................... spicy root with hot taste used in cooking: ginger
bef-tzif...................... pungent pod of capsicum: chilli
bêr............................ pertaining to first part of a period of time: early
bêr-rze....................... cause miscarriage in birth: abort
bêr.jôm..................... belonging to the earliest times: primitive
biôm .... think highly of: admire
biôm-lbu-zgu .... influence owing to success, etc.: prestige
bih .... of the darkest colour: black; difficult to understand: abstruse
bih-zel .... of colour between black and white: grey; producing gloom: depressing
bih-jzêm.................... dark, smooth substance consisting of various hydrocarbons: asphalt
bih-brat.................... soft black carbon used for pencils, etc.: black lead
bih-brat-rdêup.......... writing implement of black lead: pencil
bih-dûn.................... black-and-blue: livid
bôi............................ any matter of definite shape with firmly cohering particles: solid substance
bôi-uûk .... small, solid mass of medicine: pill
bôz .... spread out: flat; without projections: level; medial value: average (v. ba-sag)
bôz.lu.aê.................. instrument with furrowed surface for smoothing objects: file
bôz-chôud .... shallow metal vessel for cooking food: pan
bôz-gsô..................... flat strip of thin material for binding round an object: band
boa .... person or thing in question: he, she, or it
bua .... time between noon and sunset: afternoon
buên......................... change into vapour: evaporate
buû .... fine grains of rock material formed from weathering: sand

buû-jluz.................... non-metallic element very abundant in combination as in quartz: silicon
buû-bruf.................... mineral of silica and most common constituent of rocks: quartz
buf .... denoting time just passing: present
buf-chauk................. ready money: cash
buv.......................... of harmonious shape: regular shape; with parts exactly corresponding about an axis: symmetrical; alike all over: uniform
buv-zab .... plane four-sided figure of which the oppposite sides are parallel: parallelogram
buv-puô .... in Luif, an expression consisting of terms arranged in regular order from the general to the particular: regular passage
buceje....................... silicon dioxide present in quartz, etc.: silica
bûuj .... be acquainted with: know
bûuj-roiz .... make known to another by speech: tell
bûuj-hzi.................... immediate knowledge of truth without reasoning: intuition
bûuj-sor.................... having good knowledge of: familiar
bûuj-jô .... close in personal relations: intimate
bûuj-jro.................... eager to know: curious
bûuj-jzu.................... mark, gesture, etc., expressing meaning: sign
bûuj-jzu-hôj .... board displayed by shop giving its name and business: signboard
bûuj-puô .... writing conveying information, warning, etc.: notice
bûuj-drû................... with attention and caution: careful
blaiv .... frozen crystallized vapour falling through the atmosphere: snow
blaiv-jzêm................ soft white limestone: chalk
blaiv-grêun .... rain falling with snow or hail: sleet

blaf............................ soft, wet earth: mud
blaf.lu........................ make muddy: muddle
blaf-tûu...................... tropical tree growing in muddy swamp: mangrove
blac .... sodium chloride used in food: salt
blac-vric .... hog's thigh salted and dried: ham
blac-srûuf................... cured swine's flesh: bacon
bleus........................... one who believes: believer; one who adheres to the ideas of another person in religion, philosophy, etc.: disciple
blem........................... fringe of hair above eye: eyebrow
blê.............................. do not possess: haven't
blêa .... three-dimensional figure having round base and lateral surface sloping to a point: cone; gradually getting smaller towards one end: tapering
blêa-prel .... edible tapered root of a plant: carrot
blêa-bluên .... hanging mass of tapering ice produced by water dropping and freezing: icicle
blêh........................... any object, abstract or concrete, real or imaginary, living or lifeless: thing
blêh-fal...................... essential character of thing: nature
blêh-fal-suô .... in Luif, a qualifier converted from a noun: object qualifier
blêh-suô .... word used as name of a thing, whether abstract or concrete: noun
blêh-jzu..................... existence as a distinct entity: identity
bli............................... disagreeable sensation: pain; afflicted by some loss, punishment, etc.: suffering
bli.aê .... instrument of torture
bliaz .... waste matter excreted from bowels: faeces
bliaz-slôp.................. conduit for transporting away excrement, etc.: sewer
bliaz.sfas .... room used for defecation: latrine

bliaz-grê .... restricted action of bowels: constipation
bliûh .... mobile muscular organ in mouth: tongue
bliûh.lu .... pass tongue over: lick
bli-hau........................ place where wicked suffer after death: hell
bli-siab .... utter sound expressive of pain: groan
blib............................ son of one's uncle or aunt: cousin
bloek .... one engaged in unskilled physical work that does not produce goods: labourer
bloêp .... one engaged in political affairs: politician
bloim .... one versed in natural science: scientist
blou............................ sounding weak: low; of ignoble quality: vulgar
blou.siab.................... speak in low tones: murmur
blop............................ terminal portion of arm below wrist: hand
blop-al....................... inner surface of main part of hand: palm
blop-rial .... hit with palm of hand: slap
blop-roic .... covering of cloth, etc., for hand: glove
blop.mro .... writing with the hand: handwriting
blop-zfê .... joint between hand and arm: wrist
blop-cêôm .... punch with the hand held in a fist: box
blop-crul .... divination from lines on palm: palmistry
blop-czû .... enclose in hand: clasp
blop-jriap .... doctor treating patients by manual operation: surgeon
blop-plêm................... hand-propelled, two-wheeled vehicle for transporting loads: handcart
blop.khau .... amount sufficient to fill the hand: handful
bluên.......................... frozen water: ice
bluên-aif..................... cream flavoured and congealed by freezing: ice cream
bluên.lu...................... turn into ice: freeze
bluên-snuim............... footwear made for gliding on ice: skate
bluên-grêun............... frozen rain: hail

bluim .... level tract of land: plain
blûgêt........................ translucent, solid essential oil with aromatic smell obtained from a tree: camphor
brail........................... water flowing in natural channel over the land: river; continuous moving line of persons or things
brail-fri...................... give continuous account of events: narrate
brail.vluar................. channel of river: riverbed
brail-coôl.................. wade across stream or shallow part of river: ford
brail.dluô.vluar......... ground bordering river: bank
brat .... heavy metallic element, soft, malleable, dull bluish-grey in colour: lead
bre............................. mental feeling: emotion
brem.......................... part of body connecting head and trunk: neck
brem.al...................... front portion of neck: throat
brem.êh..................... back portion of neck: nape
bre-mul..................... temporary state of the emotions: mood
brem-lub .... enlargement of thyroid gland: goitre
brem-roic .... band of cloth tied round neck as clothing accessory, usually male: necktie
brem-vluar................ narrow extent of land joining two larger regions: isthmus
brem-vrôih .... narrow passage of water linking two seas: strait
brem-jaz .... part of shirt, etc., around the neck: collar
bre-sûig .... make earnest request directed at the feelings: appeal
bre-cua .... in Luif, word used to express feeling: exclamatory term
bre-cru .... having a feeling of gratitude: grateful
bre-pêa .... punctuation mark used for exclamations: exclamation mark

bre-tuê .... in Luif, sentence embodying a feeling: exclamatory sentence
bre-kôz .... feel sorry for some occurrence: regret
brian .... hard component of body: bone
brian.i .... bony framework of body: skeleton
briêt .... competitor in physical feats: athlete
briêt-drûuk............... performer of feats of physical skill: acrobat
brik .... one of terminal members of foot: toe
brik.laz .... tip of toe: tiptoe
brik-vrôih................. small inlet of sea: cove
brôn .... vapour, etc., issuing from a burning substance: smoke
brôn.lu .... emit smoke: smoke
brôn-slôp.................. passage for escape of smoke: chimney
broit .... one whose occupation is the cooking of food: cook
broig .... liquid excreted by kidneys: urine
broig-khuêj.............. receptacle for urine: urinal
broh .... brother of father or mother: uncle
bruf.......................... inorganic natural substance obtained by mining: mineral
bruf-moês................. explore for valuable mineral deposit: prospect
bhon .... entire body of persons in a locality or country: society; concerning the people generally: public; be inclined to social intercourse: sociable
bhon-oih .... member of privileged class of persons of high rank: aristocrat
bhon-siut.................. expel from society: ostracize
bhon-srah................. study of nature and development of human society: sociology
bhon-plaz................. state without a monarch with the government in the hands of the people: republic

bhon-plêm .... large public vehicle that often travels a fixed route: bus

bzê .... make entire: complete; free from restrictions: absolute

bzê-zku..................... constitute that which completes: complement

bzê-ciam................... consume entirely: exhaust

bke .... feel no interest in: indifferent

bke-stû .... pay no due attention to: neglect

-t-

tau............................. mark representing something: symbol; geometrical figure

tau-thôuh .... symbolic picture: emblem

tef.............................. as much as is required: enough

tev .... integral number just above seven: eight

tev-jlec...................... cephalopod with eight arms: octopus

tên............................. fitting in with requirements: suitable; serving ease and comfort: convenient

tiûn .... ingest food by mouth: eat

tiûn-srêm.................. place where meals are sold: restaurant

tiûn-tôm.................... sufficiently developed (as organic food) for eating: ripe

tin .... sharp sound produced by striking metal: clink

tis .... not different: same

tis-zma-vlub .... repetition of multiple words that begin with the same initial consonant: alliteration

tis-grê-vlub .... corresponding ending sound in multiple words: rhyme

tid .... all taken individually: every; every one of a number considered separately: each

tid.um .... every person who: whoever
tid.rô .... at whatever place: wherever
tid.hlan .... every day: daily
tid.sa .... no matter what: whatever
tid.su .... at every time when: whenever
tid.ca .... in whatever manner: however
tid.cel.ghal................ every two years: biennial
tid.cûg...................... every other: alternate
tid.ghal .... every year: annual
tik .... sound of clock: tick
tôm .... grownup: adult
tôk .... sound of knock on wood: rap
toif............................ move with pressure against: rub; vex playfully: tease
toif-siut .... remove hair with razor: shave
toif-shu .... rub body with hands by way of treatment: massage
toif-zgu..................... force encountered in moving one object over another: friction
toif-tbo..................... rub with sticky substance: smear
toif-kiûr.................... cleanse by rubbing: scour
toif-griu.................... bring to smooth, glossy state by rubbing: polish
tuê........................... succession of words that are complete grammatically: sentence
tuês .... seek and victimize: prey
tuês-hia .... one who seeks victims for plunder: bandit, thief
tues-suêt................... pay for release from captivity: ransom
tuês-sgiel .... voracious, long fish with mouth on underside: shark
tuê-pom .... major division of sentence with subject and predicate: clause
tuê-puô .... distinct passage of writing consisting of a number of sentences: paragraph

tuû .... any structure designed for flying: airplane
tuû.uô .... area used by aircraft for arrival and departure: airport
tuûs .... ask courteously to come: invite
tuz............................. possessed of the quality that delights the sight: beautiful
tuz-flêl....................... branch of study dealing with the beautiful: aesthetics
tuz-glup..................... hard, metallic element noted for beautiful colour of compounds: chromium
tû .... in favour of: for
tûu .... vegetable organism of whatever type or size: tree or plant
tûu-aif .... powder made from cacao seeds: cocoa
tûu-aif-jluz .... paste of cocoa with sugar, etc.: chocolate
tûu.ia......................... group of trees: grove
tûu.uô .... area of land of some extent covered with trees: wood
tûu.nio .... rind of trunk and branches of tree: bark
tûu-pleuf .... bushy-tailed rodent haunting trees: squirrel
tûu-trêf...................... fence of plants or small trees: hedge
tûu-dûn..................... blue dye from a plant: indigo
tû-lien .... commemorative structure, etc.: monument
tû mij .... for each hundred: per cent
tû-coôl....................... stick carried in walking: walking-stick
tû-jbe .... given to favouring one side: partial
tû.pa.......................... for and against: pro and con
tû ghal....................... by the year: per annum
tla............................. perform dramatic part: act; temporarily do another person's work: act in lieu
tla-lbe....................... buffoon in a circus: clown
tle .... irritating sensation in the skin: itch

tle-rnû .... contagious eruptive skin disease accompanied by intense itching: scabies
tle-cêôm .... prone to assail others: aggressive
tliô .... join one number to another: add
tliô.lu .... grow in quantity: increase
tliô-mro.................... addition to a letter after it is ostensibly completed: postscript
tliô-zfê...................... of organizations or states that join together without losing their separate identities: federate
tliô-cua..................... in Luif, word formed of letters taken from a phrase: synthetic word
tliô-bzê .... add to supply deficiency or make more thorough: supplement
tliô-tuê-pom............. in Luif, a clause merely added on to the rest of the sentence and not taking the place of a noun or qualifier: additional clause
tluat .... contrivance carried in the hand to protect against rain or sun: umbrella; protecting thing
tluem......................... sheets, blankets, pillows, etc.: bedclothes
tluin .... tool with toothed blade for cutting: saw; notched like saw: serrated
tras .... opening in wall to admit light and air: window
tres .... rounded pungent edible bulb of plant of lily family: onion
tres-tzif..................... culinary vegetable with cylindrical bulb of onion genus: leek
trê .... impute fault to: blame
trêf .... structure of brick, etc., serving as enclosing side of house: wall; structure to prevent access: barrier (v. grê.ôi)
trê-fri........................ charge with wrongdoing: accuse
trêf-poc .... shallow recess in wall of house: niche

trê-bli .... inflict suffering for offence: punish; suffer pangs of conscience: remorse

trê-bli-cto .... be deprived of by way of penalty: forfeit

trief .... eight-legged arachnid, many kinds being given to spinning webs: spider

trief-thaid .... fine network spun by spider: web

trôp .... building where vendors gather to sell provisions, etc.: market

tro .... unable to: cannot

troi .... having great force: strong; difficult to penetrate, cut, or break: tough; of colour resistant to fading or washing out: fast

troih .... edible ten-footed crustacean: shrimp or prawn

troi-hêun .... rushing stream of water: torrent

troi-fria...................... exacting rigid conformity: strict

troi-zrôp .... malleable alloy of iron with small percentage of carbon: steel

troi-jav .... with clear limits: definite

troi-phuet................... powerful musical wind instrument: trumpet

tro.rze........................ unable to bear offspring, fruit, etc.: barren

tro.vlô .... that cannot be: impossible

trot............................. cereal of genus *Triticum*: wheat

truar .... fine, soft fibre produced by silkworm: silk

truar-hiû.................... soft plumage of birds: down

truar-tûu .... tree whose leaves are food for silkworms: mulberry

truem .... toothed implement for dressing hair: comb

truôz .... shallow vessel of earthenware, etc., for holding food: plate

truôz-ba..................... central part of wheel: hub

truôz-kruod............... spindle in nave of wheel on which wheel revolves: axle truop........................ musical instrument with keys working hammers that strike wires: piano

truûv........................ any implement that magnifies objects: magnifying glass

trun........................ short literary composition on any topic: essay

thaid........................ fabric woven as mesh: net; structure forming skeleton of anything: frame

thaid-sfo........................ write in tabular form: tabulate

thaid-zfê........................ form close texture by needles: knit

thaub........................ vessel for liquids made with narrow neck and usually of glass: bottle

thêh........................ systematic knowledge of nature arrived at through observation, experimentation, and reason: science

thêt........................ one's permanent residence: home; private dwelling

thêt.blê.û........................ wanderer without fixed home: vagabond

thien........................ domestic swimming bird with short, webbed feet and long bill: duck

thiez........................ edible bivalve shellfish with grooved and ridged shell: clam

thin........................ hard, fibrous substance of tree: wood

thin-hriûp........................ one who does construction work in timber: carpenter

thin-faê........................ arrangement of fibres in wood: grain

thin-vlêr........................ wood in powdery or fragmentary form produced in sawing: sawdust

thin.siut.spuc........................ factory where timber is sawn: saw mill

thin-tûu........................ woody plant of low height: shrub

thô........................ commercial or industrial activity: business

thôuh........................ any drawing or painting: picture

thôuh.ûp........................ like a striking picture in point of beauty, vividness, etc.: picturesque

thôuh-stêk................ theatre exhibiting motion pictures: cinema
thôuh-skun............... motion picture: cinema picture; movie
thô.srêm.................. building where the administrative and clerical staff of a private organization work: office
thô.sfas..................... room where administrative or clerical work of private organization is performed: office
thô-sjie..................... small equal parts into which capital of company owned by many persons is divided: shares
thô-phuê................. method of conducting business: procedure
thô.tla....................... work as actor professionally
thôd .... unit of length
tho ....common infectious disease characterized by running nose, sore throat, etc.: cold; spread easily and rapidly
thuas .... bitter dried narcotic juice of a kind of poppy: opium
thuas-jluz .... narcotic alkaloid of opium: morphine
thuas-tûu.................. plant with showy flowers of a species from which opium is obtained: poppy
thuas-due .... tincture of opium: laudanum
thuû .... in a domesticated state: tame; ready to yield to control: submissive
thuû.iûr.................... domestic animal
thûic......................... small, industrious hymenopterous insect: ant
thûs.......................... beverage decocted from dried leaves of plant of camellia family: tea
thûs-srêm .... place where tea and light refreshments are sold for consumption on the premises: teahouse
thûs.poc.ôi .... vessel with handle and spout for brewing, holding, and pouring out tea: teapot
tsu............................ free from blame: excuse
tsu-stû .... allow to go unpunished: forgive

tziôl........................... bird of gentle nature: pigeon
tziôl.uô..................... place where pigeons live: dovecot
tzif........................... any culinary plant: vegetable
tzif.tiûn.io .... one who lives on vegetable-based food to the exclusion of meat: vegetarian
tpê............................ rule a territory: govern; direct actions of: control
tpê-lruic .... assembly for directing public affairs: council
tpê-htug .... anthropomorphic being deemed to have control over nature and humankind: god
tpê.mai..................... city in which the government of a country resides: capital
tpê-voi...................... body of persons ruling a country: government
tpê-vuô..................... centre from which operations, military or otherwise, are conducted: headquarters
tpê-suêf.................... oppose the government of country: rebel
tpê-stû...................... relinquish office as ruler: abdicate
tpê-jlec..................... chief of a department of national government: minister
tpê-gûi...................... chief minister of state: prime minister
tbo .... place in some position: put; deposit until full: fill (v. khau.lu)
tbo-seêm .... preserve from spending, loss, or danger: save
tbo-stû...................... settle and get off one's hands: dispose
tbo-cuem................... give in charge: commit
tbo-jrot..................... press under foot: tread

-d-

dau.......................... day immediately before today: yesterday
daul......................... get hot and evolve bubbles: boil; keep in restless state: agitate

daul.ius .... boiled egg
dau.guê .... night of yesterday: last night
dak .... occasion or instance: time; occurring again: repeated; not of first importance: secondary
dak-ual .... puff of air: whiff
dak-uem .... food taken at one time: meal
dak-uem.eu .... one of successive dishes of a meal: course
dak.fleu .... amount of medicine, etc., taken at one time: dose
dak-sme..................... in Luif, additional meaning of a word: secondary meaning
dak-kraut.................. periodical publication having contributions from various writers: magazine
dê .... from end to end within boundaries of: through
dêisehi .... member of Western race characterized by white skin, long nose, etc.: Caucasian
dêl .... little in depth from surface to surface: thin; without strength or firmness: flimsy; readily reacting to outside influence: sensitive
dê-lil .... capable of being distinctly seen through: transparent
dêl-rnû .... infectious disease characterized by formation of tubercles, wasting, etc.: tuberculosis
dêl-nio .... thin skin or sheet: film
dêl-siut .... cut off thin, broad piece: slice
dêl-thin .... thin slip of wood: lath; thin coating of fine wood: veneer
dêl-dê-sdôus .... thin, transparent cloth: gauze
dêl-grê .... at the usually pointed extremity: tip
dê-hmav .... radiation capable of penetrating matter opaque to ordinary light: X-ray

dê-nad........................ without deviating from the shortest course: direct
dê.vrê........................ get through: pass; force way into: penetrate
dê-siut........................ cross each other: intersect
dê-kûs........................ of lines constantly equidistant: parallel
diô........................ plural of I: we
diuk........................ desire to inflict injury in retribution: revenge
dôg........................ plane figure having more than four sides: polygon
do........................ during the time that: while; portion of time associated with an event or series of events: period
due........................ substance in flowing state of water or oil: liquid
due.uem........................ food in liquid form: soup
due-laz........................ small, serum-filled bubble on skin: blister
due-rkec........................ rice boiled with plenty of water: congee
due-htê........................ short pipe with valve for drawing liquid: tap
due-voi........................ secreting organ in living things: gland
due-vluar........................ wet, spongy land: swamp
due-vrer........................ projecting tube for liquid to flow out: spout
due-seêm........................ preseve in vinegar, etc.: pickle
due-czaf........................ machine for raising liquid: pump
due-phêuz........................ closed vessel for holding liquid: cask
dûn........................ of colour of clear sky: blue; having deep knowledge: profound
dûn-uêr-lai........................ metallic element from which a blue pigment is made: cobalt
dûn-leg........................ colour made by mixing blue and red: purple
dûn-zrar........................ precious stone of beautiful transparent blue colour: sapphire
dliôt........................ one holding a public office: official

dlos .... projecting organ on face containing sense of smell: nose; any protruding thing: protuberance
dlos-oim .... large quadruped with one or two horns on nose: rhinoceros
dlos-siab...................... make sudden explosive sound through nose: sneeze
dlos-poc .... either hole of nose: nostril
dlos-due .... slimy secration of mucous membrane of nose, etc.: mucus
dluô.......................... a flat surface of an object: side
dluô-hli .... hear without the speaker knowing of it: overhear
dluô-fri..................... indicate indirectly: hint
dluô-skêf .... gallery along side of house: veranda
dluô.jô...................... by the side of: beside
dluô-jôm .... most recent: last
dluô-jlô .... in passing: by the way
dluô-blêh-suô .... noun placed after another to describe it: appositional noun
dluô-blê-svair .... brimless headgear: cap
dluô-tbo .... place side by side: appose
dlû .... revolve ideas in the mind: think
dlû-fcô .... form explanatory supposition: theorize
dlû-vlil .... that which thinks: subject
dlû-siab .... give voice to one's thoughts without intending them to be heard by others: think aloud
dlû-zvê .... put forward idea for acceptance or rejection: suggest
dlû-ciam.................... weigh pros and cons: consider
dlû-blêh.................... thing thought of: object
dlû-khe..................... feel angry over insult or injury: resent
dlû-gsô .... haunt with fixed idea: obsess

draz .... that something in living things that acounts for their existence as such: life
draz.vê .... duration of one's life: lifetime
draz-smôn .... account of person's life: biography
draz-dhô .... that which befalls a person by chance: fortune
draz-dhô-fri .... foretelling of one's fortune: fortune-telling
draz-gsô .... predetermined lot of person: fate
drein .... part of digestive system located in abdomen from stomach to anus: intestine
drein-laz-rnû .... inflammation of appendix: appendicitis
drein-luû .... gas from stomach or intestines: flatus
dreuv .... part of nervous system enclosed in skull: brain
drês .... ductile, malleable, fusible metallic element: tin
drê-rsûh .... thin sheet of tin or similar material used as wrapper: tinfoil
drês.poc.ôi .... container of tin or tin-plate: tin
drês-brat .... alloy of tin and lead: pewter
driôs .... one who writes book, etc.: author
drin .... man to whom a woman is married: husband
drô .... change direction in moving: turn
drô.aê .... implement for turning nuts, etc.: spanner, wrench
drô-nêz .... line produced by folding: crease
drô-fiôv .... leap and roll, turning heels over head simultaneously: somersault
drô-sdôus .... strip of cloth for winding round wound, etc.: bandage
drô-bauz .... fall headlong: tumble
drô-truôz .... circular frame made to revolve on axle: wheel; turn over and over on axis: roll
drô-kruod .... pin on which a thing turns: pivot
droim .... one who plays music professionally: musician
droim.ia .... company of musicians playing together: band

drof........................... part of body where arm joins trunk: shoulder
drof-roic.................... loose covering wrapped round shoulders: shawl
drof-hsa..................... move shoulders upwards: shrug
druap .... ground covered with grass: field
druap-hsa .... art of manoeuvring military forces in presence of enemy: tactics
druin.......................... irruption of water over the ground: flood
druin.lu..................... overspread and crush: overwhelm
drû .... feel anxiety: care
drûuk .... one who performs on the stage: actor
drûuk.zriv................. wife of an actor: actor's wife
drûuk.drin................ husband of an actress: actress's husband
drû-sku...................... take care of the sick or babies: nurse
drû-sku.vriam........... one whose work is to take care of the sick or babies: nurse
drû-znû .... judicious and cautious in action: prudent
drû-cûg .... bring up child not born to oneself: foster
drûd .... one angrily opposed to another: enemy
drûd-cuem .... deliver up perfidiously: betray
dhô .... fall out indesignedly: chance; unfavourable event occurring unexpectedly: accident (v. dhô-jlô)
dhô-rud..................... having bad luck: unlucky
dhô-fôb .... having good luck: lucky
dhô-jlô .... unfavourable event occurring unexpectedly: accident
dhô.bauz .... accidentally fall
dhûiv......................... passage inside neck for food going from mouth to stomach: gullet, esophagus
dhûiv-czo .... make pass through gullet: swallow
dba............................ confine within bounds: limit
dba-nêz .... line marking limit: boundary
dba-plia.................... small, exclusive group of people: clique

dba-trêf .... wall, etc., enclosing land: fence
dba-grê .... terminating point of a route: terminus

-k-

kaê .... group of a few words not forming a complete sentence or clause: phrase
kaj .... unpleasant to the sight: ugly
kay-hpu .... make human figure ugly: deform
ken .... integral figure just above four: five
kêu .... word by which person or thing is called: name; short descriptive appellation: title (v. ûp-kêu); opinion generally held about a person or thing: reputation
kêu.ih .... by name: namely
kêu-liuz .... name unknown: anonymus
kêu.rud.lu .... defame by false malicious statements: libel
kêu-rûus .... propose for appointment: nominate
kêu-mro .... write one's own name: sign
kêu.fa .... in name only: nominal
kêu.zên .... having a great reputation: famous
kêu.zên.û .... one who is famous: celebrity
kêu.ceud .... calling over of list of names: roll call
keû-pêa .... in Luif, punctuation mark to indicate a name: name mark
kêu.blê .... without a name: nameless
kêu-blêh-suô .... in Luif, noun that is the individual name of a person or thing: name noun
kêu-thaid .... system of names or terms: nomenclature
kêg .... characteristic specimen: type; relating to all or most: general

kêg.plia..................... group of things, persons, etc., with common characteristics: type
kiaz .... speak in a loud voice: shout
kiuf .... use extravagantly or ineffectually: waste
kiuf.ôi .... waste material: refuse
kiuf.vluar.................. land not used for any purpose: wasteland
kiuf-spe .... talk or act in trifling fashion: frivolous
kiuf-coet................... spend with reckless profusion: prodigal
kiuv........................... move slowly with body near ground: creep
kiuv-tûu .... plant growing along ground or up wall: creeper
kiû............................. small citrus fruit with acid pulp: lemon
kiûr .... cleanse with water: wash; clean body with water: bathe (v. lie.kiûr); free of foreign elements: purify
kôof........................... cause to be conveyed to some destination: send
kôof-jza .... send forth like divergent rays: radiate
kôr .... of the sex that begets but does not give birth to offspring: male
kôr-vlêô.................... reproductive gland of male: testicle
kôr-phêuz................. pouch that holds testicles: scrotum
kôr-due .... male reproductive liquid: semen
kôn............................ sound of door closing forcefully: bang
kôz .... not according to what should be: wrong
kôz-hrô..................... intrude unwarrantably: trespass
kôz-hse..................... desire wrongfully: covet
kôz-mac.................... free from moral or legal wrongdoing: innocent
kôz-nrio .... quarrelsome while being unreasonable: cantankerous
kôz-troi .... obstinate in the wrong: perverse
ko............................. denoting the agent: by
kol............................ integral number just above two: three
kol.ia .... group of three: trio

ku............................ what reason: why
kul............................ of the usual kind: ordinary; pertaining equally to more than one: common
kul-dlû .... ordinary understanding: common sense
kuv........................... in accordance with fact; true; actually existing or occurring: real (v. jluz.fa)
kuv.blêh .... anything that actually occurs: fact
kus .... unhappy being in seclusion: lonely
kus.û .... one who lives away from human society: hermit
kus-fleu .... subsisting as a distinct unit: individual
kus-clu .... sole possession of some commercial line of activity: monopoly
kut .... good ethically: moral
kut.û .... one characterized by superlative virtue: saint
kut-htug.................. attendant spirit in heaven: angel
kut.sraô .... conduct judged ethically: virtue
kut-snuv.................... branch of knowledge dealing with morals: ethics
kut-gsô .... constrain morally: oblige
kûs .... same in quantity: equal
kûs-sag .... equal in value, etc.: equivalent
kûs-blêa-vêg .... curve formed by cone cut by plane parallel to its side: parabola
kûs.dlûo .... with all sides equal: equilateral
kûz .... principal or leader: chief
kûz.û .... principal person: chief
kûz-rze .... person's greatest piece of work: masterpiece
kûz-plaul .... principal figure portrayed in a story, real or fictional: hero
kleuc .... daylight lepidopterous insect with knobbed antennae: butterfly
klô............................ astonishing effects inexplicable by the known workings of nature: magic

klô.io........................ one who practises magic: wizard
klô-htug .... being of human form with supernatural powers: fairy
klô-mru.................... fascinating as though by magic: glamorous
klû........................... expel from stomach by mouth: vomit; issue suddenly: gush
kraun........................ digging tool with iron blade: spade
krauf .... covering of any kind for the body: clothing
krauf.uô.................... place for keeping clothes: wardrobe
krauf-phêuz.............. receptacle forming part of garment: pocket
krauf.blê .... not wearing any clothing: naked; without usual appurtenances: bare
krauf-kiûr................. wash, dry, and iron clothing: launder
kraut .... set of sheets of written or printed paper bound together: book
kraut-flêl .... knowledge acquired by study: learning
kraut-srêm................ building where books are kept for reading: library
kraut-jluz.................. one side of leaf of book: page
kraut-puô .... principal division of book: chapter
kraug........................ vessel used for drinking: cup
kraug-truôz .... small plate for holding cup: saucer
kran.......................... writing which is not verse: prose
krat .... building where goods are sold: shop
krat.vriam................. person engaged in selling goods in shop: shop assistant
krev .... tropical giant grass with woody stem: bamboo
krev-zma-zca .... new growth on bamboo plant: bamboo shoot
krêd......................... unit of money
kri .... be able to: can; mental capability: ability
kri.lbu .... capable of producing required result: efficient
kri.hsa .... able to move about easily: mobile

kri.vlô........................ that can be or happen: possible
kri.vzô .... possessed of insight: understanding
krô .... ask earnestly for: beg; make earnest request directed at the feelings: appeal (v. bre-sûig)
krôf........................... entrance into house or room: door
krois .... small invertebrate creature with segmented body: insect
krois.ia .... throng of insects: swarm
krois-hvau .... silky sheath of insect larva: cocoon
krois.muir.ôi............ substance for killing insects: insecticide
kruin .... mechanical device for measuring time: clock
kruod .... thin, rigid, pointed piece of metal wire for fastening things together: pin
kruod-tûu................. prickly composite plant: thistle
khau.......................... completely filled: full
khau.lu..................... deposit until full: fill
khau.ril..................... whole number: integer
khau.tiûn .... eat to the full
khau.drô................... complete turn
khe........................... injure animal tissue by external force: wound; mar qualities of: spoil
khe.aê....................... instrument for inflicting physical injury: weapon
khe-roiz.................... utter falsehood with intent to injure: slander
khe-nuap.................. deprive of physical power: disable
khe-spiû .... one who oppresses weaker persons: bully
khe-jzu .... mark left after wound or sore heals: scar
khiar......................... quadruped with sharp snout, upright ears, and bushy tail: fox
khôis .... compound of sodium or potassium with fatty acid used in washing: soap
khôn......................... science of number, magnitude, and spatial properties: mathematics

khov .... dusty residue of anything burnt: ashes
khu .... acquire by paying money: buy
khuên .... piece of cloth with design serving as emblem for various purposes: flag
khuêj .... hollow open vessel less deep than wide for holding liquid: basin
khu.io .... one who purchases goods or services: customer
khug .... unit of area
kson .... coniferous tree with evergreen needle-shaped leaves: pine
kson-gai .... oleoresin obtained from some conifers and terebinth: turpentine
kzoêp .... four-winged insect that is gregarious and produces honey: bee
kzoêp-iêt .... very small bird making humming sound with vibrating wings: hummingbird
kzoêp.uô .... structure of waxy cells made by bees for storing honey and raising young: honeycomb
kzoêp-jzêm .... sticky secretion of bees used to form cells: wax
kzoêp-jzêm-hmav ..... cylinder of wax, tallow, etc., with wick for lighting: candle
kzoêp-plif .... sweet substance manufactured by bees from nectar they gather from flowers: honey
kzoêp-phêuz .... box made for bees to live in: beehive

-g-

gai .... greasy, inflammable liquid lighter than water: oil
gai.rôûn .... cook in boiling oil: fry
gaif .... reduce to ruins: destroy
gaif-trê .... declare not guilty: acquit

gaif.krois.................. any destructive insect
gaif-krois .... migratory gregarious insect devouring vegetation on extensive scale: locust
gas.......................... of time to come: future
gas.vê...................... time to come: futurity
gêd .... four-sided figure with equal sides and all right angles: square
gêd-spe.................... game of skill played with pieces of diverse kinds on chequered board: chess
gi............................ used in comparisons to introduce the second member: than
giêf......................... regard with profound admiration and adoration: worship
giêf-cuem .... make offering to a god in worship: sacrifice
giêf-plaul................. image of a god associated with worship: idol
giêf-krô................... make reverent supplications to a deity: pray
giêf-gûin.................. promise solemnly on oath: vow
giûk........................ feel hurt by rivalry: jealous
gou......................... persons or things in question: they
gu........................... at a great distance from: far; stretch of space separating: distance (v. gu.jô)
guê .... period from sunset to sunrise: night
guê-iêt..................... small bird noted for its rich singing at night: nightingale
gûe-uem.................. meal taken about time when night falls: dinner
guê-vlaul .... water in small drops deposited from the air at night on grass, etc.: dew
guê-bluên................ frozen dew: frost
guê-krois .... small lepidopterous insect given to flying by night: moth
gun......................... little in size: small
gun-leg................... small inflamed swelling on skin: pimple

gun-khôn .... computation using infinitesimal changes of varying quantities: calculus

guz .... having shape of two lines meeting at a point: angular; spot at which sides converge: corner; point of view

guz-zfê-nêz .... line joining two nonadjacent vertices of polygon: diagonal

guz-blêa.................... solid figure with triangle, square, or polygon as base and triangular sides converging to a common point: pyramid

gu.jô .... stretch of space separating: distance

gu.jôm...................... of distant past: ancient

gu.truûv .... optical instrument for magnifying distant objects: telescope

gu.gas.vê.................. distant future

gûi........................... uppermost part of body: head; highest part of a thing: top; principal person: chief (v. kûz.û)

gûi-oic...................... large tawny carnivore with terrific roar: lion

gûi-laz .... pith of a matter: gist

gûin.......................... hold same opinion: agree; engage to do or not do: promise

gûi.nio...................... hairy skin of head: scalp

gûin-lpa.................... agreement of parts with one another: harmony

gûin-gloit .... person who binds himself to do work or furnish goods at agreed price: contractor

gûin-glu .... agree to do what is required: comply

gûi.zru...................... shake head in salutation, etc.: nod

gûi-bli .... pain in head, a complaint whose causes are numerous: headache

gûi.brian.................. body framework of head: skull

gûi-tluem .... cushion for supporting head in bed: pillow

glaif.......................... waterless, desolate region: desert; abandoned place
glaif-iûr .... large ruminant with one or two humps useful for crossing deserts: camel
glaif-druap................ fertile area in desert: oasis
gle .... agreeable sensation: pleasure
gle-lruic.................... area in town laid out with trees, etc., for public recreation: park
gle-ruam................... contest of any kind for amusement: game
gle-feur..................... get-together for amusement purposes: social gathering
gle-vriam .... one engaging in a pursuit as a pastime only, and not for pay: amateur
gle-bhon................... association formed for recreational purposes: club
gle-kiuf..................... given to wasteful pleasures: dissipated
gle-glu .... pursuit that is not one's main work and is undertaken for amusement: hobby
glied .... membranous receptacle for waste fluid of body: bladder
gliuk.......................... person employed to maintain public order: police officer
glif............................ organ of sight: eye
glif-auf .... pair of lenses worn to correct defective sight: spectacles, eye glasses
glif.hiû...................... hair on eyelid: eyelash
glif-vlêô .... ball of eye: eyeball
glif-ba....................... round opening in centre of iris of eye: pupil
glif-troi..................... power of seeing: eyesight
glif.due .... water secretion of the eye: tear
glif.drô .... cast side glances: ogle
glik........................... one of terminal members of hand: finger

glik-rie........................ nutritious, finger-shaped tropical fruit growing in clusters: banana
glik-fcô........................ show by directing finger at: point
glik-sbaun .... pronged eating utensil: fork
glik-sguit.................. musical instrument resembling lute played with fingers: guitar
glik-jui .... projecting joint at base of finger: knuckle
gloin........................... liquid secreted in mouth: saliva
gloit........................... one engaged in trade: merchant
gloit.sla...................... work of a merchant or trader: trading
glu............................. perform or bring about: do
glui............................ direction of rising sun: east
glu-lruic .... council concerned with administration: executive council
glu-lbu .... carry into effect: execute
glu-hfo .... what one is bound morally or legally to do: duty
glun........................... apparent vault over the earth: sky
glun-aiz-nêz .... line at which earth and sky seem to meet: horizon
glu-nion .... make gesture expressing recognition, etc.: salute
glun-mul .... state of a land in regard to temperature, rainfall, etc.: climate
glu.vûil...................... act of imagining: imagination
glu.sag....................... worth doing
glu-suô .... word that predicates: verb
glu-znû...................... talented in practical work: clever
glu-ceud .... rouse into action: provoke
glu-ciam .... do habitually: practise
glup........................... one of a class of substances like iron characterized by certain properties like ductility, hardness, lustre, etc.: metal
glup-chauk .... stamped piece of metal serving as currency: coin
glup-czuûb .... connected series of metal links: chain

glup-czuûb.eu........... one of the rings or loops of chain: link
glup-jzêm .... fusible alloy for joining metals: solder
glup-bruf.................. natural mineral containing metal: ore
glu-blêh.................... list of things to be done at a meeting: agenda
glûis .... one occupied with literature: literator
gren.......................... sister of father or mother: aunt
grê............................ cease to do: stop; complete the doing of: finish (v. grê-bzê)
grê.ôi........................ structure to prevent access: barrier
grêun .... water in drops falling through the atmosphere: rain
grêun-crêus.............. waterproof overcoat worn as protection against rain: raincoat
grêun-czuûb .... multicoloured arch across sky associated with rain: rainbow
grêut......................... extensive area of land naturally overgrown with trees and undergrowth: forest
grêl........................... natural phenomenon associated with heat and light: fire
grêl.û.ia .... firefighters organized as a unit: fire brigade
grêl-muir.................. extinguish fire: quench
grêl-vlair.................. mountain with crater from which lava, etc., erupts: volcano
grêl-chûp.................. burning particle: spark
grêl-troi .... resistant to fire: fireproof
grêl-thin .... wood used as fuel: firewood
grêl-gzô .... live remains of fire: embers
grê.fe .... end of
grê-frê .... discontinue meeting for resumption later: adjourn
grê-vlaul .... embankment to hold back water: dam
grê-vlû...................... with feeling temporarily in abeyance: numb
grê-vrer..................... contrivance preventing animal using its mouth: muzzle

grê-seêm .... put under restraint: detain
grê-siab .... prevent speaking by blocking mouth with something: gag
grê-slar .... iron device to keep ship at rest: anchor
grê-srêm .... house providing food and lodging for travellers: hotel
grê-zvê .... pass out of sight: disappear
grê-poc .... that which is used to block a hole: plug
grê-plêm .... device for bringing vehicle to rest: brake
grê-prus .... framework of bars serving as barrier on bridge, etc.: railings
grê-bzê .... complete the doing of: finish
grê-dluô .... last part: end
griu .... of even surface: smooth
griu.lu.aê .... tool for making woodwork smooth: plane
griu-hsa .... move smoothly along: glide
griu-zrôp .... implement for removing wrinkles from clothing: iron
griu-jzêm-jui .... hard limestone taking high polish: marble
griu-bauz .... lose footing by sliding accidentally: slip
griûs .... one whose occupation is the performance of religious duties: priest
griûs-plaz .... state ruled by priests: theocracy
griûk .... one whose business is making clothing: tailor
grib .... person with whom one associates freely on terms of mutual regard: friend
grib-zfê .... join together for particular purpose: ally
grib-zkû .... disposed to treat indulgently: favour
grôiv .... naturally formed small body of still water: pool; small artificial lake: pond
grûs .... upper front part of trunk of body: chest

grûs-brian................one of bones in chest curving round from spine: rib
ghal..........................period of days based on revolution of earth round sun: year
ghal-nêz....................lengthy division of time: era
ghal.cel.dak ....twice in a year: biannual
ghal-jzu ....annually recurring day of an event: anniversary
gsô...........................make firm: fix; bind with string or the like: tie (v. czuû.gsô); set up permanently: establish; bring to a state of finality: settle
gsô-lkô ....keep under: repress
gsô-hfo ....admit no refusal: peremptory
gsô-vêu.....................limited period of time: term
gso-spiû.....................not fixed firmly: loose
gsô-cua ....the actual words originally set down by author: text
gsô-jzêm...................substance for binding stone, etc., to make a firm mass: cement
gsô-phuê...................regular disposition in which every part is in its proper place: order
gsô-blêh....................gelatine obtained from boiling hides and bones and used as adhesive: glue
gsô-troi.....................closely fastened: tight
gsô-thin.....................board fixed horizontally on wall or in cabinet, etc.: shelf
gsô-krauf..................knob or disk used for fastening clothing: button
gsô-krôf....................bar for fastening door: bolt
gsô-kruod.................pointed piece of metal for fastening wood, etc.: nail
gsô-gzô ....attach firmly as by glue: stick
gzauf ....territory of a state: country

gzauf-hia .... the inhabitants collectively of a country sharing common characteristics in respect of descent, culture, etc.: nation
gzauf-nu .... enter a country as settler or bring goods into it: immigrate, import
gzauf.sû .... pertaining to or between different countries: international
gzauf-za .... leave a country for good or send goods out of it: emigrate, export; live outside one's country for prolonged period and not necessarily by choice: exile
gzauf-zgu .... condemn to exile: banish
gzauf-jroz .... person of same country: compatriot
gzauf-joi .... devoted to one's own country: patriotic
gziûl .... organ in chest engaged in circulation of blood: heart
gziûl-rial .... throbbing of arteries due to pumping of blood through heart: pulse
gziûl-gzô .... attach zealously: devote
gzô .... be left over from a greater quantity: remain
gzô.ôi .... that which is left over: remains
gzô-reu .... remains of plant or animal of past ages preserved in rock: fossil
gzô-cuem .... leave property for inheritance: bequeath
gzô-jzu .... mark of what has been: trace
gzô-kaê .... in Luif, a phrase not belonging to the specified types: miscellaneous phrase
gbo .... deliberately give false representation: deceive
gbo-liôl .... deceitful artifice: wile
gbo-hne .... perceive what does not exist: hallucinate
gbo-mru .... lead astray: seduce

gbo-mcu.................. produce an imitation with intent to deceive: counterfeit

gbo-zla .... one exercising an occupation on false pretences: quack

gbo-thôuh .... illusive appearance produced by atmosphere: mirage

III

English-Luif Alphabetical Dictionary

A

abacus .... sci-thaid
abandoned place .... glaif
abattoir .... iûr.muir.uô
abdicate .... tpê-stû
abeyance .... rbo-mul
ability .... kri
abolish, cancel .... pa.lva
aborigines .... hjuez-iûn
abort .... bêr-rze
about (here and there nearby) .... jaz-jô
about (more or less) .... fem-ris
about to .... vam-fem
above .... hê.êz
abscond .... fiôv-vrê
absolute .... bzê
absorb .... piev
abstract (antonym of concrete) .... zlôn.fa
abstract object .... zlôn
abstruse .... bih
absurd .... pa.nzo
abuse, misuse .... rud-ciam
abut .... zle
abutment .... stô-cêi
accelerate .... em.nru
accept .... maûs-czo
accessory .... stô-tliô
accident .... dhô, dhô-jlô
accidentally fall .... dhô.bauz
accompany .... mi-vrê
according to .... im

accordion .... svaup-flaic
account .... sci-sfo
accuse .... trê-fri
acid (noun) .... jom.ôi
acknowledge .... fri-zla
acquit .... gaif-trê
acrimonious .... nos
acrobat .... briêt-drûuk
across .... lên.dê
act (theatrical performance) .... tla
act in lieu .... tla
active .... so.glu
actor .... drûuk
actor's wife .... drûuk.zriv
actress's husband .... drûuk.drin
acute angle .... huv-guz
ad hoc .... ûpoci (tû pom-chêô ib)
add .... tliô
addict .... bauz
additional clause (Luif) .... tliô-tuê-pom
address (as a letter) .... vuô-tbo
adjourn .... grê-frê
adjust .... hsa-paz
admirable .... o.kri.biôm
admiral .... oi.vlioc-a
admire .... biôm
admit .... sto
adopt .... rûif
adopted son .... rûif.zlog
adore .... ên.jci
adult .... tôm
adultery .... car-môip

advance .... zoû.vrê
adventure .... zhi-jlô
advertise .... lên-bûuj
advise .... csa
advisory council .... csa-lruic
aerated water .... luû-vlaul
aesthetics .... tuz-flêl
affair .... jiô
affidavit .... pimrô (plal-fri mrô ô.roiz-vlô)
after .... al
after this .... jû
afternoon .... bua
again .... lrai
against, versus .... suêf.ud
age .... nôf.has
agenda .... glu-blêh
agent .... moê.io
aggregated phrase (Luif) .... zfê-kaê
aggressive .... tle-cêôm
agitate .... daul
agnosticism .... fûfel (fûl flêl fe lua)
agrarian .... vluar-sjie
agree .... gûin
agriculture .... ô.czu
ailment .... creu.rnû
aim .... jzu-rpû
air .... ual
air-conditioning .... ual-csû
airplane .... tuû
airport .... tuû.uô
alarm .... hzô-jeûp
album .... seêm-blêh-kraut

albumen .... ius-zel
algebra .... mau-khôn
alias .... cûg.kêu
alibi .... zvê-cûg-vuô
alkali .... sujôj (suêf jom.ôi jzab)
all .... cim
allege .... czû-fri
alliteration .... tis-zma-vlub
allow .... sfu
allude .... nûh-fri
alloy .... ztê-glup
ally .... grib-zfê
almond .... val-jaz-foi
alms .... viûr-chauk
along .... val.dê
aloof .... za-rêh
alphabet .... mau.i
already .... vôp
alternate .... tid.cûg
alternative .... vo
altitude .... jêh-laz
alum .... zucuhijef
aluminium .... creu-glup (cu)
always .... vrêu
amateur .... gle-vriam
ambassador .... plaz-msê-dliôt
amber .... hiz-phûl-jluz
ambiguous .... sme-niav
ambitious .... jêh, pso-hse
ambush .... cêôm-sma
amethyst .... leg-dûn-zrar
ammonia .... lûkora

ammunition .... puêr-hue
among .... sû
amuse .... ruap, zu.gle
anachronism .... vêu-kôz
anaemia .... spiû-ian
analogy .... ûp-fiem
analyse .... prel-nuap
anarchy .... fûl-tpê
ancestor .... vrih
anchor .... grê-slar
ancient .... gu.jôm
and .... ne
and immediately .... hum.jû
and not li
and the rest, etc. .... ne cûg
angel .... kut-htug
angle (for fish) .... czuûb-rpû
angry .... hiôp
angular .... guz
animal .... iûr
ankle .... jrot-zfê
anniversary .... ghal-jzu
annoy .... u.hiôp
annual .... tid.ghal
anomalous .... za-cab
anonymous .... kêu-liûz
ant .... thûic
ante meridiem (a.m.) .... êh nôu.ba
anticipate .... êh-piôs
antimony .... suz-nuap-lai (sa)
anus .... nlep-poc
anvil .... shail-zrôp

any .... sa
anything .... ar
ape .... ûp-eûk
apologise .... fri-kôz
appeal .... krô, bre-sûig
appear .... zvê.hrô-zvê
append .... ûp-tliô
appendicitis .... drein-laz-rnû
appetite .... uem.zri
applaud .... fcô-biôm
apple .... siû
apply .... moês-sûig
appoint .... rûus-zku
appose, juxtapose .... dluô-tbo
appositional noun (Luif) .... dluô-blêh-suô
appreciate .... vzû-jci
appropriate .... czo-sto
approve .... jbe-sfu
apron .... sku-krauf
aquarium .... sgiel.uô
arch .... vêg-sdu
archaeology .... nôf-blêh-thêh
archipelago .... nrôus.ia
architect .... srêm.jriêf
architecture .... srêm-crul
area (extent) .... hôj
argue .... jzi-ruam
aristocracy .... oih-plaz
aristocrat .... bhon-oih
arithmetic .... sci-khôn
arm .... jlec
armour .... zrôp-krauf

armpit .... jlec-nuê
army .... lziap.ia-mo
around .... jaz.fe
arrange .... phuê-tbo
array .... phuê.plia
arrest .... chêb-czû
arrive, reach .... hrô
arrow .... cze-chuf
arsenal .... chuf.seêm.srêm
arsenic .... fluam-lai (fa)
art (fine art) .... crul
art (practical art) .... hriûp-crul
artery .... êz-ian-czuûb
as .... ih
as fast as possible .... vaekô nru
as follows .... im sa hrô
as long as .... lêr.do
as much as possible .... vaekô (va dba fe kri.vlô)
as soon as .... hum.su
as soon as possible .... vaekô vam
ashes .... khov
ask, inquire .... sûig
asparagus .... sriol-rsûh
aspect .... zoû
asphalt .... bih-jzêm
assimilate .... ûp.lu
assistant .... stô.vriam
associated thing .... zfê-blêh
assumed person .... htug
assumed thing .... hrôz
assumed world .... hau
asthma .... fien-rnû

astray .... pue-kôz
astrology .... êol-crul
astronomy .... chav
asylum .... sku.uô
at .... va
atheism .... nêftêh (nlê fe tpê-htug)
athlete .... briêt
athletics .... sje
atlas .... aiz-thôuh-kraut
atom .... vêi
attach .... zfê
attack .... cêôm
attention .... vsud-srô
attitude .... jluê, lie-jluê
attract .... mru
attribute .... fe-tbo
auburn .... leg-poi-bih
auction .... rial-rza
audience .... hli.io.ia
aunt .... gren
author .... driôs
authority .... fe-zgu
autocracy .... mov-vliêc-plaz
automatic .... vlil-hsa
automaton .... vlil-hsa-czaf
autumn .... hnuv-ê
avail .... pci-cuem
avaricious .... chauk-jro
average .... bôz, ba-sag
avoid .... êz.sêem
awake .... sdû
away, off .... êz

awkward .... jom-jroi
awl .... fiôp-aê
axe .... ftuav
axis .... pca-nêz
axle .... truôz-kruod

B

baby .... vnên-rze
bachelor .... sê.mêus.io
back vlic
backbite .... êh-trê
background .... vlic-vluar
bacon .... blac-srûuf
bad .... rud
badge .... roic-tau
badger .... pauh-guê-iûr
bag or box .... phêuz
bail .... zvê-tbo
bait .... mru-sgiel
baker .... aif-jluz.broit
bakery .... aif-jluz.krat
balance (verb) .... lpa
balance, weighing machine .... lpa.aê
bald .... hiû.blê
ball .... vlêô.ôi
ballast .... stô-hue
balloon .... luû-vlêô
balm, ointment .... shu-gai
bamboo .... krev
bamboo shoot .... krev-zma-zca

banana .... glik-rie
band (flat strip) .... bôz-gsô
band, orchestra .... droim.ia
bandage .... drô-sdôus
bandit .... tuês-hia
bang (sound of door) .... kôn
banish .... gzauf-zgu
bank (for financial transactions) .... chauk-rgêp
bank (of river) .... brail.dluô.vluar
bankrupt .... chauk-nuap
banyan .... prel-czil
bar, pub .... aot-srêm
bar, rod .... nê.nui
barbaric .... crêe
barber .... hiû.siut.vriam
bare .... krauf.blê
bargain .... pci-khu
bark (of tree) .... tûu.nio
barley .... rjok
barometer .... ual-mrail
barren, sterile .... tro.rze
barrier .... trêf, grê.ôi
base (in value) .... ban-rud
basic word (Luif) .... prel-cua
basin .... khuêj
basket .... fluaz
bat (flying mammal) .... chiul
bat (used in sports) .... rial-blêh
bathe .... kiûr, lie.kiûr
bathroom .... lie.kiûr.sfas
baton .... czû-thin
battle .... puêr.eu

bauble .... ûp-stuûc
bay .... vrer-vrôih
bayonet .... phôs-phaiv
beacon .... jzu-hmav
beam .... fzi.prus
beam or post .... prus
bean .... rcûf
bear (animal) .... iep
bear or produce .... rze
beard .... nrûs
beat .... rial
beautiful .... tuz
because .... en
beckon .... zru-ceud
become .... of
bed .... snêul
bedclothes .... tluem
bedcover .... snêul-tluem
bedridden .... snêul-bauz
bedroom .... rbo.sfas
bee .... kzoêp
beef .... friêm.vliêl
beehive .... kzoêp-phêuz
beer .... rjok-aot
beetle .... nriô-iôm
beetroot .... plif-prel
before, previous .... êh
beg .... krô
beginning of .... zma.fe
behave .... rêh.lu
behind .... êh
believe .... lgi

believer........bleus
bell........spuin
bellows........hêun.aê
belly........zcos
belong........fe.lu
below........lô.êz
belt........stuôm-czuûb
bench........sû-ôut
bend........vêg.lu
benefit........ciam
benevolent........lûr
bequeath........gzô-cuem
berry........chim
beside........dluô.jô
besides (in addition to)........pe
bet........ûp-saic
betray........drûd-cuem
between........ba
beverage........piev.ôi
beware........niav-drû
beyond........ôv
biannual........ghal.cel.dak
bias, tendency........mru-hsa
bicycle........vric-plêm
biennial........tid.cel.ghal
big........zên
big toe........poz.brik
bile........jriol-due
bill (account of money)........clu-uam
bind........zfê-gsô
biography........draz-smôn
biology........czôn

bird .... iêt
biscuit .... nriô-uos
bisect .... cel-sjie
bismuth .... zel-dêl-glup (zê)
bite .... vhoil-siut
bitter .... nos
bivalve .... cel-zrôp-nio
black .... bih
blackbird .... chûn-iêt
black lead .... bih-brat
blacksmith .... zrôp.zboec
bladder .... glied
blade .... phaiv-jluz
blame .... trê
blank .... mro.blê
blanket .... hê-tluem
bleach .... zel.lu
bleed .... ian-stû
blemish .... rud-jzu
bless .... zri-fôb
blind .... cto-hne
blister .... due-laz
block, mass .... lub.fleu
block of wood .... lub.thin
blood .... ian
blood vessel .... ian-czuûb
blotting paper .... smuat-uam
blow (wind) .... hêun
blue .... dûn
blunder .... ên.prû
blunt (antonym of sharp) .... jziû
blush .... nio-leg

board, plank .... hôj.thin
boast .... viaf.roiz
boat .... a.slar
body .... lie
boil (disease) .... leg-cli
boil (water) .... daul
boiled egg .... daul.ius
boiler .... uêj-phêuz
bolt .... gsô-krôf
bomb .... vlêô-chuf
bombast .... fcô-rua
bond, contract .... ô.gûin
bone .... brian
book .... kraut
bookkeeper .... chauk-sfo-vreuc
boot .... jêh-snuim
booty .... puêr-tuês
bore .... roiz-jziû
borrow .... êz.pauk
both .... cim.cel
bother .... lto-beûl
bottle .... thaub
bottom .... jrot
bounce .... fiôv-nru
boundary .... dba-nêz
bouquet .... spol.ia
bourgeois .... ba-plia-hia
bow (for shooting arrows) .... vêg-chuf
bow (neck or body) .... vêg.lu
bowl (vessel) .... jaz-poc
box .... blop-cêôm
boy .... heu

boyhood .... heu.vê
bracelet .... jlec-jaz
brain .... dreuv
brake .... grê-plêm
bramble .... rvoh-thin-tûu
branch .... czil
brand .... zku-kêg
brass .... vmac-vtuk
brave .... jeûp.blê
brazier .... nuah-khuêj
bread .... aif-jluz
break .... nuap
break in pieces .... sen.nuap
breakfast .... zôa-uem
breath .... fien-ual
breathe .... fien
breeze .... a.êun
bribe .... chauk-csû
brick .... sdu-jhus
bride .... mêus.viô
bridegroom .... mêus.noê
bridge .... cêi
bright lil
bring .... vrê-rpû
brittle, fragile .... suz.nuap
broad .... lên
brocade .... sfuom-truar
broker .... ba-gloit
bromine .... leg-due (gu)
bronze .... vmac-drês
brooch .... crêus-sfuom
broom .... skêf-sruêl

brothel .... car.srêm
brother .... zten
brotherhood .... zten.mul
brother-in-law .... jzon.zten
brown .... poi-bih
bruise .... rial-khe
brush (instrument) .... sruêl
brusque .... nriô-nru
brutal .... iûr
bubble .... poc-due
bucket, pail .... jêh-khuêj
bud (noun) .... vam-zca
budget .... coet-liôl
bug .... snêul-krois
build .... sdu
bullet .... phôs-vlêô
bully (noun) .... khe-spiû
bunch, cluster .... zfê.plia
bundle .... zfê-gsô.plia
buoy (noun) .... jain-jzu
burn .... nuah
burst .... nuap.htê
bury .... sêûn
bus .... bhon-plêm
business .... thô
busy .... so.sla
but .... ze
butcher .... iûr.muir.vriam
butter .... iuv-jluz
butterfly .... kleuc
buttock .... nlep
button .... gsô-krauf

buy .... khu
by (indicating the agent) .... ko
by the way, incidentally .... dluô-jlô
bystander .... jô.fiûl.io

C

cabbage .... rfom
cabinet .... fcô-êus
cactus .... vlaul-sgon
café .... fdem-srêm
cage .... iar-sdut
cajole, coax .... mru-pra
cake .... uos
calamity .... ên.vce-jlô
calcium .... jzêm-lai (ji)
calculator .... sci.aê
calculus .... gun-khôn
calendar .... hlan-kraut
calf (of leg) .... vric-zal
call .... ceud
callous .... nriô-zpe
calm .... hpi
calyx .... spol-kraug
camel .... glaif-iûr
camera .... fbun-thôuh-phêuz
camp (noun) .... jroi-piem
camphor .... blûget (bôi lûr gai ê tûu)
can .... kri
canal .... hia.zku.brail
cancer .... frûin-vliêl

candle........kzoêp-jzêm-hmav
candy........plif-uem
cane........hsa-sgon
cannibal........hia.tiûn.io
cannon........oi.phôs
cannot........tro
cantankerous........kôz-nriô
canvas........nriô-sdôus
cap........dluô-blê-svair
cape........vluar-laz
capital (for business)........prel-chauk
capital (of country)........tpê.mai
caprice, whim........hpu-dlû
captain (of ship)........slar.kûz
captious........jom
caravan........vrê-plia
carbolic acid........picikerajera
carbon........chûn-lai (ci)
carbon dioxide........ciceje
carbonic acid........ceracikoje
cardboard........nriô-uam
care (anxiety)........drû
career........sla-vrê
careful, heedful........bûuj-drû
careless........liûz-drû
caricature........hpu-ûp
carouse........stû-piev
carpenter........thin-hriûp
carpet........skêf-sdôus
carrot........blêa-prel
carry........riam
carry by vehicle........plêm.riam

carry in arms .... jlec.riam
cart .... jroi-plêm
cartilage .... of-brian
cartoon .... ceûl-thôuh
carve .... siut, siut.zku
case .... flua-jlô
cash .... buf-chauk
casino .... saic.srêm
cask .... due-phêuz
cassia .... ûp-bef-nio
cast iron .... nriô-zrôp
castrate .... car-siut
casual .... fe-dhô
cat .... phiom
cataract (of eye) .... cto-hne-rsûh
catch .... czo-czû
caterpillar .... of-kleuc
Caucasian .... dêisehi (ldêi sehi)
cauldron .... oi.rmuêz
cauliflower .... sû-rfom
cause .... hzô
cautious .... jeûp-drû
cave .... vluar-vrer
cavil .... poc-suêf
ceiling .... sku-sfas
celebrate .... vuêl-jzu
celebrity .... kêu.zên.û
cell .... eul
cellar .... vluar-sfas
cement .... gsô-jzêm
cemetery .... sêûm-poc.uô
censor .... jbe-siut

centenarian..mij.ghal.û
centipede..sor-vric-iar
century..mij.ghal.ia
cereal..chûp
ceremony..cab-giêf
certain..raz
certificate..jzi-uam
ceteris paribus (if other things remain the same)...ocêgi (og cûg blêh gzô tis)
chaff..chûp-nio
chain..glup-czuûb
chair..ôut
chairman..csû-kûz
chalk..blaiv-jzêm
challenge..ceud-puêr
chameleon..hpu-hev
champion (in competitions)..puaf.io
chance..dhô
change..hpu
channel..vlaul-pue
chaos..lto-nuap
chapter..kraut-puô
character (in book)..plaul
character, disposition..vsud-fal
charcoal..ûp-chûn
charity..fe-zkû
charming..ên.zis
chart..vrôih-thôuh
chase..soun-czo
chaste..car-vza
chatter..hêun-roiz
cheap..pa.stui
check..fiem-csû

cheek .... jzef
cheese .... nriô-iuv
chemistry .... fbun
cheque .... suêt-uam
cherish .... jci-sku
chess .... gêd-spe
chest (of body) .... grûs
chestnut .... poi-bih-foi
chew .... vhoil-toif
chickenpox .... lô-laz-rnû
chief (adjective) .... kûz
chief (noun) .... gûi, kûz.û
chilli .... bef-tzif
chimney .... brôn-slôp
chin .... zrir
chisel .... siut-nui
chloride .... zûfue (zû zfê-hue)
chlorine .... zov-luû (zû)
chloroform .... cirakozû
chocolate .... tûu-aif-jluz
choke .... fien-faur
cholera .... ôuv-klû
choose .... rûus
chop .... nru-siut
chopping block .... siut-lub
chopsticks .... uem-sviu
chord .... flaic.czuûb
chorus .... plê.ia
chromium .... tuz-glup (tu)
chrysanthemum .... zvôt-spol
cicada .... vliê-krois
cigarette .... uam-plauf

cinema .... thôuh-stêk
cinema picture, movie .... thôuh-skun
cinnamon .... bef-nio
circulate .... jaz-hsa
circumference .... jaz-val
circumlocution .... jaz-fri
circumstances .... mi-jlô
citizen .... plaz.û
city .... oi.mai
civil engineer .... sdu.nziop
civil service .... plaz-chaêv
civil war .... nu-gzauf puêr
civilized .... prôu
claim .... fri-sto
clam .... thiez
clamour .... vliê-lto
clan .... oi.jlûv
clap .... mi-rial
clasp .... blop-czû
class (school) .... jiaz.plia
class, order .... jzu.plia
classic .... jêh-kraut
classify .... jzu.plia.lu
clause (Luif) .... tuê-pom
clay .... jhus
clean .... pa.chui
clear, distinct .... lil, hne-lil
clerk .... vreuc
clever .... glu-znû
cliff .... nad-vlair
climate .... glun-mul
climax .... jêh-laz

climb........peôn
cling........czû
clink (of metal)........tin
clip........sgêûn-siut
clique........dba-plia
clock........kruin
close........lkô
clot........fleu.rev.bôi
cloth........sdôus
clothing........krauf
cloud........jrual
clown........tla-lbe
club........gle-bhon
clue........pca-laz
coagulate........zal.lu
coal........chûn
coat or upper garment........crêus
cobalt........dûn-uêr-lai (da)
cobbler........snuim.luam.io
cobra........crum-chiûs
cockatoo........sû-mrean
cockroach........chiat
cocoa........tûu-aif
coconut........rûo
cocoon........krois-hvau
code........ûp-slôn
coffee........fdem
coffeepot........fdem.poc.ôi
coffin........sêûm-thin
coil........jaz-drô
coin........glup-chauk
cold (antonym of hot)........lûk

cold (disease) .... tho
colic .... zcos-zên-bli
collar .... brem-jaz
colleague .... sla-jroz
collide .... srô-rial
colony .... lruic-gzauf
colour .... hev
comb (for hair) .... truem
come .... hrô
comedy .... zsû-skun
comet .... euf-êol
comfortable .... u.zsû
comma .... nôh-pêa
command .... zgu-pra
comment .... jzu-roiz
commit .... tbo-cuem
committee .... csû-lruic
common .... kul
common sense .... kul-dlû
communicate .... vrê-hrô
communicating instrument .... sgam
companion .... mi.û
company (presence in association) .... mi
company (business firm) .... mi-thô
compare .... fiem
compass .... vlôi-mrail
compasses .... jaz.rnê.aê
compatriot .... gzauf-jroz
compensate .... lpa-suêt
compete .... ruam
compile .... feur-mro
complain .... fri-vce

complement .... bzê-zku
complete .... bzê
complete turn .... khau.drô
complex sentence .... ztê-tuê
complexion .... zoû-hev
complicate .... pa.fêz.lu
compliment .... fri-biôm
comply, conform .... gûin-glu
component .... lai
compose .... ûp-mro
composer .... mro-droim
composite word (Luif) .... ztê-cua
compound (chemical) .... zfê-hue
compound word .... zfê-cua
comprehensive .... lên
compromise .... rev-rev
comrade .... sû-grib
concave .... nu-vêg
conceited .... viaf
concentrate .... laz-dba
concerning .... es
concoct .... rôûn
concrete (antonym of abstract) .... hôi.fa
concrete (building material) .... sdu-ztê
concrete object .... hôi
condemn .... fe-trê
condescend .... jêh-zkû
condition (state) .... mul
cone .... blêa
conference .... ô.frê
confess .... stû-roiz
confide .... lgi-roiz

confident .... lgi-raz
confined .... kuv
confirm .... fri-gsô
confiscate .... plaz-czo
confuse .... beûl, plo-ztê
congee .... due-rkee
congratulate .... fri-zsû
connective (Luif) .... zfê-suô
connoisseur .... crul.flêl.û
conquer .... puaf
conscience .... suô.kut
conscious .... vle, sdû-bûuj
conservative .... mru-seêm
consider .... dlû-ciam
considering .... hne.ih
consistent .... rôef-gûin
consonant .... lkô-mau
consonant group (Luif) .... lkô-mau-plia
conspicuous .... vliê
conspire .... mi-liôl
constant .... pa.hpu
constellation .... êol.ia
constipation .... bliaz-grê
constitution .... plaz-rêh
consult .... csa-sûig
consumption, tuberculosis .... dêl-rnû
contact .... zle-zfê
contagious, infectious .... rnû-cuem
contemplate .... nriô-dlû
contented .... zmo
contents .... czû.ôi
continent .... oi.jluêm

continual, endless .... sê.grê
continue .... seêm
continue raining .... seêm.grêun.lu
continuous .... vêu
continuous expanse .... vrôih
continuous moving line .... brail
contractor .... gûin-gloit
contradict .... suêf-fri
contribute .... sû-cuem
control .... tpê
convenient .... tên
converse .... sû-roiz
convex .... za-vêg
convince .... lbu-lgi
cook (noun) .... broit
cook (verb) .... rôûn
cooked rice .... rôûn.rkec
cooking vessel .... chôud
cooperate .... zfê-stô
copper .... vmac (va)
copperas .... rôhipoje
copy .... mcu-mro
copyright .... jza-rza-paz
coral .... vrôih-jzêm
cormorant .... czo-sgiel
corner .... guz
corpse .... mli.lie
correspond .... pruv.lu
corridor .... sfas-pue
cosmetic .... chaim
cost .... rpû-suêt
cost of living .... cofse (coet fe sne)

cotton .... sruêm
cough .... cvo
council .... tpê-lruic
count, reckon .... sci
countenance .... zoû-fri
counter .... clu-ôêp
counterfeit, forge .... gbo-mcu
country .... gzauf
countryside .... jraim
course (of meal) .... dak-uem.eu
court (of justice) .... jbe.rgêp
court (enclosed space) .... lkô-nuê
cousin (female) .... jlûd
cousin (male) .... blib
cove .... brik-vrôih
cover (verb) .... lkô
covering .... nio
covet .... kôz-hse
coward .... jeûp.û
cowherd .... friêm.seêm.io
crab .... frûin
cradle .... zma-snêul
craftsman .... hriûp
craftsmanship .... hriûp.sla
crane .... val-vric
creaking .... jroi-jloi
cream .... iuv-gai
crease .... drô-nêz
create .... mjê
creature (excluding human) .... iar
credulous .... suz.lgi
creep .... kiuv

creeper.................... kiuv-tûu
crêpe.................... huûl-sdôus
crescent.................... vêg.ôin
crest (of bird).................... iêt-hê
cricket (insect).................... phiôk
crime.................... ckô
cringe.................... pleuf-vêg
crisis.................... jbe-gsô-laz
criticize.................... jbe-fri
crockery.................... jhus.poc.ôi
crocodile.................... vric-chiûs
crop.................... fe-siut
crossroad.................... pue-guz
crow (bird).................... fnoôl
crowd.................... plia.hia
crude.................... paf-jroi
cruise.................... hêun-vrê
crumple.................... zgu-nêz
crush.................... zgu-nuap
crustacean.................... fi.frûin
cry.................... roih.siab
crystal.................... lil-buv-jui
cube.................... hlua
cuckoo.................... suz-ûuc
cucumber.................... sû-smer
cuff, wristband.................... crêus-blop-zfê
culture.................... lil-czu
cunning.................... vêg-znû
cup.................... kraug
cupboard.................... êus
cure.................... shu
curfew (restriction).................... ûp-grê

curio .... côh-nui
curious, inquisitive .... bûuj-jro
current .... soun-vlaul
curry .... bef-hiz
curse .... zri-rud
curtain .... fiôf-sdôus
curved .... vêg
cushion .... cgi-zoc
custom .... ûp-pre
customer, client .... khu.io
cut .... siut
cuttlefish .... ftiûn
cycle .... vêu-slôn
cylinder .... hvau.ôi
cylindrical .... hvau
cymbals .... rial-flaic

D

dagger .... fiôp-chuf
daily .... tid.hlan
dam .... grê-vlaul
damp .... u.snôi
dance .... chê
dangerous .... pa.sôp
dare .... pa.jeûp
dark .... nûh
dash .... nuap-pêa
data .... cuem-kuv
date (time) .... hlan
daughter .... jzez

dawn .... zma.zôa
day .... hlan
daytime .... nôu
dazzle .... vuêl-beûl
dead person .... mli.hia
deaf .... cto-hli
dear (beloved) .... o.jci
dear (costly) .... stui, rôef-jêh
debt, liability .... pa.suêt.ôi
decay, rot .... ke-kiuf
deceased .... la.lva
deceive .... gbo
decide .... jbe-gsô
decimal fraction .... foz-sen
decimal mark (Luif) .... foz-sen-tau
decimal system .... foz-phuê
declare .... roiz-vlô
decline .... bauz
decrease .... czûa.lu
deduce, infer .... nzo-rpû
deep .... jêh, cûg-jêh
deer .... iot
defective .... prû-kôz
defend .... sku
deficient .... nôh
define .... sme-gsô
definite .... troi-jav
deform .... kaj-hpu
degree, grade .... peôn-jzu
delay .... lêr-tbo
deliberate .... nzo-dlû
delicate .... zis

delirious .... ûp-plo
deliver .... fe-stû
demand .... nriô-pra
democracy .... iûn-plaz
demonstrate .... fcô-jzi
demote .... pa.hues
den .... iûr.uô
denominator .... sjie.pom
dense .... zal
deny .... fûl.lu
depart .... vrê
department .... lai
deplorable .... o.kri.vce
deposit, pledge .... czû-tbo
depot .... seêm-vuô
depreciate .... sag-ris
depressing .... bih-zel
deprive .... pa.zla
deputize .... msê
derive .... êz-hrô
descend .... pa.peôn
descendant .... lrob
describe .... chêô-fri
descriptive title .... chêô-fri-kêu
desert .... glaif
design .... liôl-rnê
desk .... mro-ôêp
destination .... ô.ud
destroy .... gaif
destructive insect .... gaif.krois
detail .... chêô
detain .... grê-seêm

detect crime .... ckô-moês
detective .... ckô-moês.io
determine .... lfe, nriô-lfe
detour .... vêg-vrê
develop, evolve .... zca, htê-zca
devil .... sraô-htug
devise .... liôl-zku
devote .... gziûl-gzô
dew .... guê-vlaul
diagonal .... guz-zfê-nêz
dialect .... rua-sjie
diameter .... jaz-lên
diamond .... jsôm
diaphragm .... sjie-voi-nio
diarrhoea .... vlaul-bliaz
diary .... hlan-sfo
dice .... saic-hlua
dictate .... mro-roiz
dictator .... zgu-vliêc
diction .... rua-rêh
dictionary .... cua-kraut
die .... mli
different, various .... sê.tis
difficult .... nriô, pa.suz
dig .... pauh
digest .... lreon-luav
dignity .... vlair-mul
dilemma .... vo-nriô
diligent .... pa.mlê
dilute .... em.dêl.lu
dim .... an.lil
dimension .... val-lên-zal

dimple .... u.poc
dinner .... guê-uem
dip .... vam-bauz
diphthong .... sviu-htê-mau
direct .... nad, dê-nad
direction .... êz-ud
direct speech .... nad-roiz-puô
dirt .... chui.ôi
dirty .... chui
disable .... khe-nuap
disappear, vanish .... grê-zvê
disciple .... bleus
discipline .... phuê-tpê
discrete unit .... ril.fleu
disease .... rnû
disguise .... hpu-fcô
dish .... ûp-truôz
dishevel .... mac-jza
disk .... jaz, sik-jaz
dismiss .... za.lu
disordered .... jzû
disperse .... nuap-vrê
dispirit .... pa.jro
dispose .... tbo-stû
dissect .... sjie-siut
dissipated .... gle-kiuf
distance .... gu, gu.jô
distant future .... gu.gas.vê
distil .... laz-rpû
distiniguish .... jzu-nion
distort, wry .... huûl-hpu
distribute .... sjie-cuem

district.......... lô.rêe
district or division of country.......... rêe
disturb.......... beûl-lto
ditch.......... lhôm-plat
dive.......... vlaul-lô
divide.......... sjie
divorce.......... pa.mêus
do.......... glu
do not exist.......... nlê
dock.......... slar.uô
doctor (medical).......... jriap
document.......... jzi-uam
doer.......... iob
dog.......... flier
doll.......... hia-stuûc
domestic animal.......... thuû.iûr
donkey.......... ûp-czûus
don't do.......... vza
don't know.......... liûz
don't want.......... vri
door.......... krôf
dose.......... dak.fleu
dote.......... lbe.jci
double consonant (Luif).......... sviu-lkô-mau
doubt.......... niav
dovecot.......... tziôl.uô
down (preposition).......... hsa-lô
down (soft feathers).......... truar-hiû
downstairs.......... lô-rtam
doze.......... u.rbo
dragon.......... chiûs-hrôz
dragonfly.......... val-euf-krois

drain (channel for refuse water) .... plat
drama .... skun
draw or paint .... rnê
drawer (receptacle) .... uac
dream .... niûh
drill (instrument) .... poc-zku.aê
drill (bore a hole) .... phuê-drô
drink .... piev
drive, steer .... sla-hsa
driver .... jleûp
drizzle .... a.grêun
droop .... fe-jain-tbo
drought .... vlaul-hse
drowsy .... mru.rbo
drug .... uûk
drum .... chôik
drunk .... aot-jzû
dry .... pa.snôi
duck .... thien
dull (re sound) .... jziû
dumb .... cto-roiz
dust .... vlêr
duster .... hsa-vlêr
duty (levied by government) .... clu-cuit
duty, obligation .... glu-hfo
dwarf .... ban.û
dwell .... piem
dye .... hev-jzab
dynamo .... zku-vzôn
dynasty .... vliêc-nêz
dysentery .... ian-bliaz

E

each .... tid
eager .... jro
eagle .... euk
ear .... beo
early .... bêr
earn .... rpû, chauk.pci
earth (planet) .... aiz
earth or soil .... lhôm
earthquake .... aiz-zru
earthworm .... lhôm-smiûp
earwax .... beo-rze
east .... glui
easy .... suz
eat .... tiûn
eat to the full .... khau.tiûn
eaves .... crum.dluô
ebb and flow .... cel-pue-hêun
ebony .... chûn-thin
eccentric .... pa.cab
echo .... lrai-vlub
eclipse .... hmav-cto
economical .... coet-creu
economics .... rze-srah
edge .... nêz-dluô
edit .... mro-piôs
edition .... jzu-mro-ril
editor .... mro-piôs.io
eel .... hvau-sgiel
effect .... lbu
efficient .... kri.lbu

egg .... ius
eight .... tev
either .... cel.vo
eject, expel .... cvo, zgu-za
elaborate .... chêô-sla
elastic .... mlûhum (mru lrai-rpû hjuez mul)
elbow .... jelc-zfê
elder, senior .... em.nôf.û
elect .... lên-rûus
electric bulb .... vzôn-auf
electric light .... vzôn.svuan
electrical engineer .... vzôn.nziop
electricity .... vzôn
elegant, graceful .... zis-tuz
element (chemical) .... lai
elementary .... zma-jroi
elephant .... ûif
élite .... oih.i
ellipse .... val-jaz
eloquent .... cfe.roiz
embark .... vrê-nu-slar
embers .... grêl-gzô
emblem .... tau-thôuh
embrace .... lie-czû
embroidery .... sdôus-sfuom
embryo .... zma-sia
emerald .... rsûh-zrar
emerge .... za.vrê, vrê za
emigrate, export .... gzauf-za
emit .... za-kôof
emotion .... bre
emphasis mark (Luif) .... zgu-pêa

emphasize.................jzu-siab
empire.................oi.gzauf
employ.................sla-ciam
empty.................pa.khau
en masse.................iolia (ih mov lub.plia)
enamel.................vuêl-crêus
enchanting.................pliz
enclose.................nu.lkô
encourage.................hêun-hsa
encroach.................ôv-hsa
encyclopaedia.................cim-flêl-kraut
end.................grê-dluô
end of.................grê.fe
endure.................zlu
enemy.................drûd
energetic.................jloi
engage (re marriage).................mêus-gûin
engine.................czaf
engineer (professional person).................nziop
engineeering.................sgô
engrave.................nêz-siut
enhance.................sag-pci
enlist, enrol.................zfê-glu
enough.................tef
entangle.................ztê-zfê
enter.................nu.vrê, vrê nu
enterprise.................jzu-sla
entertain.................ruap
enthusiastic.................jro
entice.................jfi-cri
entrance.................vrer, nu.vrê.uô
envelope.................pruv-nio

environment.. ual
envy .... ûp-giûk
epidemic .... lên-rnû
episode .... fi.smôn.eu
equal .... kûs
equator .... aiz-ba-jaz
equilateral.. kûs.dluô
equip .... fe-frê-cuem
equivalent... kûs-sag
era .... ghal-nêz
eradicate .... prel-siut
escape .... stû
escort, see off.. zfê-vrê
essay (literary composition) .... trun
essence .... nu-fal
essential... jae, lva-sko
establish .... gsô
estimate .... sag-jbe
eternal .... vêu.sê.dba
ethics .... kut-snuv
etiquette .... rêh-chêb
eunuch .... car-cto-noê
evaporate .... buên
even (adverb).. sê.ris
even (antonym of odd) .... cel-poh
event .... ô.jlô
ever .... su
every.. tid
exact .... cav
exaggerate.. ôv.lu
examine (by questioning) .... sûig-jbe
examine carefully in detail .... vluar-rti

example .... flua
exceed .... fem-vlô, vlô fem gi
excel .... jêh-pci
except ci
exchange .... rôef
excited .... pa.hpi
exclamation mark .... bre-pêa
exclamatory sentence (Luif) .... bre-tuê
exclamatory term (Luif) .... bre-cua
exclude .... pa.ro.lu
excluding .... pa.ro
excrescence .... sko-blê-zca
excuse .... tsu
execute (carry into effect) .... glu-lbu
execute (put to death) .... jbe-muir
executive council .... glu-lruic
exercise (physical) .... flo-hsa
exercise (school) .... mro-fleu
exhaust .... bzê-ciam
exile .... gzauf-za
exist .... lva
exit .... za.vrê.uô
expanded phrase (Luif) .... jza-kaê
expect .... jfi-sma
expenditure .... coet-chauk
experience .... frê-bûuj
experiment .... csû-cri
expert .... fe-cfe
explain .... hne-lil
explanatory noun (Luif) .... hne-lil-blêh-suô
explode .... nuap.htê
explore .... moês-bûuj

expose .... fcô, htê-fcô
ex-president .... jôm.rûus-vliêc
express (in words) .... fri
extempore .... siêpi (sê.mi êh piôs)
extinct .... reu.fa
extinct thing .... reu
entinguish .... zu.nlê
extravagant .... ôv-cab
extremely .... rûm
eye .... glif
eyeball .... glif-vlêô
eyebrow .... blem
eyelash .... glif-hiû
eyesight .... glif-troi

F

face .... zoû
face-to-face .... izuz (mi zoû ud zoû)
face upwards .... zoû-hê
fact .... kuv.blêh
factory .... spuc
faculty (bodily or mental) .... suô
fade .... lil-cto
faeces .... bliaz
fail .... pa.pso
fairy .... klô-htug
faith .... hzi-lgi
fall .... bauz, lô-vrê
false .... pa.kuv
familiar .... bûuj-sor

family .... jlûv
famine .... uem-hse
famous .... kêu.zên
fan (noun) .... svaup
far .... gu
farewell .... fôb-mul
farm .... suo
farmer .... zmeop
fashion .... lva-rêh
fast (of colour) .... troi
fast, starve .... pa.tiûn
fastidious .... hvo-nriô
fat (substance) .... jliun
fatal .... zu.mli
fate .... draz-gsô
father .... nrûn
fatherhood .... nrûn.mul
favour .... grib-zkû
favourable .... lûr
fear .... jeûp
feast .... stui-uem
feather .... hiû, rsûh-hiû
feature, characteristic .... pêa
federate .... tliô-zfê
feel (physically) .... vlû
fell .... zu.bauz
fellow, mate .... jroz-grib
fellow human .... jroz-hia
fellow citizen .... mai-jroz
felt .... êz-hiû
female .... pêm
fence .... dba-trêf

ferment .... sla-jza
ferry .... vlaul-riam
fertile, luxuriant .... zca-stui
festival .... jzu-hlan
fever .... phi
fibre .... sia-czuûb
fickle .... suz.hpu
fiction .... fkal
field .... druap
fierce .... oic
fight .... rial-pfê
fight one another .... rôef.rial-pfê
figure (numerical symbol) .... rôu
figure of speech .... vêg-fri
file (for papers) .... sfo-nui
file (instrument) .... bôz.lu.aê
filial love .... zlog.jzez.jci
fill .... tbo, khau.lu
film .... dêl-nio
filter .... hêun-kiûr
fin .... iôm
finance .... fe-chauk
find .... moês, moês.rpû
find fault .... moês-trê
fine (impose monetary penalty) .... chauk-bli
fine, excellent .... fôb-sag
finger .... glik
finish .... grê, grê-bzê
fire .... grêl
fire brigade .... grêl.û.ia
firecracker .... vlub-uam
firefly, glow worm .... hmav-krois

fireproof .... grêl-troi
firewood .... grêl-thin
firework .... stuûc-grêl
firm .... zrôp
first .... poz
First Cause .... lua
fish .... sgiel
fist .... lkô-blop
fit .... vzû
five .... ken
fix .... gsô
fixed to one place .... vuô-gsô
flag .... khuên
flap, flutter .... iôm-hsa
flash .... az.vuêl
flat .... bôz
flat side .... hôj-dluô
flatter .... rpê.biôm
flatus .... drein-luû
flax .... smuas.tûu
flea .... ian-krois
flee .... cze
fleet .... slar.ia
flesh .... vliêl
flicker .... nuah-zru
flimsy .... dêl
float .... jain
flood .... druin
floor .... skêf
flour .... aif
flourishing .... zal
flow .... hêun

flower .... spol
fluctuate .... huûl-hsa
fluent .... hêun-roiz
flute .... sû-phuet
fly (insect) .... rseut
fly (verb) .... cze
foam .... ual-vlaul
focus .... ûp-ba
foible .... u.spiû
fold .... cel-drô
follow (in place) .... êh.vrê
follow (in time) .... al.jlô
follower .... êh.vrê.io
food .... uem
food eaten with rice .... mi-rkec
fool .... ûp-czûus
foolish .... lbe
foot .... jrot
football .... jrot-vlêô
footpath, pavement .... coôl-pue
footprint .... jrot-jzu
for (in favour of) .... fû
for example .... flua.ro
forbid, prohibit .... fri-vza
force .... zgu
forced labour .... zgu-sla
ford .... brail-coôl
forehead .... vlûr
foreign .... za-gzauf
foresee .... êh-hne
forest .... grêut
forfeit .... trê-bli-cto

forget .... pa.lien
forgive, pardon .... tsu-stû
fork (eating utensil) .... glik-sbaun
fork, bifurcate .... czil-sjie
form of parts .... sdu
formal .... phuê-cab
former .... fot
formidable .... jeûp.rze
formula .... flêl-fri
fort, stronghold .... zrôp-vuô
fortune .... draz-dhô
fortune and misfortune .... lif.nos
fortune-telling .... draz-dhô-fri
fossil .... gzô-reu
foster .... drû-cûg
foul (in smell) .... hem
found, originate .... zma-zku
foundation, base .... prel, stô-nui
founder, originator .... nliôr
foundry .... luav-spuc
fountain .... zku-hjuez
four .... poh
fourfold, quadruple .... poh.mloû
fowl (common domestic type) .... chiûv
fox .... khiar
fraction .... sen
fragment .... sen
fragrant .... lûr
frame .... thaid
frank, blunt .... roiz-htê
freckle .... nio-hev-laz
free .... mac

freeze .... bluên.lu
frequent .... so.vrê
frequently repeated .... mloû
fresh .... zov
friction .... toif-zgu
friend .... grib
frivolous .... kiuf-spe
frog .... fries
from .... êz
front .... al
frost .... guê-bluên
fruit .... rie
fruit season .... rie.vê
frustrate .... rze-fûl
fry .... gai.rôûn
fuel .... nuah-hue
fugitive .... soun-cze
fulfil .... lbu
full .... khau
full stop, period (punctuation) .... val-pêa
fumble .... rud-hsa
fun .... spe-gle
function .... fe-ciam
funeral .... cietûem (cab-giêf es tbo-stû es mli.hia)
fungus .... fi.spom
funnel .... stû-blêa
funny .... o.kri.ceûl
fur .... zal-iûr-hiû
furnace, kiln .... oi.flêc
furniture .... fi.ôêp
fury .... ên.hiôp
fuse .... luav-glup

fusillade .... nê.cze-fiôp
fuss .... rseut-lto
futile, vain .... poc, lbu.blê
future .... gas
futurity .... gas.vê

G

gadfly .... friêm-rseut
gag .... grê-siab
gain .... pci
gait .... coôl-rêh
gallop .... fiôv-soun
gamble .... saic
game .... gle-ruam
garage .... plêm-uô
garden .... fuû
garland .... spol-jaz
garlic .... ûp-tres
gas .... luû
gasoline, petrol .... hsa-gai
gasp .... zgu-fien
gather .... feur
gauze .... dêl-dê-sdôus
gaze, stare .... ên.hne
gel .... rev.bôi
general (antonym of particular) .... kêg
general (of army) .... oi.lziap-a
generation .... nrel
generous .... cuem-zkû
genius .... mjê-znû

gentle .... lûur
genuine .... sik
geography .... hôj.czal
geology .... jzab.czal
geology or geography .... czal
geometrical figure .... tau
geometry .... jav-khôn
germ .... proic
gesture .... sme-hsa
get .... rpû
geyser .... cze-hjuez
ghost .... mli-htug
giant .... jêh-htug
giddy .... plo
gift .... cuem.ôi
gild .... zvôt-gsô
gill .... fien-voi
ginger .... bef-prel
giraffe .... val-brem
girl .... liu
gist .... gûi-laz
give .... cuem
give back .... lrai.cuem
gizzard .... vrouh-lreon
glamorous .... klô-mru
glance .... az.hne
gland .... due-voi
glare .... ên.vuêl
glass (material) .... auf
glass (tumbler) .... auf.kraug
glide, slide .... griu-hsa
glimmer .... u.vuêl

glimpse........u.hne
gloomy........nos
glorious........mêj
glove........blop-roic
glue........gsô-blêh
gnat........ian-rseut
go........vrê
go back........lrai.vrê
goat........criôm
god........tpê-htug
goitre........brem-lub
gold........zvôt (zô)
goldfish........zvôt-sgiel
goldsmith........zvôt.hriûp
gong........ûp-spuin
good........fôb
goods........clu.ôi
goose........ploil
gorilla........oic-eûk
gossip........poc-roiz
gourd........smer
govern........tpê
government........tpê-voi
governor........rêe.kûz
gown, robe........val-crêus
gradual........fleu-hsa
graduate........pci-zdoaf
graft........hsa-zfê
grain (of wood)........thin-faê
grammar........faê
gramophone........vlub.rze.aê
granary........chûp.srêm

grandfather .... hron.nrûn
granite .... zrôp-jui
grape .... pler
graph .... nêz-fcô
grass .... fjûb
grasshopper .... fpies
grateful .... bre-cru
grating, gridiron .... zrôp-thaid
grave (for burial) .... sêûm-poc
gravitate .... mru-hsa
gravy .... uem-due
grey .... bih-zel
grey-haired .... hiû.zêl
great .... zên
greedy .... uem-jro
green .... zov
greet .... frê-ceud
gregarious .... plia-mru
grimace .... zoû-hsa
grin .... lên-ceûl
grind .... aif-nuap
groan, moan .... bli-siab
grocer .... srêm-sko-gloit
groin .... zcos-vric-nêz
groove, furrow .... val-poc
grope .... zle-hsa
gross .... ro-ril
grotesque .... vûil-plo
ground nut .... vluar-foi
group .... plia
group spread over a surface .... hôj.plia
grove .... tûu.ia

grovel .... jeûp-kiuv
grow .... zca
growl .... hiôp-miôz
grumble .... lto-siab
guarantee .... sôp-gûin
guess .... heun
guest .... ruap.e
guide .... pue-pca
guilty .... ckô-jzu
guitar .... glik-sguit
gulf .... jlec-vrôih
gullet .... dhûiv
gum (of mouth) .... vhoil-vliêl
gum (of tree) .... jhus-phûl
gun .... phôs
gunpowder .... phôs-vlêr
gush .... klû

H

habitat .... pan.thêt
habitual practice .... pre-seêm
habituate .... pre
hail .... bluên-grêun
hair .... hiû
hairpin .... hiû-kruod
half .... rev
half-blooded .... ztê-rze
half brother .... rev.zten
hall .... oi.sfas
hallucinate .... gbo-hne

ham .... blac-vric
hammer .... shail
hand .... blop
handcart .... blop-plêm
handcuffs, fetters .... ckô-zrôp
handful .... blop.khau
handkerchief .... riam-sdôus
handle .... sbaun
handwriting .... blop.mro
hang .... jain-tbo
haphazard .... pa.liôl
happen .... jlô
happy .... zsû
harass .... mloû.lto
harbour .... rui
hard .... nriô
hard (of water) .... nriô
hare .... sjie-lrim-iûr
harmony (of parts) .... lpa, gûin-lpa
harvest .... chûp-feur
haste .... nru-hsa
hat or headgear .... svair
hatch .... ius-rze
hate .... zto
have .... zla
haven't .... blê
hawk .... ûp-euk
hay .... siut-fjûb
he, she, or it .... boa
head .... gûi
headache .... gûi-bli
headquarters .... tpê-vuô

healthy .... flo
heap, amass .... feur
heap, mass .... lub.plia
hear .... hli
hearing .... beo-troi
hearsay .... hli-cua
heart .... gziûl
heat .... not.lûk
heaven .... zsû-hau
heavenly body .... fi.êol
heavy .... fria
hedge .... tûu-trêf
hedgehog .... rvoh-srûuf
heel .... jrot-êh
helium .... creu-luû (rû)
hell .... bli-hau
helm, rudder .... sla-hsa.aê
helmet .... sku-svair
help, aid .... stô
helpful .... jci.stô
helpless .... stô.blê
hemp .... czuûb-tûu
herb .... fi.fjûb
here .... zlêu
hermit .... kus.û
hero (brave man) .... pa.jeûp.û
hero (of book) .... kûz-plaul
heroin .... ûp-thuas
heron .... jivoi (jloi.kiaz vlaul-coôl iêt)
hesitate .... u.grê
heterosexual .... car-cûg
hew .... rial-siut

hiccup .... ûp-cvo
hide .... fiôf
hide-and-seek .... fiôf-moês
high .... jêh
hill .... vlair
hinge .... zfê-krôf
hint .... dluô-fri
hip .... vric-zma
hire, rent .... suêt-ciam
his, her, or its .... rum
history .... smôn
hither (on this side) .... un
hoax .... spe-gbo
hobby .... gle-glu
hoe .... pauk.aê
hold .... czû
hold in mouth .... vrer-czû
hold in slight regard .... creu.lu
holding article, receptacle .... fi.phêuz
hole .... poc, poc.uô
holiday .... mac-hlan
hollow .... poc
holy .... plal-kut
home .... thêt
homicide .... hia-muir
homosexual .... car-tis
honest .... pa.gbo
honey .... kzoêp-plif
honeycomb .... kzoêp.uô
honour, respect .... fe-biôm
hood .... ûp-crum
hook .... vêg.ôi

hope .... jfi
horizon .... glun-aiz-nêz
horizontal .... fzi
horn .... oim
horse .... czûus
hospital .... mrak
host .... ruap.io
hostage .... czo-czû.e
hostel .... vam-thêt
hot .... not
hotel .... grê-srêm
hour .... vlul
house .... srêm
hover .... jain, jêh-jain
how .... ca
how many .... sa.ril
how much .... sa.sor
however .... tid.ca
hub .... truôz-ba
hulled rice .... nio.blê.rkec
hum (sound of mosquito) .... ni
human being .... hia
humankind .... hia.i
humble, modest .... pa.viaf
hummingbird .... kzoêp-iêt
humour .... fe-ceûl
hump .... ôv-fiûl-blêh
hunchback .... lub-vlic
hundred .... mij
hundred million .... cez
hundredth (part) .... mûn
hunger .... jlo

hunt .... moês
husband .... drin
hut .... a.srêm
hydrangea .... sfuom-vlêô-spol
hydrate .... vlaul-zfê
hydrocarbon .... racip
hydrochloric acid .... razû
hydrogen .... creu-lai (ra)
hydrogen peroxide .... ceraceje
hyena .... ceûl-siab-flier
hygiene .... seêm-flo
hyphen .... zfê-pêa
hypnosis .... rbo-piûj

I

I .... nûu
ice .... bluên
ice cream .... bluên-aif
ichthyosaur .... priog-reu
icicle .... blêa-bluên
idea .... ô.dlû
ideal .... cun-cab
idealism (devotion to ideals) .... cun-cab.jci
idealist (one given to ideals) .... cun-cab.û
identity .... blêh-jzu
idiom .... cab-fri
idiosyncracy .... vlil-fal
idle .... sê.sla
idol .... giêf-plaul
if .... og

ignoramus .... fûl.flêl.û
ignore .... fe-bke
illustrate .... rnê-fri
image .... ûp-blêh
imaginary .... vûil, o.vûil
imagination (act) .... glu.vûil
imagination (faculty) .... suô.vûil
imaginative .... vûil, vûil.zla
imagine .... vûil
imbue .... vlû
imitate .... mcu
immature .... paf
immediately .... hum
immigrate, import .... gzauf-nu
imminent, impending .... jô-hrô
immoral .... sraô
impede .... fe-faur
implore .... ên-krô
imply .... vêg-sme
important .... sag, sag-zên
impossible .... tro.vlô
impress .... jzu-gsô
impromptu .... piôs-blê
improve .... hues
impulse .... vsud-hsa
in .... nu
in a word, in short .... ifu (im fef cua)
in general .... isô (im sê.chêô)
in order to .... ib
in presence of .... zvê.mi
in the long run .... im lêr
incense .... lûr-brôn

incentive .... hsa-glu
incite .... fois
incline .... mru
including .... ro
income .... rpû-chauk
increase .... tliô.lu
inculcate .... mloû-tbo
index .... feur-sfo
indicate .... fe-fcô
indifferent .... bke
indigenous (antonym of exotic) .... pan-rze
indigo .... tûu-dûn
indirect speech .... vêg-roiz-puô
indispensable .... hfo-zla
individual .... kus-fleu
indiction .... vle-nzo
indulge .... stû
industry (economic activity) .... clu-rze
inert .... hsa-vza
inevitable .... hfo.jlô
inferior .... lô.û
infinite .... pa.dba
infinitesimal .... pa.dba.gun
inflammation .... slû-nuah
inflate .... ual-jza
influence .... lbu-zgu
influenza .... ûp-tho
inform .... cuem-bûuj
inhabitant .... iûn
inherit .... rpû-gzô
initial .... poz-mau
inject .... nu-zgu

injure, harm .... ûp-khe
ink .... smuat
inland .... nu-vluar
inmate .... srêm.iûn
innocent .... kôz-mac
insect .... krois
insecticide .... krois.muir.ôi
insensitive .... zal
insert .... sû.tbo
inside out .... nu-za
insist .... nriô-fri
inspect .... jzu-hne
inspire .... fois, hêun-lbu
instant, moment .... az.vêu
instead .... vuô.tû
instinct .... hzi
instrument .... chaêv
instrument of torture .... bli.aê
instrument of war .... chuf
insult .... fri-rud
insure .... zku-raz
integer .... khau.ril
intelligent lil
intense .... val
interest (engage attention) .... pci-mru
interest (re money) .... rie-chauk
interfere .... es-ztê
interim .... ba-vêu
intermediate or neutral .... man
intermingle .... mi.ztê
intermittent .... mloû-grê
international .... gzauf.sû

interpose .... ba.tbo
interrogative sentence (Luif) .... sûig-tuê
interrogatory term (Luif) .... sûig-cua
interrupt .... nuap
intersect .... dê-siut
interval (of space) .... nuap-nuê
interval (of time) .... nuap-vêu
interview .... frê-sûig
intestine (in body) .... drein
intestine (internal affairs relating to state or country) .... nu-gzauf
intimate .... bûuj-jô
into .... ud.nu
intrinsic .... pan-nu
introduce .... zvê, czo-bûuj
intuition .... bûuj-hzi
invade .... fe-cêôm
invent .... mjê
investigate .... moês
invite .... tuûs
involve .... srô
iodine .... leg-dûn-lai (la)
iron (metal) .... zrôp (rô)
iron (for clothing) .... griu-zrôp
irrigate .... vlual-pca
irritating thing .... priêk
is .... vlô
island .... nrôus
isn't .... hlu
issue .... za-cuem
isthmus .... brem-vluar
itch .... tle
item .... plia.fleu

itinerary .... hsa.liôl

J

jackal .... ûp-flier
jackdaw .... rseut-fnoôl
jade, nag (horse) .... rud.mul.czûus
jade (stone) .... zov-sfuom-jui
jagged .... jroi-dluô
jailer .... sdut.seêm.io
jam .... rie-jluz
jar .... hvau-khuêj
jaundice .... hiz-rnû
jaw .... vrer-brian
jealous .... giûk
jelly .... zoc-griu
jellyfish .... zoc-lie
jerk .... nôh-hsa
jewel (precious stone) .... zrar
job, post .... fe-sla
join .... zfê
joint, junction .... zfe.uô
joke, jest .... ceûl-spe
jostle .... zle-zru
judge (verb) .... jbe
jug .... sbaun-khuêj
juice .... phûl
jump .... fiôv
junior .... ri.nôf.û
just (a little while ago) .... vam-ris
just (equitable) .... hiêm

jut .... ôv-fiûl

K

keep .... seêm
keepsake .... seêm.cuem.ôi
kernel .... foi-vliêl
kerosene .... raciz-jluz
kettle .... rmuêz
key .... htê-kruod
kick .... moil
kidnap .... zgu-czo
kidney .... vriôb
kill .... muir
kind, benevolent .... zkû
kiss .... pûen
kitchen .... rôûn.sfas
kite .... êun-uam
knee .... vric-zfê
kneel .... vric-zfê.lu
knife .... phaiv
knit .... thaid-zfê
knock, hit .... rial
knot .... czuûb-zfê
know .... bûuj
knowledge .... flêl
knuckle .... glik-jui

L

label .... sfo-uam

labour.......lie-sla
labourer (unskilled).......bloek
lack.......hse
ladder.......ûp-rtam
ladle.......rôûn-pluiz
lake.......jruûn
lame.......cto-coôl
lament.......fri-vce
lamp.......svuan
land (noun).......vluar
land (verb).......vluar.lu
landlord.......srêm.gûi
landowner.......vluar.sto.io
landscape.......jzuis
lane, path.......a.pue
language.......rua
languish.......jziû-spiû
lantern.......hmav-phêuz
lap.......cgi-vric
larva, grub.......zma-krois
last (antonym of first).......peb
last (most recent).......dluô-jôm
last night.......dau.guê
late.......zam
lath.......dêl-thin
lathe.......jav-czaf
lather.......êz-khôis
latitude.......lên-aiz-nêz
latrine.......bliaz.sfas
latter.......mip
laudanum.......thuas-due
laugh.......ceûl.siab

launder .... krauf-kiûr
lava .... luav-jui
law .... chêb
layer .... plia.hôj.fleu
layman, civilian .... sêv-vriam
lazy .... mlê
lead (metal) .... brat (ba)
lead (verb) .... pca
leaf .... rsûh
leak .... poc-hêun
learn .... jiaz
learned .... jiaz-zên
learning, scholarship .... kraut-flêl
least .... per
leather .... nio
lecture .... rlu-roiz
leech .... ian-smiûp
leek .... tres-tzif
left side .... nlai
leg .... vric
leg below knee .... lô-vric
legend, myth .... smôn-hrôz
legerdemain .... cfe-nru
legislative council .... chêb-lruic
leisure .... sla.mac
lemon .... kiû
lend .... ud.pauk
length (long piece) .... nêz.fleu
lengthen, stretch .... val.lu
lenient .... zoc-zkû
lens .... hpu-auf
leopard .... laz-oic

leprosy.......sriol-nio
less.......ris
lesson.......rlu.eu
lest.......jeûp.ih
let go.......stû
letter (missive).......pruv
letter (of alphabet).......mau
lettuce.......iuv-phûl-tzif
level.......bôz
lever.......zgu-sgon
libel.......kêu-rud.lu
library.......kraut-srêm
lick.......bliûh.lu
lid, cover.......lkô.ôi
lie (horizontal posture).......fzi
lie (utter falsehood).......roiz-gbo
life.......draz
lifebuoy.......vrôih-stô
lifeless object.......nui
lifetime.......draz.vê
light (in weight).......creu
light (phenomenon).......hmav
light or set fire.......fois
light work.......u.sla
lighthouse.......vrôih-hmav
like (similar).......ûp
like (verb).......u.jci
lily.......rhez
lime (calcium oxide or hydroxide).......jzêm
limestone.......jzêm.jui
limit.......dba
line.......nêz

linen .... smuas
linger .... piem, lêr.gzô
link .... glup-czuûb.eu
lintel .... htê-prus
lion .... gûi-oic
lip .... lrim
lipstick .... pliz-chaim
liquid substance .... due
list (of things) .... fleu-puô
literary circle .... prôh.jaz
literate .... srû-bûuj
literator .... glûis
literature .... prôh
little (in quantity) .... fef
live .... sne
live person .... sne.hia
liver (gland) .... jriol
livid .... bih-dûn
living thing .... sia
lizard .... sboif
load .... riam-ôi
loam .... sû-lhôm
loan .... pauk
loathe, disgust .... ên.zto
lobster .... frûin-troih
locality .... az.vuô
lock (device) .... lkô-truôz
locust .... gaif-krois
lodging house .... ûuc-srêm
logic .... nzo-flêl
lonely .... kus
long .... val

long afterwards....lêr.jû
long time....lêr
longitude....val-aiz-nêz
look (appear)....fcô
loop....nuê-czuûb
loose....gsô-spiû
lorry, truck....clu-plêm
lose....cto
lottery....czo-saic
lotus....jain-rhez
loud....vliê
louse....hiû-krois
love....jci
low (antonym of high)....ban
low (re sound)....blou
loyal, faithful....lgi-kuv
lucky....dhô-fôb
luggage....vrê-phêuz
lukewarm....u.not
lunch....ba-uem
lung....lbion
lust....car.zri
luxury....stui-gle
lyric....flêz-stôh

M

machine....czaf
mad....jzû
madder....rze-leg
magazine, periodical....dak-kraut

maggot .... of-rseut
magic .... klô
magnesium .... zel-nuah (za)
magnesium suplhate .... zahipoje
magnet .... vlôi-zrôp
magnifying glass .... truûv
magpie .... ûp-fnoôl
main part .... sgon
mainland .... sgon-vluar
maintain .... mul-seêm
maize .... phit
majestic .... mêj
major .... hê
major vocabulary division (Luif) .... hê-cua-sjie
majority .... fem-ril
make .... zku
make the best of .... fôb-zku
maker .... zku.io
malaria .... lûk-phi
male .... kôr
malicious .... hem
mammoth .... ûif-reu
man .... noê
manage .... csû
manager .... csû.io
manganese .... nriô-suz-nuap (nu)
mangrove .... blaf-tûu
manhood .... noê.mul
manner .... rêh
mansion .... oi.srêm
manufacture .... czaf-zku
manure, fertilizer .... lhôm-uem

manuscript .... mro-kraut
many sorts of .... mij
map .... aiz-thôuh
marble .... griu-jzêm-jui
mark .... jzu
mark well, *nota bene*, N.B. .... jloi-jzu
market .... trôp
married man .... ôr.mêus.io
marry .... mêus
martyr (noun) .... lgi-mli
mask .... lkô-zoû
massacre .... ôuv-muir
massage .... toif-shu
mast .... slar-sgon
master .... iov
masterpiece .... kûz-rze
mat .... ûp-sdôus
match .... zku-grêl
materialism .... hue.sô
materialist .... hue.be
mathematics .... khôn
matter (physical substance) .... hue
matter (subject engaging attention) .... ô.es
mattress .... lô-tluem
maxim .... rlu-tuê
maximum .... rûm-laz
may .... lro
maybe, perhaps .... lro.vlô
mayor .... mai.kûz
meal .... dak-uem
mean (re behaviour) .... ban, pleuf
mean (re words) .... sme

means .... lbu-blêh
means of solving a difficulty .... cêi
measles .... leg-laz
measure .... rti
measuring instrument .... czuel
meat-seller .... vliêl.gloit
mechanic (engineering and allied trades) .... zboec
mechanical engineer .... czaf.nziop
medal .... jzu-glup
medicine .... uûk
meet .... frê
melon .... phûl-smer
melt .... luav
member (of a group or society) .... iûn
membrane .... voi-nio
memorandum .... lien-puô
memory .... suô.lien
mental faculty .... vsud-suô
mention .... es-fri
menu .... uem-fleu-puô
merchant or trader .... gloit
mercury .... hêun-jzêk (hê)
merit .... fe-sag
merry .... vliê-zsû
message .... sca
metal .... glup
metaphor .... fiem-kaê
metaphysics .... vaê-snuv
meteor .... hêun-êol
methane .... cipora
method .... phuê
metre .... vlub-thaid

miasma....rud-za-fien
microphone....vliê.lu.aê
microscope....jô.truûv
middle....ba
middleman....ba.û
midwifery....rze-sma
milk....iuv
Milky Way....êol-brail
mill....aif-nuap.czaf
millipede....hvau-sor-vric
mince, chop....chûp-siut
mincemeat....chûp-vliêl
mind....vsud
mine (explosive)....fiôf-nuap-chuf
mine (minerals)....hkiap
mineral....bruf
miniature....rseut-kêg
minimum....per-laz
minister....tpê-jlec
ministry....plaz-lai
minor....lô
minor vocabulary division (Luif)....lô-cua-sjie
minority....ris-ril
mint....lûr-lrim
minute (of time)....hê.pom.vlul
minute (very small)....vêi
mirage....gbo-thôuh
mirror....spôis
miscellaneous....ztê, ztê.kêg
miscellaneous phrase (Luif)....gzô-kaê
miserly....coet-bli
miss....pa.rpû

mist .... vluar-jrual
mistake .... prû
mistress, concubine .... seêm-viô
mix .... ztê
mixture (product of mixing) .... ztê-jzab
mobile .... kri.hsa
mobilize .... ceud-piôs
mock, ridicule .... ceûl-spe
model, pattern .... mcu-flua
moderate .... an.sor
modern .... fe-buf
mole .... nio-laz
molecule .... hue-laz
monarch .... rze.vliêc
monarchy .... rze-vliêc-plaz
Monday .... hlan-a
money .... chauk
Mongolian .... luisehi (glui sehi)
mongrel .... ztê-iar
monkey .... eûk
monogamy .... mov-drin-zriv
monopoly .... kus-clu
monotheism .... lemtêh (lva fe mov tpê-htug)
monotonous .... jziû.tis
monster .... zên-hrôz
month .... vnên
monument .... tû-lien
mood .... bre-mul
moon .... ôin
moral .... kut
more .... fem
morning .... zôa

morphine .... thuas-jluz
mosquito .... priêk
mosquito net .... priêk-thaid
moss .... rmed
most .... rûm
mote .... az.vlêr
moth .... guê-krois
mother .... zrel
mother-of-pearl .... ûp-cheud
motionless .... pa.hsa
motive .... hjuez, nzo-hsa
motley .... mloû-hev
motor .... hsa-czaf
motorcar .... czaf-plêm
motorcycle .... lpa-plêm
mould (woolly growth) .... vlêr-rmed
mound .... a.vlair
mourn .... roic-vce
mouse .... ûp-pleuf
mouth .... vrer
move .... hsa
move from place to place .... vuô-hpu
move house .... hpu-piem
move quietly .... môip
mow .... fjûb-siut
much .... sor
mucus .... dlos-due
mud .... blaf
muddle .... blaf.lu
mulberry .... truar-tûu
mule .... ztê-czûus
multiply .... mloû

multitudinous .... rûg
murder .... sraô-muir
murmur, mutter .... blou.siab
muscle .... vrouh
museum .... fcô-hôi-srêm
mushroom .... spom
music .... sluj
musical instrument .... flaic
musician .... droim
must .... hfo
mustard .... zvôt-aif
mutatis mutandis
(the necessary changes having been made) .... azoh (al zku sko hpu)
mutual, one another .... mov-cûg
muzzle .... grê-vrer
my .... fêr
mysterious .... nûh

N

nag, jade (horse) .... rud.mul.czûus
nail (of fingers and toes) .... vgep
nail (of metal) .... gsô-kruod
naked .... krauf.blê
name .... kêu
name mark (Luif) .... kêu-pêa
name noun (Luif) .... kêu-blêh-suô
nameless .... kêu.blê
namely, viz. .... kêu.ih
nape .... brem.êh
naphthalene .... focitera

narcotic .... fi.thuas
narrate .... brail-fri
narrow .... huv
nation, people .... gzauf-hia
nationalize .... plaz.lu
native (born in the place) .... vuô-rze
natural .... pan
natural calamity .... pan-gaif
nature (of a thing) .... blêh-fal
nature (world of nature) .... pan.blêh
nausea .... vlû.klû
navel .... zcos-laz
navy .... slar.ia
near .... jô
nearly .... jô.fa
neat, tidy .... phuê-fôb
nebula .... êol-jrual
neck .... brem
necktie .... brem-roic
need .... sko
needle .... pûuk.aê
negative .... nlê.fa
neglect .... bke-stû
negotiate .... roiz-liôl
Negroid .... zusehi (zluû sehi)
neighbour .... jroz
neighbourhood .... jroz.uô
neither .... cel.fûl
neon .... leg-luû (lu)
nephew .... jzod
nerve .... ouz
nest .... ûuc

nestle .... ûuc-fzi
net (antonym of gross) .... ci-ril
net (noun) .... thaid
nettle .... fiôp-tûu
never .... jrôû
nevertheless, notwithstanding .... sê.ris.tû
new .... vam, hrô.vam
New Year .... zma.ghal
new-born kitten .... rze.vam.phiom
news .... vam-jlô
newspaper .... ftuêp
next .... jû
next night .... nlôl.guê
nib .... rdêup-jluz
niche .... trêf-poc
nickel .... ûp-jzêk (pê)
nickname .... spe-kêu
niece .... vriz
night .... guê
nightingale .... guê-iêt
nightmare .... jeûp-niûh
nimble .... nru-creu
nine .... rez
nipple .... hpim
nitric acid .... ralûkoje
nitrogen .... ual-luû (lû)
noble, lofty .... jêh
nobody .... fûl.hia
nod .... gûi.zru
noisy .... vlub.sor
nolens volens (without any choice) .... lfe.pa
nomenclature, terminology .... kêu-thaid

nominal........kêu.fa
nominate........kêu-rûus
nonsense........fûl.sme
noodle........czuûb-aif
noon........nôu.ba
north........vlôi
nose........dlos
nostril........dlos-poc
not........sêv
notch........u.siut
note........sû-puô
nothing........fûl.blêh
notice........bûuj-puô
noumenon........vaê.jluz
noun........blêh-suô
nourish........stô-zca
novelist........fkal.driôs
nozzle........za-slôp
nucleus........ba-jzab
nuisance........rseut
numb........grê-vlû
number........ril
numerator........o.sjie.pom
nurse (noun)........drû-sku.vriam
nurse (verb)........drû-sku
nut........foi
nutmeg........lûr-foi

O

oak........zrôp-tûu

oar .... hsa-slar
oasis .... glaif-druap
oats .... fsep
obey .... nrû
object (antonym of subject) .... dlû-blêh
object (of sentence) .... eûd-cua
object qualifier (Luif) .... blêh-fal-suô
oblige .... kut-gsô
oblique, leaning .... êz-nad
obscene jest .... car.ceûl-spe
obsess .... dlû-gsô
obstacle .... fe-faur.ôi
obstinate .... nriô-lfe
obtrusive .... vliê
obtuse angle .... lên-guz
obvious lil
occupation .... sla
occupy .... rpû-czû
occupy office or post .... czû-sla
ocean .... oi.vrôih
ochre .... jhus-zrôp
octopus .... tev-jlec
odd (antonym of even) .... mov-kol
of (belonging to) .... fe
of course .... pan.raz
offend .... hiôp-lto
offer .... piôs-cuem
office (building) .... thô.srêm
office (public) .... rgêp
office (room) .... thô.sfas
officer (military) .... oi.lziap
official (government) .... dliôt

official (private) .... plia-jlec
often .... so.dak
ogle .... glif-drô
ogre .... jeûp-htug
oil .... gai
old (in years) .... nôf
old (long in use) .... lêr, hrô.lêr
olive .... ius-rie
omelette .... rsûh-ius
omen .... fcô-jlô
omit .... pa.ro.lu
omniscient .... cim.bûuj
on .... hê.mi
on or above .... hê
one .... mov
one at same table .... ôêp-jroz
one characterized by a certain quality .... ûil
one practising intellectual art .... jriêf
onion .... tres
only .... cûf
onomatopoeia .... vlub-cua
opal .... iuv-zrar
open .... htê
open space .... htê-hôj
operate .... sla, sla-lbu
opinion .... jbe-lgi
opium .... thuas
opportunity .... ciam-dak
oppose .... suêf
opposite (in kind) .... pal
opposite (in position) .... vuô.ud
oppress .... zgu-bauz

optimistic .... jfi-hrô
or .... vo
orangutan .... hia-eûk
orange (fruit) .... poi
orange (in colour) .... poi
oratory .... roiz-crul
orbit .... jaz-soun
orchard .... rie.lruic
order .... gsô-phuê
ordinary .... kul
ore .... glup-bruf
organ (internal or external) .... voi
organize .... csû-zfê
origin .... ô.êz
original .... hjuez
original part of speech (Luif) .... poz-suô
oriole .... zvôt-iêt
ornament (ornamental article) .... sfuom
orphan .... sviu-blê
orthodox .... cab, fe-cab
osprey .... sgiel-euk
ostensible .... lnu.fa
ostentatious .... fcô-vuêl
ostracize .... bhon-siut
ostrich .... ûif-iêt
other .... cûg
otter .... vrôih-phiom
ought, should .... paz.hfo
our .... sêf
outlaw .... chêb-siut
outline, draft .... jav-rnê
outrage .... ôuv-khe

outside .... za
outspread .... ên-jza
oval .... ius
ovary .... ius-voi
oven .... flêc
overcoat .... lûk-crêûs
overhear, eavesdrop .... dluô-hli
overtake .... hsa-rpû
overwhelm .... druin.lu
owe .... pa.suêt
owl .... phûun
own .... sto
owner .... sto.io
ox .... friêm
oxygen .... jae (je)
oyster .... phoôz
oyster bed .... phoôz-uô
ozone .... sû-jae

P

pack .... pa.jza
paddy .... nio.rkec
page .... kraut-jluz
pageant, spectacle .... mru-fcô
pain .... bli
paint (substance) .... uêr
painter (of picture) .... hfios
pair .... sviu
palace .... vliêc.srêm
palate .... vrer-crum

pale, wan .... slû-hev
palm (of hand) .... blop-al
palmistry .... blop-crul
palm tree .... svaup-rsûh
pamper .... stû-ruap
pan .... bôz-chôud
pancreas .... jô-lreon
pant .... fien-zru
pantheism .... leliv (lva fe lua ih vaê)
paper .... uam
parabola .... kûs-blêa-vêg
parachute .... sôp-tluat
paragraph .... tuê-puô
parallel .... dê-kûs
parallelogram .... buv-zab
paralyse .... cto-vle
parapet .... sû-trêf
parasite .... ciam-sia
parch .... vlaul-cto
parental love .... nrûn.zrel.jci
park .... gle-lruic
parlour .... cgi.sfas
parrot .... mrean
part .... pom
part of speech .... suô
partake .... zla-pom
partial .... tû-jbe
particle .... laz.fleu
particular .... pom-chêô
partner .... zfê-thô.io
part-of-speech division (Luif) .... suô-cua-sjie
party (political) .... plaz-bhon

party, organization .... hia.ia
pass (mountain) .... vlair-pue
pass (verb) .... dê.vrê
pass time .... vêu-ciam
passenger .... plêm.cgi.io
passion .... leg, ên.bre
passport .... vrê-uam
past (time) .... jôm
pat .... ûp-zle
patient .... hpi-zlu
patriotic .... gzauf-jci
patrol .... hsa-sku
pavilion .... creu-srêm
pawn .... hôi-pauk
pay .... suêt
payee .... suêt.e
pea .... ûp-rcûf
peach .... pliz-rie
peacock .... svaup-iêt
peak .... vlair-laz
pear .... ûp-siû
pearl .... dheud
peasant .... jraim.û
peck .... rial-tiûn
peculiar .... fe-sto
peel .... rie.nio
peep .... fiôf-hne
peg .... ûp-kruod
pelican .... phêuz-vrer
pelvis .... lô-zcos
pen or any writing implement .... rdêup
pencil .... bih-brat-rdêup

pendant .... jain-tbo-sfuom
pendulum .... huûl-jui
penetrate .... dê.vrê
penholder .... rdêup-sgon
peninsula .... jô-nrôus
penis .... ôr.hlût
penknife .... a.phaiv
pension .... lkô-chauk
peony .... vlêô-mêj-spol
pepper .... flec
peppermint (plant) .... bef-lûr
per annum .... tû ghal
per cent .... tû mij
peremptory .... gsô-hfo
perfect .... cun
perfume .... phuûf
period, full stop (punctuation) .... val-pêa
period (of time) .... do
permanent .... vrêu, zlu.lêr
permit (noun) .... sfu-uam
perpendicular .... fiûl-guz-nêz
perpetuate .... zlu-lva
perplex .... bêul
persecute .... zto-lto
person (re words) .... cua-hia
person above ordinary grade .... oih
personal vlil
perspective .... fcô-ûp-kuv
persuade .... hzô-lgi
pervade .... puaf
perverse .... kôz-troi
petal .... spol.eu

petition .... mro-pra
petrol, gasoline .... hsa-gai
petroleum........ raciz
petty........ rud.gun
pewter .... drês-brat
phenomenon .... vle.blêh
philosopher .... hlier
philosophy .... snuv
phlegm .... cvo-phûl
phoenix .... iêt-hrôz
phosphoresce........ nûh-vuêl
phosphorus .... nûh-hmav (na)
photograph........ fbun-thôuh
phrase........ kaê
physics .... phun
piano........ truop
pick, pluck .... meuh
pickaxe .... vluar-ftuav
pickle .... due-seêm
pickpocket........ lie.môip.io
picnic .... jraim-ruap
picture........ thôuh
picturesque........ thôuh.ûp
piece (detached portion)........ pom.fleu
piece (flat) .... hôj-fleu
pier, jetty........ ud-vrôih-cêi
pierce, bore........ poc-zku
pig........ srûuf
pigeon .... tziôl
pigsty .... srûuf.uô
pill, tablet........ bôi-uûk
pillow........ gûi-tluem

pilot (guide ship) .... pca-csû
pilot (of airplane) .... zpiat
pimple .... gun-leg
pin .... kruod
pincers .... meuh.aê
pine (tree) .... kson
pineapple .... sriol-rie
pioneer .... pca-zma
pipe (musical instrument) .... phuet
pipe (tube for fluids) .... slôp
pirate (verb) .... vrôih-môip
pistil .... spol-pêm
piston .... hsa-hvau
pit .... vluar-poc
pitfall .... sma-poc
pith, marrow .... nu-lifûe
pity .... viûr
pivot .... drô-kruod
place .... vuô
plague .... pleuf-rnû
plain (level tract of land) .... bluim
plain, unembellished .... zel, sê.sfuom
plan .... liôl
plane .... griu.lu.aê
plane figure .... hôj
planet .... hsa-êol
plant .... lô.tûu
plantation .... lruic
plaster .... jzêm-buû
plastic (adjective) .... jhus
plastic (noun) .... jhus-jzab
plate .... truôz

plateau .... jêh-bluim
platform, stage.. jêh-skêf
platinum .... sag-fria (si)
play .... spe
play music .... flô
plead .... stô-roiz
pleasant to senses .... zis
pleasure .... gle
plesiosaur .... chiûs-reu
pliant .... suz-vêg
pliers .... czû.siut.aê
plough .... czu.aê
plug (noun) .... grê-poc
plunge .... vlaul-fiôv
plural .... snou
pocket .... krauf-phêuz
poet .... jziem
poetry .... stôh
point (dot) .... laz
point (with finger) .... glik-fco
point of view .... guz
poison .... fluem
poison gas .... muir-luû
pole .... aiz-laz
police officer .... gliuk
policy .... liôl
polish .... toif-griu
polite .... cua-lûur
politician .... bloêp
politics .... plaz-blêh
polygamy .... snou-drin-zriv
polygon .... dôg

polytheism ....lesotêh (lva fe snou tpê-htug)
pomegranate.. sor-snil
pomelo..ûif-poi
pomp .... coet-fcô
pond ....grôiv
pony... rseut-czûus
pool (of water)..grôiv
pool (re resources) .... mloû.lu
poor .... pa.stui
poppy..thuas-tûu
popular.. lên.o.jci
population..iûn-ril
porch...ud-krôf
pore... vêi-poc
pork .... srûuf.vliêl
porpoise .... srûuf-priog
port .... rui.mai
porter .... riam.bloek
portrait.. hia-thôuh
position ....jluê
positive.. lva.fa
possessive noun (Luif) ....sto-blêh-suô
possible ....kri.vlô
post ....fiûl.prus
post meridiem (p.m.) .... al nôu.ba
postage ....pruv-suêt
poster .... roiz-gsô-uam
posthumous... al-mli
post office..pruv.rgêp
postscript..tliô-mro
pot .... vlêô-chôud
potassium .... zoc-glup (zu)

potato.......... crif
pour.......... stû
pout.......... vrer-val
powder.......... aif
power.......... zgu-kri
practise.......... glu-ciam
praise.......... siab-biôm
praiseworthy.......... siab-biôm.sag
pray.......... giêf-krô
preach.......... csa-rlu
precede (in place).......... al.vrê
precede (in time).......... êh.jlô
precedent.......... êh-flua
precious.......... hiz
predecessor.......... êh.jlô.io
predicament.......... lto-jluê
predict, foretell.......... êh-fri
preface.......... zma-cua
prefer.......... fe-rûus
pregnant.......... mi-paf
prejudice.......... êh-dlû
premature.......... êh-vêu
prepare.......... piôs
prescribe.......... shu-fri
presence of mind.......... vsud-zvê
present, attend.......... zvê
present, now.......... buf
preserve.......... sôp.seêm
president (of country).......... rûus-vliêc
prestige.......... biôm-lbu-zgu
pretend.......... rpê
prevaricate.......... hpu-drô

prevent .... faur
prey .... tuês
price .... rôef
prick .... fiôp
priest .... griûs
primarily .... poz
primary meaning (Luif) .... poz-sme
prime minister .... tpê-gûi
primitive .... bêr.jôm
principal word (Luif) .... iov-cua
principle .... slôn-mau
print .... jzu-mro
printing press .... jzu-mro-czaf
prism .... liûgued (lub mi ûp grê-dluô ne dluô)
prison .... sdut
prisoner .... sdut.û
private vlil
private dwelling .... thêt
privilege .... jzu-côh-pci
prize .... ruam.ôi
pro and con .... tû.pa
probable .... jô.raz
problem .... sûig-blêh
procedure .... thô-phuê
process .... phuê, jlô-nêz
procession .... vrê-nêz
proclaim .... lên-roiz
prodigal .... kiuf-coet
product .... rze.ôi
profound (knowledge) .... dûn
programme .... liôl-uam
project .... sla-liôl

promise .... gûin
promote .... hues, stô-al
prompt .... piôs-nru
pronounce .... cua-siab
propagandise .... lgi-jza
propeller .... sla-hsa-nui
property, assets .... sto.ôi
proportion, ratio .... pom-fiem
propriety .... paz-buv
prose .... kran
prospect (for minerals) .... bruf-moês
prostitute .... rza-viô
protect .... sku
protecting thing .... tluat
protest .... fri-suêf
protuberance, knob .... dlos
proud .... viaf-rêh
prove .... jzi
proverb .... flêl-tuê
province .... hê.rêe
proviso .... puô-og
provoke .... glu-ceud
prudent .... drû-znû
prune .... siut-jav
pseudonym .... fkal-kêu
psychiatry .... vsud.rnû.flêl
psychology .... mrêl
pterodactyl .... iêt-reu
public .... bhon
publish .... jza-rza
puddle .... a.grôiv
pull .... meuh

pulley, windlass ....meuh-drô-truôz
pulp .... rie-zoc
pulse (of heart) ....gziûl-rial
pulse (of plants).. fi.rcûf
pumice ....poc-luav-jui
pump ....due-czaf
punctual..cav, vêu.cav
punctuation mark... pêa
pungent (in taste) ....bef
punish .... trê-bli
pupa, chrysalis...vza-krois
pupil (of eye) ....glif-ba
pure.. fêz
purify .... kiûr
purple..dûn-leg
purpose, aim ....ib
purse ....chauk-phêuz
pus .... cli-jluz
push .... pa.meuh
pustule ....cli-jluz-laz
put .... tbo
put out of sight.. sêûm
pyjamas ....rbo-krauf
pyramid...guz-blêa
python, boa .... nuap-chiûs

Q

quack, charlatan .... gbo-zla
quadrilateral .... zab
quaint..zis-côh

qualification ....sla-fal
qualifier.. fal-suô
quality..fal
quantity.. sor.fef
quarrel...pfê
quarry .... jui.uô
quarter ....fe.poh
quartz..buû-bruf
quasi... lnu-kuv
quench ....grêl-muir
question mark ....sûig-pêa
queue ....sma-nêz
quick..nru
quick to understand ....jloi
quiet .... hpi
quinine... phi-nos-uûk
quorum ....hse-ril
quota...rpû-pom
quote.. czo-roiz
quotient .... sjie-lbu

R

rabbit ....pauh-iar
race (competitive running) ....ruam-soun
race (human group)..sehi (sjie fe hia.i)
radiate .... kôof-jza
radiation..huûl-zgu
radio..nuê-sgam
radioactive...hue-nuap
radium ....vlil-nuap-lai (vi)

radius .... ba-nad
raft .... jain-bôz
rafter .... êfpec (êz-fzi prus fe crum)
rag .... nuap-sdôus
ragged .... nuap-jroi
raid .... jzêl-cêôm
railings .... grê-prus
railway .... zrôp-pue
rain .... grêun
rainbow .... grêun-czuûb
raincoat .... grêun-crêus
raisin .... cto-phûl-pler
rake .... vhoil.lu.aê
ram .... zgu-tbo
ramble .... zlêu-jzua-coôl
rambutan .... hiû-rie
rank, grade .... fal-plia
ransom .... tuês-suêt
rap (sound of knock on wood) .... tôk
rape .... car-zgu
rare .... côh
rash (behaviour) .... fiôv-glu
rash (disease) .... nio-laz-plia
rat .... pleuf
rather .... fem-lfe
rattan .... val-sgon-tuû
raw .... pa.rôûn
ray .... nê.hmav
rayon .... zku.truar
razor .... nrûs-phaiv
react .... piûj-glu
read .... srû

ready .... piôs-bzê
real .... kuv, jluz.fa
real thing .... jluz
reap .... siut-czo
rear .... zca-csû
reason .... nzo
rebel .... tpê-suêf
receipt .... maûs-uam
receive .... maûs
receiver .... eûd
recent .... vam.jôm
receptive (to ideas) .... vsud-maûs
recite .... ûp-srû
reckless .... vsud-stû
recognise .... nion
recoil .... vlic-hsa
recommend .... zvê-fôb
reconcile .... zu.gûin
record .... sfo
recording meter .... mrail
recover (get back) .... lrai.rpû
recover (return to former condition) .... shu
recreation .... fe-ruap
recruit .... vam.lziap
rectangle .... val-gêd
rectify .... paz.lu
red .... leg
redress .... nad.lu
redundant .... ôv-sko
reed .... vlaul-fjûb
refer .... es-jzu
refine .... piôs-hues

reflect .... vlic-vuêl
reform .... hpu-fôb
refreshments .... creu-uem
refuge .... ûuc
refuse, reject .... pa.hse
refuse, rubbish .... kiuf.ôi
regain .... lrai.pci
region .... jluêm
regret .... bre-kôz
regular passage (Luif) .... buv-puô
regular shape .... buv
reign .... vliêc.vê
rein .... pca-czuûb
related .... fe-mi
relative (any kind) .... hbel.jzon
relative (by blood) .... hbel
relative (by marriage) .... jzon
relative apart by one more generation .... hron
relax .... stû-jain
relent .... zoc.lu
relevant .... es-zle
relieve .... czûa-stô
religion .... plal
religious organization .... plal-bhon
reluctant .... pa.jro
rely, depend .... piem, stô-sko
remain .... gzô
remains .... gzô.ôi
remember .... lien
remorse .... trê-bli
remove .... êz.hsa
renegade .... siut-hpu.io

renounce, give up .... vri-stû
repair .... luam
repeat .... lrai.lu
repeated .... dak
repellent .... hem
repent .... vce-kôz
reply .... piûj
report .... cûg-fri
reporter .... cûg-fri.vriam
represent .... msê
repress .... gsô-lkô
reptile .... fi.chiûs
republic .... bhon-plaz
repulse .... vlic.zgu
reputation .... kêu
request .... pra
request mark (Luif) .... pra-pêa
request sentence (Luif) .... pra-tuê
require .... pra-hse
requite .... lrai.suêt
rescue .... sôp.lu
research .... flêl-cri
resent .... dlû-khe
reserve .... seêm-czû
reservoir .... vlaul.uô
resign .... sla-stû
resin .... phûl-jluz
resist .... fe-suêf
resolute .... vsud-raz
resort .... jci-vuô
respectable man or Mister. .... iûh
respectable woman or Madam .... oin

respectively .... uput (rum pom ud tid)
responsible .... ceud-piûj
rest .... pa.sla
restaurant .... tiûn-srêm
restore .... lrai.tbo
resultant word (Luif) .... lbu-cua
resume .... lrai.zma
retail .... u.rza
retinue, suite .... ûp-euf
retire .... siut-stû
retract .... lrai.czo
retreat .... vlic.vrê
retrench .... coet-siut
retrospect .... vlic-hne
return .... lrai.drô
reveal .... htê-roiz
revenge .... diuk
revenue .... plaz-maûs
reverse .... cûg, cûg-drô
revise .... jbe-hpu
revive .... lrai.sne
revolt .... nriô-suêf
revolutionise .... prel-hpu
revolve .... jaz-hsa
revolve round and round .... mloû.jaz-hsa
reward, give prize .... cuem-ruap
rheumatism .... vrouh-bli
rhinoceros .... dlos-oim
rhombus .... ûp-gêd
rhyme .... tis-grê-vlub
rhythm .... sluj-buv
rib .... grûs-brian

ribbon .... nê.sdôus
rice .... rkec
ricefield .... rkec.druap
rich .... stui
ride .... cgi, cgi-vrê
riddle .... beûl-sûig
ridge .... ôv-fiûl-nêz
right (antonym of wrong) .... paz
right angle .... fiûl-guz
right side .... jzêu
ring (for finger) .... jaz-sfuom
ring (sound of bell) .... rin
ring, hoop .... poc-jaz
ringworn .... jaz-rnû
rinse .... creu.kiûr
riot .... lto-suêf
ripe .... tiûn-tôm
ripple .... u.huûl
rise .... pa.bauz, hê-vrê
rival .... ruam.io
river .... brail
riverbed .... brail.vluar
road .... pue
roast .... nuah.rôûn
robber .... zgu.môip.io
rock .... oi.jui
rocket .... cze-hvau
roll .... drô-truôz
roll call .... kêu-ceud
romantic .... vûil-mêj
roof .... crum
room .... sfas

root .... prel
rope .... oi.czuûb
rose (flower) .... pliz
rosy .... pliz
rotate .... jaz-drô
rough .... jroi
round (circular) .... jaz
rouse .... sdû
routine .... jaz
row, series .... nêz.plia
rub .... toif
rubber .... nriô-phûl
ruby .... leg-zrar
rude .... roiz-jroi
rudiments .... mau
rugged .... jroi
ruin .... nuap-gaif
rule .... cab
ruler (for lines) .... nêz.zku.aê
ruler (of country) .... vliêc
rumour .... êun, êun-roiz
run .... soun
rush (plant) .... ûp-fjûb
rush (verb) .... zgu-hsa
rust (noun) .... zrôp-zca

S

sacrifice .... giêf-cuem
sad .... vce
saddle .... czûus.cgi.ôi

safe .... sôp
saffron .... spol-hiz
sag .... ba-vêg
sage .... znû.û
sail (noun) .... hsa-sdôus
sail (verb) .... vlaul-hsa
sailor .... vlioc
saint .... kut.û
sake, behalf .... pci
sal ammoniac .... lûporazû
salad .... sêv-rôûn-tzif
salary, wages .... suêt, sla-suêt
saliva .... gloin
salt (ionic compound) .... jôzue (jom.ôi zfê-hue)
salt (sodium chloride) .... blac
saltpetre .... zulûkoje
salty (in taste) .... zûr
salty delicacy .... zûr.zis.uem
salute .... glu-nion
same .... tis
sample .... fcô-flua
sand .... buû
sandalwood .... lûr-thin
sapphire .... dûn-zrar
sarcastic .... bef
sarong .... sgon-stuôm
satellite .... mi-hsa-êol
satin .... sû-truar
satire .... pal-biôm-prôh
satisfy .... fe-zmo
sauce .... ôip
saucer .... kraug-truôz

sausage .... hvau-vliêl
savage .... zma-hia
save .... seêm, tbo-seêm
saw (instrument) .... tluin
sawdust .... thin-vlêr
sawmill .... thin.siut.spuc
scab .... cli-sriol
scabies .... tle-rnû
scaffolding .... peôn-thaid
scale (of degrees) .... rtam
scale (of fish) .... sriol
scalp .... gûi.nio
scandal .... lkû-jlô
scar .... khe-jzu
scarcely .... jô.sêv
scare .... zu.jeûp
scarecrow .... iêt-jeûp
scatter .... sen.cze-stû
scene .... jzuis
sceptical .... flêl-niav
scepticism .... neufla (niav es kuv fe lva plal)
schedule .... chêô.plia
scholar .... jiaz.û
school .... fruc
schoolfellow .... fruc-jroz
school time .... fruc.vê
science .... thêh
scientist .... bloim
scissors .... sgêûn
scold .... siab-trê
scope .... hôj
scorpion .... fiôp-troih

scour ....toif-kiûr
scowl .... jom
scrape ....jloi-toif
scratch..vgep-toif
screen .... sku
screw ....czuûb-hvau
scroll ....hvau.lkô.fleu
scrotum ....kôr-phêuz
scruple..sraô-drû
scrutinise .... chêô-sûig-jbe
sculptor ....plaul.jriêf
sculpture .... plaul-zku
scum ....jain-hue
scythe .... fjûb-siut.aê
sea .... vrôih
sea animal.. priog
seal (animal) .... vrôih-flier
seal (for stamping) ....jzu.ôi
sea level ....vrôih-bôz
seam ....zfê-nêz
seasick ....vrôih-slû
season..hnuv
seat.. cgi.ôi
second (of time) ....lô.pom.vlul
secondary .... dak
secondary meaning (Luif) ....dak-sme
secret ....fiôf, fiôf-nûh
secret danger.. fjûb-chiûs
secretary ....piôs-iûn
secretion .... phûl
sediment.. vlaul-hue
seduce ....gbo-mru

see .... hne
seed .... snil
seek .... moês
seem .... lnu
segment of fruit .... rie-pom
seize .... zgu-czû
seldom .... côh
self vlil
selfish .... zpe
self-noun (Luif) .... vlil-blêh-suô
sell .... rza
semen .... kôr-due
send .... kôof
sensation .... vle
sense (faculty) .... hue.suô
sense of humour .... ceûl-suô
sensible, judicious .... fôb-dlû
sensitive .... dêl
sentence .... tuê
sentry .... sku-lziap
sepal .... spol-kraug.eu
separate .... pa.zfê
sequel .... lbu-pom
serial word (Luif) .... czuûb-cua
series of points .... nê.laz
serious, earnest .... pa.spe
serious disease .... fria.rnû
sermon .... plal-roiz
serrated .... tluin
servant .... eiz
serve .... eiz.lu
set (associated things) .... lpa.plia

set, frame .... sku-tbo
set of rules .... faê
settle.......... gsô
seven .... cûn
several .... ef.ril
severe, grim .... nriô-lûk
sew .... pûuk
sewer .... bliaz-slôp
sex .... car
sexual intercourse .... car.lu
sexual love .... car.jci
sexual organ.......... hlût
shady .... von
shake .... zru
shallow .... ban, cûg-ban
shame .... lkû
shame concerning sexual matters .... car.lkû
shape .... jav
share.......... sjie.lu
shares (of company).......... thô-sjie
shark .... tuês-sgiel
sharp (re sound) .... jloi
sharp, cutting .... jloi
shave .... toif-siut
shawl .... drof-roic
sheath.......... poc.czû.ôi
shed.......... jroi-srêm
sheep .... ûp-criôm
shelf .... gsô-thin
shell.......... zrôp-nio
shellfish .... znaisib (zrôp-nio vlaul iar sê.mi vlic.brian)
shelter .... sku.uô

shin .... lô-vric-al
shine .... vuêl
ship .... slar
shirt .... nu-crêus
shiver .... fe-zru
shock .... zgu-frê
shoe or outer foot covering .... snuim
shoot .... fiôp, cze-fiôp
shop .... krat
shop assistant .... krat.vriam
shore .... vrôih.dluô.vluar
short (in length) .... nôh
short (in stature) .... ban
shortcut .... em.nôh.pue
short pants .... nôh-stuôm
short story .... a.fkal
short time .... vam
shorten .... nôh.lu
shorthand .... nru-mro
shoulder .... drof
shout .... kiaz
shovel .... ûp-kraun
show .... fcô
shrimp or prawn .... troih
shrink .... lub-feur
shrub .... thin-tûu
shrug .... drof-hsa
shy .... u.lkû
sick .... slû
side .... dluô
siege .... cêôm-lkô
sieve .... ûp-fluaz

sigh .... vlub-fien
sight (something seen) .... hne.ôi
sign (expressing meaning) .... bûuj-jzu
sign (name) .... kêu-mro
signboard .... bûuj-jzu-hôj
silent .... jûz
silica .... buceje
silicon .... buû-jluz (bu)
silk .... truar
sill .... fe-tras
silver .... jzêk (jê)
silverfish (fish) .... jzêk-sgiel
silverfish (insect) .... jzêk-krois
simple .... fêz
simple sentence .... fêz-tuê
simultaneous .... vêu.tis
sin .... plal-sraô
since .... vêu.êz
sine qua non (indispensable condition) .... hozôo (hfo-zla ô.og)
sinew, tendon .... zfê-vrouh
sing .... plê
singer .... plê.io
sink .... bauz
sip .... lrim-piev
sister .... vlez
sit .... cgi
sit together .... mi.cgi
site .... srêm.uô
situate .... fzi
six .... pin
size .... zên.gun
skate .... bluên-snuim

skeleton .... brian.i
skill .... cfe
skin .... nio
skip .... u.fiôv
skirt .... jza-stuôm
skull .... gûi.brian
sky .... glun
skylark .... jrual-iêt
slander .... khe-roiz
slap .... blop-rial
slate .... hmaf
slave .... zgu-eiz
sleep .... rbo
sleet .... blaiv-grêun
sleeve .... crêus-jlec
slice (noun) .... siut.hôj.fleu
slice (verb) .... dêl-siut
slip .... griu-bauz
slippers .... suz-snuim
slit .... sjie-siut
slogan .... mru-cua
sloping .... êz-fzi
slow .... jra
small .... gun
smallpox .... hê-laz-rnû
smear .... toif-tbo
smell (odour) .... ô.nlo
smell (sense) .... suô.nlo
smell (verb) .... nlo
smile .... ceûl
smoke (noun) .... brôn
smoke (verb) .... brôn.lu

smooth .... griu
smoulder .... fe-nuah
snail .... priûm
snake .... chiûs
snarl .... pfê-miôz
sneer .... bef
sneeze .... dlos-siab
snore .... rbo-siab
snout .... srûuf.dlos
snow .... blaiv
so .... rec
soak .... vlaul-seêm
so-and-so .... rec-fleu
soap .... khôis
soar .... jêh-cze
sociable .... bhon
social gathering .... gle-feur
social science or philosophy .... srah
society or community .... bhon
sociology .... bhon-srah
sock, stocking .... jrot-roic
socket .... czû-poc
sodium .... hiz-hmav (ha)
sodium bicarbonate .... haracikoje
sodium cabronate .... cehacikoje
sodium hydroxide .... hajera
sofa .... val-ôut
soft .... zoc
softly captivating .... lif
sojourn .... vam.piem
solder .... glup-jzêm
soldier .... lziap

sole..jrot-lô
solemn .... phûun
solid (antonym of hollow) .... sik
solid figure .... lub
solid substance ....bôi
soliloquy...vlil.roiz
solution (of problem) ....htê-kruod
solve ....rpû-piûj
some, a certain ....fleu
somersault .... drô-fiôv
something .... fleu.blêh
sometimes .... ef.dak
son .... zlog
song .... flêz
soon ....hum-vam
soot ....ûp-khov
soothe .... ûp-hpi
sordid ....chui-ban
sore cli
soul .... ûp-vsud
sound, noise ....vlub
sound made by living thing other than human ....miôz
sound of footsteps ....pet
sound of splashing water .... ses
sound sleep..ên.rbo
soup .... due.uem
sour.. jom
source (of river) .... hjuez
source of supply.......................................hkaip
south..zluû
souvenir...lien.ôi
sow..snil-tbo

soya bean .... zvôt-rcûf
space .... nuê
space taken .... czo-nuê
spade .... kraun
span .... zfê-nuê
spanner, wrench .... drô.aê
spark .... grêl-chûp
sparrow .... ftûuv
spasm, convulsion .... vrouh-hsa
spatter .... laz.lu
spear .... laz-chuf
special .... jzu-côh
species .... sia.ia
spectacles .... glif-auf
spectrum .... hev.ia
speech .... nê.roiz
speech mark (Luif) .... roiz-pêa
speed, rate .... nru.jra
spell (re words) .... mau-srû
spend .... coet
sphere .... vlêô
spheroid .... jô-vlêô
spice .... fi.flec
spider .... trief
spin .... czuûb-zku
spine .... vlic.brian
spiral .... fe-vêg
spirit .... vsud-htug
splash .... jza-stû
spleen .... lbu-ian-voi
splinter .... az.thin
split, crack .... sjie-nuap

spoil .... khe
spoke .... ba-nad
sponge .... roic-vlaul
spoon .... pluiz
sport (physical play) .... sje
spout .... due-vrer
sprain .... nuap-khe
spread .... jza
spread easily and rapidly .... tho
spring (elastic contrivance) .... mlûhum-glup
spring (water) .... hjuez
spring (season) .... hnuv-a
sprout (verb) .... zma-zca
spurt .... jzêl-hêun
spy .... nûh-zvê
square .... gêd
squat .... ûp-cgi
squeeze .... lkô-zgu
squint .... hne-dluô
squirrel .... tûu-pleuf
stab .... ên.fiôp
stable .... czûus.srêm
staff, personnel .... vriam.ia
stagger .... fe-zru
stain, discolour .... hev-hpu
stairs .... rtam
stalk, stem .... rseut-sgon
stamen .... spol-kôr
stammer, stutter .... nuap-siab
stamp (noun) .... jzu-nui
stampede .... jeûp-soun
stand .... fiûl

standard, criterion .... cab
star .... êol
starch .... chûp-hue
start .... zma
startle .... jeûp-nius
state (political community) .... plaz
statement sentence (Luif) .... fri-tuê
station (building like police station) .... prêc
statistics .... ril-kuv
statue .... plaul
steal .... môip
steam (noun) .... uêj
steam (to cook) .... uêj.rôûn
steamship .... uêj.slar
steed .... fôb.fal.czûus
steel .... troi-zrôp
steep .... nad-jêh
step (in walking) .... coôl.eu
step (of stairs) .... rtam.eu
stepson .... lrai.zlog
stern, austere .... nriô
stew (mode of cooking) .... lkô-daul
stick, adhere .... gsô-gzô
stick, pole .... nê.thin
sticky .... jzêm, fe-gsô
stiff .... nad-nriô
stigma .... rud-jzu
sting .... sia-fiôp
stitch .... fe-pûuk
stock (keep goods) .... rza-seêm
stolen goods .... môip.ôi
stomach .... lreon

stomach ache....................zcos-bli
stone....................jui
stool....................vlic-blê-ôut
stoop....................lie-vêg
stop....................grê
stopper, cork....................lkô.ôi
storehouse....................seêm-srêm
storekeeper....................seêm-srêm.vriam
storey....................skêf
stork....................leg-vric
storm....................ôuv
story....................fi.smôn
stove....................ûp-flêc
straight....................nad
strait....................brem-vrôih
strange....................pa.bûuj-sor
stranger....................liûz.e
strangle....................fien-gaif
stratagem....................rial-liôl
strategy....................puêr-csû
straw....................chûp-sgon
stray....................pue-cto
street....................srêm-pue
strict....................troi-fria
strike (of workers)....................plia-grê
string....................czuûb
strip....................meuh-stû
strive, struggle....................fe-cri
stroll....................mlê-coôl
strong....................troi
structure (engineering)....................sdu.ôi
structure (organization)....................faê

student .... zdoaf
stumble .... rev-bauz
stump .... sgon-gzô
stun .... nuap-vle
stunt .... fcô-glu
style .... mro-rêh
subdivision .... pom.plia
subdue .... lô-tbo
subject (antonym of object) .... dlû-vlil
subject (of sentence) .... iob-cua
subject (of study) .... flêl-czil
subject matter .... flêl-blêh
sublime .... jêh-mêj
submarine .... lô-vlaul-slar
submissive .... thuû
submit .... lô.lu
subordinate word (Luif) .... eiz-cua
subscribe .... sû-suêt
subserve .... lô-stô
subsidiary device .... pêa
substance .... jzab
substitute .... msê
subtract .... czûa
suburbs .... mai.dluô
succeed (antonym of fail) .... pso
success and failure .... pso.pa
such .... rec
suck .... vrer-meuh
sudden .... jzêl-nru
suddenly realise .... fiôv-bûuj
sue .... chêb-moês
suffer .... bli

sugar .... plif
sugarcane .... plif-krev
suggest, propose .... dlû-zvê
suicide .... vlil.muir
suitable .... tên
sulphur .... hiz-lai (hi)
sulphuretted hydrogen .... cerahi
sulphuric acid .... cerahipoje
summarise .... nôh.lu
summer .... hnuv.e
summon .... ceud-glu
sun .... ueh
sunstroke .... ueh-rial
superior .... hê.û
supernatural .... ôv.pan
superstition .... nûh-lgi
supper .... zam-uem
supplement .... tliô-bzê
supply .... frê-cuem
support, prop .... stô, stô-czû
suppose .... czo-dlû
surface .... hôj
surgeon .... blop-jriap
surly .... iep
surname .... jlûv.kêu
surpass .... vrê-ôv
surplus .... czûa-gzô
surprise .... nius
surprise attack .... nius.cêôm
surrender .... cuem-cto
surround .... jaz.lu
survey (re land) .... vluar-rti

survive .... ôv.sne
suspect .... niav
swallow (bird) .... priôh
swallow, gulp .... dhûiv-czo
swamp .... due-vluar
swan .... ûp-thien
swarm .... krois.ia
swear .... plal-fri
sweat .... lie-vlaul
sweep .... rial-hsa
sweet (in taste) .... lif
swell .... lub-zca
swim .... pdi
swing .... zru-nui
swoon, faint .... pa.vle
sword .... phaiv-chuf
syllable .... cua-pom
symbol .... tau
symmetrical .... buv
sympathy .... mi-bre
symptom .... rnû-jzu
synthetic word (Luif) .... tliô-cua
syphilis .... car-rnû
syringe .... nu-zgu.aê
syrup .... plif-due
system (of ideas) .... slôn

T

table .... ôep
tablecloth .... ôêp-sdôus

tabulate .... thaid-sfo
tact .... vzû-csû
tactics .... druap-hsa
tadpole .... of-fries
tail .... euf
tailor .... griûk
take .... czo
take away .... czo-vrê
talent .... pan-kri
talk .... roiz
talkative .... jci.roiz
tall .... jêh
tally, match .... fe-gûin
tame .... thuû
tank .... oi.khuêj
tap (for fluid) .... due-htê
tap (knock gently) .... zoc-rial
tapering .... blêa
tapestry .... sfuom-sdôus
tar .... chûn-jluz
target .... jzu-blêh
taste .... hvo
tasteless .... hvo-blê
tasty .... hvo.zis
tax .... cuit
taxi .... suêt-plêm
tea .... thûs
teach .... rlu
teacher .... jzûut
teahouse .... thûs-srêm
teak .... jui-tûu
teapot .... thûs.poc.ôi

tear (of eye) .... glif.due
tear (verb) .... ôuv-sjie
tease .... toif
technical .... fe-sgô
telegraph .... sca-sgam
telephone .... roiz-sgam
telescope .... gu.truûv
television .... hne-sgam
tell .... bûuj-roiz
temper .... vsud-mul
temperature .... not.lûk
temple or place of religious worship .... chôk
temple (of head) .... jô-vlûr
temporary .... zlu.vam
tempt .... mru
ten .... foz
ten thousand .... rûg
tenacious .... jhus
tenant .... srêm.ciam.io
tendril .... peôn-voi
tensely active .... bef
tent .... nrio-sdôus-srêm
tenth .... fe.foz
term .... gsô-vêu
terminus .... dba-grê
terrace .... htê-skêf
test .... jzi, ûp-cri
testicle .... kôr-vlêô
tetanus .... rilvafvi (rnû mi bli vrouh-hsa fe vrer-brian)
text .... gsô-cua
textbook .... jiaz-kraut
than .... gi

thank...cru
that (antonym of this) .... fot
that (denoting the idea following) .... ih
that is, i.e. (*id est*) .... sme.ih
thatch..crum-fjûb
theatre...stêk
their .... fus
theme...roiz-blêh
then.. lac
theocracy...griûs-plaz
theorem...jzi-flêl
theorise .... dlû-fcô
there.. jzua
therefore...nzo.ûz
thermometer ....not-mrail
they...gou
thick.. zal
thigh ....hê-vric
thimble .... sku-glik
thin ....dêl
thing (any kind) .... blêh
thing held.. czû.ôi
think .... dlû
think aloud.. dlû-siab
third .... fe.kol
thirst ....vlaul-jlo
this .... mip
thistle..kruod-tûu
thorn .... rvoh
thou .... jea
though .... hû
thousand .... sod

thread .... a.czuûb
threaten .... fri-khe
three .... kol
threshold .... fe-krôf
thrill .... zhi
throat .... brem.al
throb .... rial-zru
throne .... zrar-ôut
through .... dê
throw .... cze-stû
thrush .... flêz-iêt
thrust .... zgu-vrê
thumb .... poz.glik
thunder or lightning .... jzêl
thus .... ûz
thy .... sam
tick (sound of clock) .... tik
ticket .... nu-vrê-uam
tickle .... zle-lto
tide .... nu-za-vlaul
tie .... gsô, czuûb.gsô
tiger .... oic
tight .... gsô-troi
tile .... crum-jhus
till (cultivate) .... czu
time .... vêu
time, occasion .... dak
time taken .... czo-vêu
tin (container) .... drês.poc.ôi
tin (metal) .... drês (dê)
tinfoil .... drês-rsûh
tingle .... vlû-fiôp

tip .... dêl-grê
tiptoe .... brik.laz
tired .... jziû, lie.jziû
tissue .... lifûe (lub.plia fe ûp eul)
title .... kêu, ûp-kêu
to .... ud
to and fro .... al-êh
toad .... ûp-fries
toast .... ud-piev
tobacco .... plauf
today .... jêu
toe .... brik
together .... mi
toil .... ên.sla
tomato .... zoc-siû
tomorrow .... nlôl
tone .... vlub-fal
tongs .... czû.aê
tongue .... bliûh
tonight .... jêu.guê
too .... fem-rec
tooth .... vhoil
top .... gûi
topography .... vluar-pêa
torch, flashlight .... riam-hmav
torpedo .... lô-vrôih-chuf
torpid .... fe-rbo
torrent .... troi-hêun
tortoise .... smior
torture .... chaêv-bli
total, sum .... feur-cim
touch .... zle

touching .... zle.va
tough .... troi
towel .... vlaul-sdôus
tower .... sgon-srêm
town .... mai
toy (noun) .... stuûc
trace, vestige .... gzô-jzu
trade .... clu
trademark .... clu-tau
trade union .... sla-bhon
trading .... gloit.sla
tradition .... vrih-lgi
traffic .... lub-hsa
tragedy .... vce-jlô
train (railway) .... nê.plêm
transfer .... ûp-hsa
transformed part of speech (Luif) .... hpu-suô
translate .... rua-hpu
transliterate .... hpu-mro
transparent .... dê-lil
transplant .... hsa-zca
trap .... czo-czû.aê
travel .... vuô-vrê
tray .... riam-truôz
tread, trample .... tbo-jrot
treasure .... sag.ôi
treasury .... chauk.seêm.uô
treat (behave towards) .... ruap
treat (medically) .... uûk-csû
tree .... hê.tûu
tree or plant .... tûu
trellis, lattice .... nriô-thaid

trench (noun) .... vluar-siut
trespass .... kôz-hrô
trial (in court) .... jbe
triangular .... zêj
trick .... vêg-cfe
trickle .... u.hêun
trifling .... u.sag
trigger .... stû-phôs
trigonometry .... zêj-khôn
trim .... jav-siut
trinket .... ef.sag.sfuom
trio .... kol.ia
triumph .... pso-zsû
troop .... lziap.ia
tropics .... not-jaz
trouble .... lto
trousers or lower garment .... stuôm
trowel .... jzêm-buû.lu.aê
true .... kuv
trumpet .... troi-phuet
trunk (of tree) .... sgon
truss (for roof) .... stô-crum
trust .... lgi, fe-lgi
try .... cri
tub .... ûp-khuêj
tube .... fi.slôp
tumble .... drô-bauz
tumour .... eul-fiûl
tungsten .... jêh-luav-laz (ja)
tunnel .... lô-vluar-pue
turkey .... leg-chiûv
turn .... drô

turn about .... rev.drô
turnip .... siû-prel
turpentine .... kson-gai
turtle .... ûp-smior
tusk, ivory .... ûif-vhoil
tweezers .... a.meuh.aê
twig .... rseut-czil
twilight .... ôv-hmav
twin .... mi-rze
twinkle .... mloû.vuêl
twist .... vêg-drô
twitter (sound of bird) .... chuit
two .... cel
two by two .... cel jû cel
type (characteristic specimen) .... kêg
type, kind .... kêg.plia
typewriter .... mro-czaf
typhoid .... leg-phi
tyrant .... zgu-bauz-vliêc
tyre, tire (rubber) .... phûl-jaz

U

ugly .... kaj
umbrella .... tluat
unanimous .... cim-gûin
uncle .... broh
under (touching) .... lô.mi
under (touching or apart) .... lô
undergrowth .... zca-lô
undersell .... lô-rza

understand .... vzû
understanding .... kri.vzû
undertake .... czo-glu
undulating, zigzag .... mloû.vêg
unfeeling, harsh .... nriô
unfix .... pa.gsô
uniform (adjective) .... buv
uniform (noun) .... plia-krauf
unify .... mov.lu
unit (quantity serving as standard of measurement) .... fi.thôd
unit or piece .... fleu
unit of area .... khug
unit of length .... thôd
unit of money .... krêd
unit of volume .... sbaz
unit of weight .... frôj
univalve .... mov-zrôp-nio
universe .... vaê
university .... oi.fruc
unless ci
unlucky .... dhô-rud
unpleasant to senses .... hec
unravel .... pa.pûuk
unskilled .... jroi
until .... ol
unusual .... pa.kul
up .... hsa-hê
upright .... paz-fôb
upside down .... hê-lô
upstairs .... hê-rtam
uranium .... fria-lai (fi)
urge .... zgu-csa

urinal .... broig-khuêj
urine .... broig
use .... ciam
useful and agreeable .... zûr
using, by means of .... mi
usurp .... zgu-czû

V

vaccine .... rnû-due
vacuum .... fûl-hue-nuê
vacuum cleaner .... mru-vlêr
vagabond .... thêt.blê.û
vague .... jrual
valley .... pa.vlair
valuable .... sag
value .... sag.pa
vane .... êun.fcô.aê
variant (noun) .... sû-plia
varnish (noun) .... uêr-vuêl
vase .... spol.czû.ôi
vault .... vêg-crum
vegetable (any sort) .... piô
vegetable (edible) .... tzif
vegetarian .... tzif.tiûn.io
vehement .... not
vehicle (all types) .... fi.plêm
vehicle (land carriage) .... plêm
veil .... zoû-sdôus
vein .... ud-ian-czuûb
velvet .... hiû-truar

veneer........ dêl-thin
ventilate........ ual-htê
veranda, balcony........ dluô-skêf
verb........ glu-suô
verbatim........ itcioc (mi tid cua ih o.ciam)
versatile........ jza-znû
vertical........ fiûl
very........ sor
vessel........ poc.ôi
via, by way of........ pue.dê
viand........ uem.eu
vice versa........ ijoh (mi jluê o.hpu)
vice president........ msê.rûus-vliêc
vicious horse........ rud.rêh.czûus
village........ a.mai
villain........ sraô.û
vine........ pler.tûu
vinegar........ jom-ôip
violent........ ên.zgu
violet........ leg-dûn
violin........ sguit
viper, adder........ fluam-chiûs
virgin........ car-vza-liu
virtue........ kut.sraô
viscera........ zcos-voi
viscous........ nriô-hêun
visit........ vrê-hne
vitamin........ flo-jzab
vivid........ ên.lil
vocabulary........ cua.i
vocabulary division (Luif)........ cua-sjie
vocative noun (Luif)........ ceud-blêh-suô

voice (human) .... siab
volcano .... grêl-vlair
volume (content) .... lub
voluntary .... vlil.lfe
vomit .... klû
vote .... ril-rûus
vow .... giêf-gûin
vowel .... htê-mau
vowel group (Luif) .... htê-mau-plia
vulcanite .... nûmhi (nriô-phûl mi hiz-lai)
vulgar .... blou
vulgar fraction .... sjie-sen
vulgar fraction mark (Luif) .... sjie-sen-tau
vulture .... hem-vliêl
vulva .... ê.hlût

W

wade .... vlaul-coôl
waist .... lie-ba
wait .... sma
waiter .... sma.vriam
walk .... coôl
walk to and fro irresolutely .... plo-coôl
walking stick .... tû-coôl
wall .... trêf
walrus .... ûif-priog
wander .... mac-vrê
want .... hse
wanton .... stû-spe
war .... pûer

wardrobe .... krauf.uô
warn .... csa-pra
warship .... puêr.slar
wash .... kiûr
wasp .... ûp-kzoêp
waste .... kiuf
wasteland .... kiuf.vluar
watch (timepiece) .... a.kruin
watch, guard .... sku, seêm-sku
water .... vlaul
waterfall .... fiôv-brail
waterlogged .... vlaul.khau
watermelon .... vlaul-smer
waterproof .... vlaul-troi
wave (of water) .... huûl
wax .... kzoêp-jzêm
wax and wane .... zca.pa
we .... diô
weak .... spiû
wealth .... stui.ôi
weapon .... khe.aê
wear .... roic
weasel .... fiôf-tuês-iar
weather .... ual-mul
weave .... sdôus-zku
web (of spider) .... trief-thaid
wedge .... ûp-ftuav
weed .... pleuf-fjûb
week .... vnên-jluz
weep .... roih
weigh .... rti
weight .... fria.creu

welcome .... zsû-maûs
weld .... zgu-zfê
well (adjective) .... fôb-mul
well (of water) .... vraid
well-meaning .... cuem-fôb
werewolf .... oic-flier-htug
west .... ldêi
wet .... snôi
whale .... nrôus-priog
wharf .... vluar-glu-skêf
what .... sa
what cause .... sa.hzô
what condition .... sa.mul
what result .... sa.lbu
what type .... sa.kêg
whatever .... tid.sa
wheat .... trot
wheel .... drô-truôz
wheelbarrow .... phêuz-plêm
when .... su
whenever .... tid.su
where .... rô
whereabouts .... jô.rô
wherever .... tid.rô
whether .... fê
whetstone .... jloi.lu.jui
which .... ar
which one .... sa.fleu
whiff .... dak-ual
while .... do
whip .... rial-czuûb
whirlpool, eddy .... jaz-vlaul

whisper .... fien-siab
whistle (instrument) .... jloi.lu.aê
whistle (sound) .... hui
white .... zel
who .... um
whoever .... tid.um
whole .... mov, cim.mov
wholesale .... ên.rza
whose .... ôs
why .... ku
wick .... svuan-czuûb
widow .... siut-mêus.viô
wife .... zriv
wild .... pa.thuû
wild animal .... pa.thuû.iûr
wile .... gbo-liôl
will (exercise choice) .... lfe
will (testament) .... cuem-uam
willing .... lfe-zri
willow .... huûl-tûu
wind (moving air) .... êun
window .... tras
windpipe .... fien-dhûiv
wine or any alcoholic beverage .... aot
wine-seller's shop .... aot.krat
wing .... iôm
wink .... mloû.vuêl
winter .... hnuv-i
wipe .... êz-toif
wire .... nê.glup
wise .... znû
wiseacre .... lnu-znû.û

wish.......zri
wit.......ceûl-znû
with.......mi
wither.......vlaul-cto
without.......sê.mi
witness.......hne-bûuj
wizard.......klô.io
wolf.......oic-flier
woman.......viô
womb.......rze-voi
wonder.......nius, nius-dlû
woo.......moês-jci
wood (wooded country).......tûu.uô
wood, timber.......thin
wool.......ûp-criôm.hiû
word.......cua
work.......sla
work as actor professionally.......thô.tla
work of art.......crul.eu
worker (one who works).......vriam
world.......uûd
worm.......smiûp
wormwood.......nos-tûu
worsen.......pa.hues
worship (revere).......giêf
worth (equal in value to).......sag-tû
worth doing.......glu.sag
would-be.......zri.vlô
wound.......khe
wrapper.......za.ôi
wreck.......nuap-gaif
wrestle.......czû-ruam

wriggle .... vêg-hsa
wrinkle .... zoû-nêz
wrist .... blop-zfê
write .... mro
writer .... mro.io
written passage .... puô
wrong .... kôz
wrought iron .... zoc-zrôp

X

X-ray .... dê-hmav

Y

yam .... ûp-crif
yawn .... vrer-htê
year .... ghal
yearn .... jlo
yeast .... sla-piô
yell, scream .... jloi.kiaz
yellow .... hiz
yesterday .... dau
yolk .... ius-hiz
you .... zeu
young .... has
your .... rôs

Z

zebra..nêz-czûus
zero .... fûl
zinc .... vtuk (vu)
zoo .... iar.seêm.uô

About the Author

Born around the time of the foundation of the Republic of China in the former English colony of British Malaya, Tan Kheng Yeang was educated in an English school. His father was from China but emigrated to Malaya and became a successful businessman, involved in various activities, including as a rubber merchant. From his early days, the author was interested in literature and philosophy, and as his interest evolved to science, he decided to study civil engineering at the University of Hong Kong, as he felt he needed a practical career.

After the Japanese occupied Hong Kong, the author fled into free China where he found work in the office of a company that constructed roads, and later an airfield in Guangxi Province. After the war ended in 1945, he returned to Malaya and became an engineer in the city council of Georgetown, Penang. After his retirement, he worked as an engineering consultant. He is the author of twelve books that reflect the broad range of his interests and talents.